AGE OF ~~TRUST~~ DOUBT

AGE OF ~~TRUST~~ DOUBT

Building Trust in a World of Misinformation

Edited by
TRACEY KIRKLAND
& GAVIN FANG

This book was written on many lands of the Aboriginal and Torres Strait Islander peoples and other indigenous peoples around the world. We acknowledge the original storytellers of these lands and pay our respects to Elders past and present, including our many brilliant colleagues who keep this tradition alive.

Age of Doubt: Building Trust in a World of Misinformation
© Copyright 2025
Copyright of this collection in its entirety is held by the editors, Tracey Kirkland and Gavin Fang. Copyright of the individual essays is held by the respective author/s. All rights reserved. Apart from any uses permitted by Australia's *Copyright Act 1968*, no part of this book may be reproduced by any process without prior written permission from the copyright owners. Inquiries should be directed to the publisher.

Monash University Publishing
Matheson Library Annexe
40 Exhibition Walk
Monash University
Clayton, Victoria 3800, Australia
https://publishing.monash.edu

ISBN: 9781923192133 (paperback)
ISBN: 9781923192140 (PDF)
ISBN: 9781923192157 (epub)

Editor: Paul Smitz
Design: Phil Campbell Design
Typesetter: Cannon Typesetting
Proofreader: Gillian Armitage

A catalogue record for this book is available from the National Library of Australia.

Printed in Australia by Griffin Press

The paper this book is printed on is certified against the Forest Stewardship Council® Standards. Griffin Press holds chain of custody certification SCS-COC-001185. FSC® promotes environmentally responsible, socially beneficial and economically viable management of the world's forests.

For people who love to explore new ideas.

Contents

Introduction   xiii

PART I   TRUST, WHERE HAS IT GONE?

The Long Age of Forgetting   3
Simon Longstaff, Executive Director, The Ethics Centre, Australia

Finding Truth in Ourselves   13
Gavin Fang, Editorial Director, ABC, Australia

Technology Didn't Give Rise to Misinformation—We Did   24
Ben Decker, Founder and CEO of Memetica, United States

Discourse Collapse: How Disinformation Erodes Public Trust   32
Layla Mashkoor, the Atlantic Council's Digital Forensic Research Lab, Canada

Agree to Disagree: Trust and Civic Debate   41
Tracey Kirkland, Continuous News Editor, ABC, Australia

PART II   TRUST AND DEMOCRACY

Trust in Government and Radical Impartiality   57
Patricia Karvelas, journalist and broadcaster, ABC, Australia

Trust in Science: Strengthening Peer Review to Build Resilience   67
Cathy Foley, Chief Scientist, Australia

Trust in Religion: We Are Like Cut Flowers   76
Michael Stead, Anglican Bishop of South Sydney, Australia

Trust in Policing: Force and Our Freedom   88
Graham Ashton, former chief commissioner of Victoria Police, Australia

An Indigenous Perspective on Community Trust   97
A Q&A with Yalmay Yunupingu, Yolŋu Elder, teacher and Senior Australian of the Year 2024, Australia

PART III TRUST AND THE MESSENGERS

Trust in the News Media: A Global and Audience Perspective   105
Nic Newman and Amy Ross Arguedas, Reuters Institute for the Study of Journalism, United Kingdom

Fact-Checking and the Golden Age of Journalism   117
Fergus McIntosh, Head Research Editor, *The New Yorker*, United States

How Constructive Journalism Can Restore Trust in Democracy   127
Ulrik Haagerup, founder and CEO of Constructive Institute, Denmark

There Is No Middle Ground: Reclaiming the Public Square   137
Catherine Tait, former president and CEO, CBC/Radio-Canada, Canada, and Eli Pariser, co-founder of New_ Public, United States

Strengthening Global Trust   147
Kristian Porter, CEO, Public Media Alliance, United Kingdom

Trust and the Danish Experience   155
Gert Tingghaard Svendsen, author and Professor of Public Policy, Aarhus University, Denmark

PART IV TRUST, CORPORATES AND LEADERSHIP

Trust and Distrust: The Existential Tension 167
Ross Honeywill, social scientist, and Michele Levine, CEO,
Roy Morgan, Australia

Trust and Corporate Leadership: Operating 'Outside
the Building' 176
A Q&A with Rosabeth Moss Kanter, Harvard Business School,
United States

Rebuilding Trust after a Crisis 182
Michael Smith, former chairman, 7-Eleven, Australia

Engaging People in Change 192
A Q&A with Subramanian Rangan, Professor of Strategy and
Management, European Institute for Business Administration
(INSEAD), France

The Currency of Trust 199
Louise Mahler, executive adviser and coach, Australia

PART V TRUST AND THE FUTURE

In AI We Trust? What to Expect in Our Technological Future 211
Toby Walsh, Chief Scientist, UNSW AI Institute, Australia

Bots and Moral Panic 225
Timothy Graham, Associate Professor in Digital Media,
Queensland University of Technology, Australia

Understanding Conspiracies and Their Theorists 235
Kaz Ross, researcher into far-right extremism and conspiracy
theories, Australia

Living with Uncertainty 244
A Q&A with Julia Baird, author, broadcaster and journalist, Australia

Acknowledgements 255
Contributor Bios 258
Notes 267

Introduction

WE ALL INSTINCTIVELY feel that we know the value of trust. It underpins our faith in each other, our communal values, our willingness to cede power to governments and institutions, our sense of a shared truth. It is fundamental to our society. History shows us that when we have it, when we are working side by side instead of at odds with each other, we make our world better.

But without trust, the Nobel Prize–winning journalist Maria Ressa tells us, 'we have no shared reality, no democracy, and it becomes impossible to deal with our world's existential problems'.[1]

Without trust, we are lost.

That is arguably the case today, with many of us feeling that trust is elusive. Across industrialised societies, the search for answers to complex problems—poverty, famine, war, climate change, rising rates of mental illness—often spiral into recriminations, fear, toxic politics. Political leaders appear to be more focused on personal point-scoring and staying in power than the hard work of creating policy solutions.

In the corporate world, too, business titans often talk a good game about corporate responsibility and a social licence, sustainability and social justice, while their actions demonstrate that making money still speaks the loudest.

And the media can hardly claim the high moral ground. Its empire-building conglomerates are often just as polarised as the politicians, serving stories tailored to the bubbles their audiences inhabit, and competing desperately for diminishing returns on social media platforms owned by tech companies that publish more and more misinformation (the unintentional spreading of falsehoods) and disinformation (the deliberate spreading of falsehoods)—while simultaneously claiming not to be responsible for tainted content.

Survey after survey of the community bears this out. In 2024, the global Edelman survey found that almost two-thirds of respondents believed government, business and journalists couldn't be trusted because they were purposely trying to mislead people by saying things they knew were either false or grossly exaggerated.[2] In Australia, Roy Morgan has found that many people hold the view that companies are explicitly motivated by profit while individuals struggle with rising living costs, leading to distrust of our economic system.

It is hardly surprising, then, that the community's faith in these bedrock institutions, particularly in democratic societies, seems weak, if not fractured. Many of us are asking: 'Who and what can I trust?' It is an Age of Doubt.

What is the cause of this modern morass? Is it perhaps the rise of misinformation that is undermining trust?

If you want to know the answer to a question, what do you do? Most of us have two go-to options. We either ask someone we know or turn to the internet—even if we do phone a friend, most of us are still inclined to retreat to the internet to fact-check their answer. Yet, for all the collective knowledge stored on the internet, definitive answers can be tough to find. Many of us are troubled by the lack of trust we can place in the facts we encounter. We are troubled in the search for truth.

There is a dark side to having access to a depthless reservoir of information. Amid the vast stores of knowledge available to us online lurks misinformation and disinformation at an enormous scale.

INTRODUCTION

Facts seem malleable, subject to manipulation by trolls and their tweets. Our erratic online culture in turn fuels a media and political discourse that is shrill and divisive.

Technology, of course, is not the only factor eroding our sense of trust. After all, the bots and AI avatars that roam the internet are of our own making. They can't be blamed for the tendency of some to deliberately distort knowledge for individual gain, or for the advancement of one group over another.

As the various, continuing missteps of the public institutions once trusted to lead and guide us have been brought to our attention, have we lost a sense of the core values that are meant to underpin them, and more broadly our society? Have we lost touch with the bedrock beliefs that support the fair, open, democratic and free society many of us want?

If this all sounds grim, it's because it is. But we cannot succumb to the doubt and lose all hope. There are crucial choices ahead of us, and if we are to build trust, we must all play a role.

A problem this big can't be solved in a collection of essays. But as journalists who have worked in the media for decades, we have spent much of our professional lives finding and elevating the voices of those with the ideas, expertise and acuity to help bring a new perspective to such problems, and to seek solutions. It is our sincere hope that the essays that follow spark new ways of thinking and open up a conversational space that is the opposite of what we often see in society currently—respectful, engaging and curious, truthful.

In these pages, you will hear from philosophers and scientists, business and religious leaders, journalists, futurists and psychologists, all at the forefront of their fields. Part I discusses how strong ethics lead to improved trust and better decision-making. It looks at how truth is subjective and what that means for how we engage with each other. It explores the origins of misinformation and disinformation, and analyses how they are deployed today for political and commercial gain. It also asserts the importance of public discourse.

Part II takes a closer look at the erosion of trust in institutions that is impacting the community's faith in democratic government, and asks what can be done about it. It puts politicians under the spotlight, seeking to understand what role they can play in the regaining of trust. It examines new ideas about how science and scientists can help build a society more grounded in research and facts, and explores the foundational part religion has played in the development of our democratic principles. It looks at the use of force and the role of trust in policing, and assesses trust from an Indigenous perspective at the community level.

Part III examines the loss of trust in the mainstream media, the impact social media is having on the fourth estate, and what all this means for a democratic and pluralistic society. It presents lessons on fact-checking from the legendary *New Yorker* magazine, takes us to Canada to look at how publicly funded media organisations there are trying to build their own social media ecosystem, and goes to the source of the constructive news trend that has seen many media organisations turn to 'solutions journalism'—asking not just 'Who, what, when and why?', but also 'What now?'. And it explains why the Danes remain some of the world's most trusting people and how that makes them happy—spoiler: it has something to do with the Vikings.

Part IV offers the firsthand experiences of leaders in business in regards to how companies can so easily lose trust and how difficult it is to regain it. It traces the links between economic hardship and the recent loss of faith and trust in government. It sets out the case for how to better lead in difficult times, and goes inside a business in trouble to see how to recover from a trust crisis.

Part V looks at the role of generative artificial intelligence (none of which was used in the creation of these essays!) and web crawlers in shaping the information environment that we rely on to discover facts and truth. It peers into the future to see whether *2001: A Space Odyssey*'s HAL 9000 or the T-800 Terminator are waiting for us, or if our AI future is similarly profound but much less as Hollywood has envisioned. It journeys into the world of bots to shed light on what they are and how they're already dominating our online world. And it looks at what makes conspiracies stick and why they seem to have a hold on so many of us. It ends with insights into how to navigate it all and emerge still full of hope.

The process of commissioning this collection has felt a bit like bringing a group of trusted people together around a table and hearing from them in turn. We hope that you will feel like you have been given a seat at this table: to listen and form your own ideas, stress-test solutions, and ultimately feel more empowered about how to value and rebuild trust in this Age of Doubt.

Gavin Fang and Tracey Kirkland

PART I
TRUST, WHERE HAS IT GONE?

The Long Age of Forgetting

Simon Longstaff, Executive Director, The Ethics Centre, Australia

IMAGINE THAT YOU are the printer laying down the type for René Descartes's *Meditations*, a book that will usher in a revolution in thinking that will challenge the certainties of previous millennia. Would you have any sense the world was about to shift? Or would you simply share, with others, a growing sense of 'unease'? What lies before you? A world in which science triumphs over prevailing superstition. A world in which the 'divine right of kings' is contested by the idea that it is better to be a 'citizen' than a 'subject'. A world in which protected economies will increasingly be opened up to trade. A world of ... doubt.

We are at a similar juncture. The settled, rules-based international order is once again under threat. Unthinkable for a generation, the possibility of war in Europe and the Pacific is under active consideration. The impetus for globalisation is in retreat. Advances in science and technology are poised either to enhance or diminish the human condition.

And yet, at precisely the time when we might hope to look to public and private institutions to offer guidance and the confidence to embrace an uncertain future, we find them weakened, in some cases entirely broken.

What has caused this precipitous decline in trust? And how might this be remedied?

The Foundations of Trust

The formation and maintenance of trust depends on two conditions being maintained. First, individuals and organisations need to publicly declare the basis on which they will act in the world. That is, they need to make explicit the 'standard of judgement' by which their conduct is to be assessed. The most powerful expression of such a standard is found in statements of core values and principles. Once espoused, they provide a reliable indication of the choices to be made—both in terms of the ends pursued and the means applied in pursuit of those ends.

Second, trust is either built or eroded depending on the degree of alignment between what the individual or organisation *espouses* and what it actually does in *practice*. Close alignment builds trust. Misalignment is experienced as hypocrisy of a kind that leads to ongoing scepticism and ultimately cynicism. The latter state is like an acid that eats away at the bonds of any human community. As those bonds are dissolved, common goals are set aside in favour of the preferences of the individual or small groups. The whole becomes weaker and far more susceptible to corruption—in all its forms.

In recent years, the most spectacular example of misalignment, and its effects, has been exemplified by a number of Christian churches in their response to the sexual abuse of children and other vulnerable people by their clergy and others. I realise there are many other examples that could serve, but the case of the relevant churches is especially telling. That is because, for over 2000 years, the churches had preached that 'love is more important than the law', 'people are more important than property' and that 'you should stand up for and face into the truth'. Yet, when confronted by evidence of abuse, how did these churches respond? With some important exceptions, too many rejected two millennia of pious teaching and instead chose 'the law over love', 'property over people' and 'protecting one's back [from scandal] rather than facing the truth'. The damage caused to victims and survivors by the abuse was terrible, but the inverted response made things so much worse for the larger group of the faithful. If church leaders do not believe in and apply what they preach, why should anyone else have faith in what is proclaimed?

This is at the heart of why integrity is so widely valued in its two major forms. The first of these is captured in the familiar declaration that 'I am who I say I am. I will do what I say I will do'. However, there is a second sense of integrity—captured most easily in the idea of bodily integrity—in which each of the parts is in a healthy relationship with the whole. The importance of this latter sense of integrity was noticed over thirty years ago by the noted Australian social researcher and author Hugh Mackay. When exploring the issue of trust, Mackay reported that people no longer relied on their direct experience as a sufficient indication of who (or what) should be trusted. That data was necessary, but not sufficient.[1] Additionally, members of the public gave weight to their perception of how others were treated; that is, espoused core values and principles needed to be applied consistently across the full spectrum of relationships. Selective application was understood to be evidence of hypocrisy and an attempt to build trust through manipulation rather than through integrity.

Now, some people assume that examples of ethical failure leading to a loss of trust are, for the most part, evidence of deliberate acts of hypocrisy rooted in vices such as greed, arrogance and indifference. Too often it is assumed that behind every 'bad' act is a 'bad' person. So we tend to vilify the leaders of public and private institutions on the assumption that they must have been deliberate in their intent to do wrong. While such leaders are ultimately responsible—and must be held so, no matter how complex their operating environment—it is more likely than not that the individuals concerned are genuinely 'good' people who have made (or have enabled) genuinely 'bad' decisions. In other words, one need not look for a villain in a black hat to explain most of the misery in the world. Indeed, when one asks those most intimately involved in examples of ethical failure to explain what they were thinking at the time of their active involvement, the most common response is, 'I don't know. I just didn't see it at the time.'

In the case of some respondents, this is a disingenuous response. If they did not 'see it' at the time, it was because of wilful blindness on their part, or deliberately turning a blind eye to conduct that they knew to be 'wrong'—even according to their own standards. However, this involves a minority of people. Far more common are those who reply, when asked why they did not see things then as they do now, by saying, 'Because, everyone was doing it. That's just the way things were done back then.'

Shocking and inexcusable as it may be, the loss of trust is produced by a hypocrisy that is less a product of careful thought than an absence of any thought at all. And this phenomenon is not merely present in individuals. It is also at work undermining the foundations of our institutions. The world has drifted into its present predicament, largely as a result of having forgotten the underlying purposes for which institutions were created and originally sustained.

A Long Age of Forgetting

As I have argued elsewhere, it's easy to understand how basic purposes might be forgotten over time.[2] Like values and principles, they are the building blocks of institutions. We might imagine these institutions in the form of great buildings: cathedrals, parliaments, universities, office blocks. Their foundations lie buried, out of sight and out of mind. Instead, interest is focused on each soaring edifice. Layer upon layer of meaning and practice offer endless fascination. They glitter; they beguile. Over time, the foundations crumble simply through neglect.

In calm times, these great buildings stand tall. However, should the forces of change shake the ground, even just a little, then the proud towers may fall. Those at the heart of a failing institution are often at a loss to explain the collapse. Yet, nearly always, the cause will be this: having forgotten—and then having unwittingly betrayed—their fundamental purposes, institutions progressively lose the trust of the community, and even of their own adherents. Perceptions of hypocrisy generate cynicism, the acid earlier described that eats into and ultimately destroys the bonds of community on which social institutions rely.

For example, the institutions of 'the market' have no intrinsic value. These include artefacts such as the right to incorporation of non-natural, legal 'persons'; the privilege of 'limited liability' for shareholders and owners; global trade agreements; banking systems; and so on. Yet, the original ideal of the market is captured in the image of two people who meet at a ford in a stream. One person has wool, one has wheat. One person is hungry, the other is cold. They exchange: freely, openly and honestly, for the betterment of both. The market has no intrinsic value. It is merely a tool to increase the stock of common good. If it fails to achieve this end, then it fails to achieve its own defining purpose.

Adam Smith understood that the market is only 'free' if it is based on a solid ethical foundation that prohibits lying, cheating or the unconscionable use of power to the detriment of others. All such conduct distorts an otherwise free market. Those who forget the underlying purpose of the market, or who treat its core values and principles as optional extras, ensure that the promise of the market rings hollow.

In response, there is a growing number of people who wish to reject 'free trade', who question the role of the banks, who believe that corporations take more than they give. Some may be tempted to dismiss such complaints as naive and simplistic. However, to do so would be to ignore the depth of underlying feeling—especially the feeling of fear.

People are fearful that the fruits of science and technology may be about to displace them from their jobs, through the employment of robots and expert systems. They sense profound social changes just around the corner, driven by evolving demographics, new patterns of engagement and the like. Instead of feeling optimistic about the transformative power of science and technology, people are inclined to anticipate a dystopian future. As such, innovations that could prove to be a massive boon to humanity risk being blocked—along with those that would be better set aside. This indiscriminate opposition risks being at the cost of all.

With all of this in mind, let us consider the exemplary circumstances of contemporary Australia.

Paradise Won or Lost?

Australia stands on the cusp of a brilliant future. It has everything any society could need: vast natural resources, abundant clean energy, and an unrivalled repository of wisdom held in trust by the world's oldest continuous culture, and supplemented by a richly diverse people drawn from every corner of the planet. Whether this future can be grasped depends not on our natural resources, our financial capital or our technical nous. The ultimate determinant lies in the quality of our ethical infrastructure and the trust it engenders.

Despite the remarkable opportunity Australia has to become one of the most just and prosperous nations the world has ever seen, the Australian people are feeling insecure. In an increasingly uncertain and belligerent geopolitical environment, they feel that national security is at risk. Australia's potential foes are already committed to a strategy of divide and conquer, and will exploit all forms of division by the increasingly potent means at their disposal.

In the economic sphere, there is a growing sense that the world is changing in ways that will undermine job security. As such, there is little appetite for reform—even if, in the medium to long term, it will increase prosperity for all. People fear an unknown future, and they are reluctant to embrace innovation where the outcome of doing so is, for them, uncertain and full of risk.

And in the social sphere, the aftermath of the colonisation of our continent has eroded a sense of 'belonging' to the place where we live, a loss that can only be restored when the question of legitimacy is resolved.

Yet, in the face of this, rather than growing trust in our public and private institutions, there has been a steady decline in trust. Worse still, the drop-off has been both consistently and concurrently affecting most institutions. That is, our society has suffered the equivalent of multiple organ failure just at the time when we need it to be at its most healthy and resilient.

Recovering Purpose and the 'Ecology of Meaning'

One might be feeling a little depressed by this point of the essay. If everything has fallen out of memory such that institutions inadvertently betray their own purposes, is there not going to be an irreversible slide into that acid pool of cynicism?

'No'—a resounding 'No!', I say.

This is a time of remarkable opportunity—if we choose to seize it. For the first time in centuries, perhaps millennia, we have before us the possibility of *rethinking* the foundations of our society. What is the purpose of a parliament, a university, a profession, a market, a corporation, a trade union, a political party, a theatre company, an ethics centre, a public broadcaster ? Even if, after reflection, we come up with the same answers as those who first addressed these questions, the crucial difference will be this: the answers will be ours. They will be invested with new life! Rather than the dead hand of history resting on our shoulders, along with its legacy of unthinking custom and practice, we will be able to build and sustain institutions that are refreshed and vital. With their underlying purpose, values and principles having been restored to the point that they are actively supporting what has been built, our institutions will be proofed against corruption—whether it be deliberate or otherwise.

Furthermore, our revitalised institutions (public and private) need not be refashioned in terms of uniform, beige monotony. The modern world calls out for authentic differentiation. As Hugh Mackay noted three decades ago, the challenge is not to be more or less like someone else, but rather to be true to your own particular character. The world in which we live no longer distinguishes between individuals and entities according to what they *do* but according to what they *mean*.

Modern technology makes it easy for anyone to identify, copy and replicate the physical and technical attributes of others, not least competitors for resources (however defined). What cannot be so easily copied is the culture of another organisation, itself an artefact of the deeper structure defined by core values and principles.

So it is that we should expect to see emerge a new ecology of meaning, with different types of organisations each defining and occupying a different niche according to their underlying ethos. In turn, they will attract key stakeholders who have a general affinity with their approach. As in nature, some will flourish due to the quality, character and relative attractiveness of what they offer, while others will founder, unable to secure a niche that others wish to share.

In all cases of flourishing, the key to success will lie in a life of *integrity*, in both senses outlined above, and the trust it produces.

The Role of Ethics in Uncertain Times

Accused of the twin crimes of impiety and of 'corrupting the youth' of Athens, Socrates was condemned to be executed. Refusing the option to escape with his life into exile, Socrates insisted that the sentence be carried out, choosing an exemplary death by drinking hemlock. Now, imagine if one could have sat with Socrates on the night before his death. Knowing his fate, how would he have evaluated his life?

All that Socrates could have known for certain was that, come the next day, he would die. As far as he knew, his impact on the world was grounded in the failure that represented.

That is, Socrates could not have known that he would become one of the most consequential people ever to live. He could not know that his life and thinking would still be shaping the world thousands of years after his death. Indeed, Socrates was declared by the Delphic oracle to be the 'wisest man in Greece' precisely because he knew how little he knew!

We are all in the same situation as Socrates. Even at the best of times, the future is uncertain. The outcomes of our choices might have a certain measure of probability, but that is something less than 'certainty'. Socrates, unable to know for certain, and therefore unable to evaluate the lasting impact of his life, would have had no choice but to reply by pointing out that his life should be judged not according to outcomes but in terms of the intrinsic quality of the choices he made. That is, he would have argued that he had led a 'good' life—in and of itself.

That is the great strength of ethics: it helps us to make good decisions even in conditions of radical uncertainty. One of the tools it provides for doing so concerns the *telos* (ends or purposes) for which we act. For example, the purpose of a knife is to cut. It follows from this that a 'good' knife is one that can cut well. Entailed in this idea is that a 'good' knife will have a sharp blade, a handle that fits the hand of its user, and so on. Such a knife will be deemed 'good' not because of any outcome it has produced; for example, it may never have been used to cut anything. Yet, the fact that it is fit for its purpose will be enough.

This leads us back to how we might remedy the long age of forgetting, by recalling the purpose of our public and private institutions. It also leads us back to the issue of trust, based on the kind of integrity that is only possible when one goes beyond living a 'moral life' (in which blind habit can rule—even the apparently virtuous), to instead live an 'ethical life'—which is, as Socrates defined, the 'examined life' of a reflective practitioner.

There is a causal connection between 'trust' and 'ethics'. Improved ethics leads to improved trust and vice versa. Thus, the quality of a nation's ethics is directly related to the realisation of these objectives. Furthermore, improved trust drives increased prosperity. Deloitte Access Economics has estimated that a 10 per cent increase in ethics would lead to an increase in Australia's GDP of $45 billion per annum.[3]

The evidence is clear. Increased trust across society will produce greater social cohesion—a form of defensive 'soft power' that can neutralise the efforts of those who wish to divide and conquer. It will also produce a permissive economic environment in which all manner of reforms (including in the energy sector) become possible because the community can believe in a process of transformation and transition that is, at its heart, both just and orderly.

This is why ethics matters. It is humanity's best tool for the avoidance of disastrously bad decisions, and the nightmare worlds that emerge from them. More optimistically, ethics equips us to make brilliantly good decisions, and the wonderous possibilities they entail.

Finding Truth in Ourselves

Gavin Fang, Editorial Director, ABC, Australia

WHAT IS REAL, what is fact and fiction—what is truth? How do we tell the difference? Our world seems more complicated than ever before, with more and more sources of information bombarding our brain. While this is neither inherently good nor bad, how do we make sense of it all? How do we find the facts amid the falsehoods? And what is our role in helping others to do the same? One thing is clear: ultimately, to have trust, we must first have truth.

Me

Do you ever feel like you are inside your own body looking out? That your eyes are windows, and you are perceiving the world by looking out of them? Look at your hands as they move. Are they you, or are they part of a machine that houses you and does your bidding? You feel pain. Is that you, or is it the body-machine letting you know that it has a problem and you'd better do something about it?

Sometimes I feel like that. I have a sense that I'm observing rather than acting. My feet feel the ground, the point where my body and the world touch. My body moves, taking me where I tell it to go. It feels, views, smells and hears the world around me, sending me signals that I must interpret. And it is through those signals that I discern the world around me, my facts, my subjective truth.

That feeling is something philosophers have talked about for centuries. It even has a name. It's called Plato's Cave, an allegory written by the ancient Greek philosopher to describe how people perceive reality.

Dr Dan Feuerriegel at the University of Melbourne explains it this way: 'Plato's allegory of the cave is useful for understanding the fundamental problem that we face when trying to figure out what is true. In this fictional cave, we have a prisoner who's chained to a rock and is facing a wall. There is a fire behind the prisoner but they can't get up to look behind them to see what else is in the cave, and they must try to figure out what is happening based on the patterns of light and dark that are dancing across the wall in front of them. This exemplifies the idea that we're always trying to figure out what is happening based on the patterns of information that we receive through our senses.'

The implication of Plato's Cave is this: if we are all in our own caves perceiving the world differently, then our own view of the world must be different to the views held by others. Taken a step further, the idea is that if we all view the world differently, then how do we know what is really true or false?

Mum and Dad used to have a debate at the family dinner table when I was a child about whether we all saw the same colours. Was the colour red the same for everyone? My dad the scientist believed it was. My mum the educator believed we all just called it red because that was what we'd learnt, which meant it was possible we were all seeing different things.

No-one ever seemed to win the dinner table debate, and it seems that similar questions have also stumped philosophers and physiologists. Feuerriegel says the famous philosopher Thomas Nagel once wondered what it was like to be a bat. 'We can't accurately imagine what a conscious experience of being a bat would be,' he says, 'and we can't fully understand the conscious experience of anybody else for that matter as well, because we've got no way of experiencing exactly what it is like to be another being.'

Back, then, to Plato's Cave. How does our brain work to make sense of what we observe in the shadows? And in a world where there is now more information—or more shadows—than there has ever been, how do our brains cope?

'In these instances, the brain needs to figure out how to make a best guess, or how to settle on one interpretation, when there are competing sources of information,' says Feuerriegel. 'We can only consciously experience one reality at any given instant, and so we need to collapse everything down to one coherent experience and cut off all of the other alternatives.'

He continues: 'There's thought to be a network involving the parietal cortex and frontal cortex, as well as a broad network of other brain areas, that essentially tries to integrate different sources of information from our senses, our beliefs and our memories until it reaches a certain amount of evidence where we can be confident to say, "I'm committing to this decision now and I'm going to act on it as well."'

You

So truth is in part what I discern from the world around me. But *you* have a huge role to play in *my* pursuit of truth as well, because in our interactions we shape each other's worlds. We do this largely through language, our main tool for sharing knowledge and experiences. And that both frames and distorts our idea of the truth.

Nick Enfield is a professor of linguistics, the scientific study of language. He explains how we use language to convey different meanings. 'The problem is that words have meanings, and they introduce all kinds of implications. Words draw your attention to certain aspects of what you are seeing and not other aspects,' he says.

An extreme example, according to Professor Enfield, is the different ways in which we might use the words 'militant', 'freedom fighter' or 'terrorist'. But he says that even something as simple as how we talk about a dog can have an impact. Interchanging the words 'dog', 'mutt', 'pet', 'mongrel' or 'my good boy' can in turn change how this canine example would be viewed.

'There's never any really neutral way to speak. That is just inherent in language. You are always making a choice to frame what you're saying in a certain way,' says Enfield. 'It is psychologically directing the attention of who you are speaking to, to certain things away from others. And it's just an unavoidable fact of language.'

Truth, then, is more than what *I* perceive in Plato's Cave. It is also the view from where *you* sit and how you describe that to me. The problem is that if you tell me something that's false or I do the same to you, we distort our view of the truth and potentially change the way we act. In our pursuit of the truth, it is a problem as old as language itself.

'How do we protect ourselves from falsehoods given that this language device is untrustworthy in its essence? We depend on other people not to abuse it,' says Enfield. 'This problem with falsehood and misinformation is ancient, but it's supercharged in this day and age by the scale and nature of our communication. So you don't want falsehoods, and when they are reasons for action, that is when they're really dangerous.'

Enfield goes on to say that this is where the big problem lies in this day and age: 'If you get involved in conspiracy theorising and actually act on those things, like you get in a fight with someone or have a falling out with people in your family over some belief that you have, then the consequences come into the real world.'

Conspiracy theories aren't new, of course, just as falsehoods communicated through language aren't. But today, thanks to the internet, we are bombarded with a far greater number of viewpoints. That said, just because people say they believe something doesn't mean they do. Sometimes the truth isn't as important as identifying with a group.

'Making statements about your beliefs is not always [about how] you really believe them and you're going to act on them, but because that belief marks who you are,' says Enfield. 'There's a big grey zone between really believing something and saying you believe it because that's who you are.'

We

So, now we have at least two factors shaping our search for subjective truth. It is what we can discern by observing the world, and it is strongly influenced by how people around us interpret and describe the world. But there's another factor we bring to bear as we seek truth: the very idea of who we are.

To understand how people can view the same information in distinct, rather dynamic ways, it is useful to think in terms of a lens—specifically, that we are all unique and apply a different lens to what is being perceived.

Associate Professor Eryn Newman is a psychologist who has been studying the idea of truth for over fifteen years. As part of that work, she has looked at how, in the search for truth, people's feelings often trump the facts.

'When you think about how we make a decision of truth, when we encounter information, when we recall information, we're making a subjective assessment of the information that's come to mind,' she says. 'A number of relevant inputs feed into that process. The weight of evidence I take on a particular issue is influenced by my attitudes, beliefs and experiences, and so it then shapes the lens I have on a particular issue.'

How does the lens we each bring at any given moment impact the subjective assessment of truth? Maybe people with similar backgrounds and experiences might share a sense of the truth?

Well, it turns out that there's some truth in that, but our individuality works against it. We each bring our own complicated set of experiences to the information around us, experiences that have been shaped by the interactions we've had with each other across our lives.

'There's the accumulation of general knowledge over time. Then there's the experiences we have over the course of our lives that then may impact the way we're encoding events and information around us, and then how we actually end up making sense of those events,' explains Newman. 'Social psychologists have shown that we have different social identities and, depending on a given moment in time, we may make judgements through the lens of a given social identity. So my Kiwi identity may be primed when watching Rugby and shape how fair I perceive the referee to be during an All Blacks match. But I might see something through the lens of my identity as a mother in other situations which can also then shape the way I interpret information in that context.'

Newman adds: 'Understanding the various cognitive and social forces that can shape how we make sense of our information environments helps us to understand how we might arrive at different conclusions after viewing similar content, whether or not we are from similar backgrounds.'

There's one more idea worth zeroing in on here, and that's the interplay between language and our lenses. As linguist Nick Enfield explained earlier, the words we use to share knowledge with each other distort our subjective assessment of truth. A lie is an extreme example of how we create falsehood from our words. But we also bring a lens to every conversation that further complicates our perception of information. Psychologists have some simple tests to demonstrate how this works.

'I give [one person] a piece of text describing a house and I say, "Okay, read this piece of text as a potential home buyer,"' says Eryn Newman. 'I tell another person, "Read this piece of text and you're a burglar." They each read the piece of text and then I test their memory.

People will remember different features about the house depending on whether they were the home buyer or the burglar. That's a really nice, basic example from psychology that highlights the fact that the lens you take with you or that you have in a given situation affects how you encode the information, but also what information you attend to, and then ... what you remember later on.'

Us

Truth is what I can observe. It is what you tell me through language. It is influenced by my lens, which is, in part, my memories and beliefs. It's complex and complicated and subjective. And to find the truth, we rely not just on ourselves but on each other. There's even scientific research to show that our brains are plastic enough to physically change over time depending on the information we take in.

By some estimates, more than 95 per cent of all the available written information has now been put on the internet.[1] There are more than 200 million active websites, and globally we do 3.5 billion searches a day just on Google.[2] We each spend an estimated six hours and thirty-five minutes online every day.[3]

It is predicted that by the end of 2024, there will be enough data on the internet to fill so many old-fashioned DVDs that, if stacked, they would circle the Earth 222 times. That amounts to 175 zetabytes of data, which is a number that I bet means absolutely nothing to most of us but sure sounds impressive.[4]

No wonder so many of us are suffering from information overload. The scale of the information we receive, and the speed at which it's coming at us, are arguably too much for our human brains to keep up with.

Scientists will tell you that our brains are biologically prone to being frugal. We have a limited set of resources to deploy at any given time, which doesn't always leave much computational brain power for critical analysis.

Dan Feuerriegel explains it like this: 'Humans are inherently lazy in a very adaptive way. We'll try to minimise effort wherever we can. All animals do this because they try not to waste energy. So it might be the case that, in contemporary society, fact-checking or figuring out the truth is so effortful that it is easier to just let it be and not evaluate whether something is correct or not.'

On top of that, our brains are wired by all the information and experiences we've ever had. Once we hold particular views and beliefs, they are often very hard to shake, making the search for truth that little bit more difficult.

'Part of the picture with truth assessment is that people aren't always attending critically to the content they encounter,' Eryn Newman says. 'Especially in online environments, we don't have time to dig in, check out the facts, engage in lateral reading, so people often go with an intuitive sense about whether something feels right. And, as it turns out, this feeling-based assessment of truth is really difficult to override.'

These factors make our brains open to exploitation—and to feeling a sense of distrust particularly in an environment where so much information is accompanied by falsehoods.

Nick Enfield points to a quote from Donald Trump adviser Steven Bannon to make the case that this is often deliberate. 'The famous comment from Bannon was to "flood the zone with shit",' says Enfield. 'That means the more you muddy the waters, the harder it is to see what's going on. It's not that they want you to believe things, it's that they want to destabilise what you currently believe so that you don't know what to believe. That is really a destroyer of trust.'

Shared Truth

So what do the complexities associated with the way in which we search for and find the truth mean for our society and for how we trust? Well, without a shared sense of truth we can have doubt, but not trust. As Nobel Prize–winning journalist Maria Ressa says, we must have truth and trust to enable us to work together to solve the tough problems confronting our societies.

'Without facts, you can't have truth. Without truth, you can't have trust. Without trust, we have no shared reality,' says Ressa.[5]

Two clear strands of thought are emerging on how to tackle this.

One is to examine the overall information environment and attempt to scour the falsehoods and disinformation within it. People talk about this as the creation of a healthier online environment. It means actively attending to the regular debunking and fact-checking of the internet to increase trust in online information.

That isn't a new idea. Fact-checking is at the core of most traditional media companies, although in recent years there's been a push to communicate more clearly to audiences the use of fact-checking or verification teams in the making of stories. 'If there's a problematic piece of content, we can develop effective corrections that mitigate its impact. That is the science of debunking,' says Eryn Newman.

But it's debatable whether this type of case-by-case debunking of misinformation and disinformation can in itself have a significant impact. 'The problem is you can't scale up. With the amount of information that is out there, you can't get around to it all,' says Newman.

The second measure to improve the information environment involves government regulation. In 2018, for example, the European Union (EU) introduced a code of practice on disinformation. The code calls out the harm disinformation can do to society by 'eroding trust in institutions and media, putting elections at risk, hampering citizens' ability to make informed decisions and impairing freedom of expression'.[6] In an update to the European code three years ago, the EU added measures aimed at increasing the transparency of political advertising, providing more data to disinformation researchers, and supporting fact-checking across EU countries.

Whether or not this is working remains to be seen. Currently, adherence to the code is voluntary, and many countries are waiting to see if the EU can get it right before deciding whether to follow suit. But if a healthier information environment is not yet a solution, then maybe the answer lies in looking inward, at our own behaviour.

A recent study in Australia found most adults aren't confident in identifying false or misleading online information, even as they encounter more of it. It also found people struggle with other common online tasks. Those who don't struggle tend to be media-literate, defined by the same study as 'the ability to critically engage with media in all aspects of life. It is a form of lifelong literacy that is essential for full participation in society'.[7] But many of us aren't, especially those of us in older and poorer groups.

Some countries have media literacy strategies aimed at educating adults. But Nick Enfield says we should take it even further. 'My view now is that what we need is a new kind of literacy, which includes literacy around our own limitations. So cognitive literacy around what language is and how biased it really is,' he says.

Enfield believes we should all become seekers of the truth, rather than defending what we already think we know. 'You should know your way around your own kind of thinking patterns as someone with an imperfect kind of system of knowledge gathering and processing,' he says. 'I'm committed to basic enlightenment values which say that probably the highest value is self-correction and an openness to being wrong ... [not an] insistence on ... proving others wrong, but proving yourself wrong; not questioning what other people tell you, but questioning what you yourself think is probably true.'

If it is the case that we cannot rediscover trust without truth, then perhaps the place to start is by doing more to discover ourselves. We could start by asking ourselves how we search for subjective truth. How and what do we observe, and how do we use language and interpret it? How do we conquer our own biases and beliefs? How do we emerge from the dark of Plato's Cave to truly see the world around us?

If we can understand how we think, how we find truth and how we can open up our own minds to other ideas, then surely we'll be better equipped to help others do the same.

A huge thanks to Dan Feuerriegel, Nick Enfield and Eryn Newman for freely giving up their time to explain in simple terms some of their complicated work.

Dan Feuerriegel is an ARC DECRA Fellow at the Melbourne School of Psychological Sciences at the University of Melbourne.

Nick Enfield is Professor of Linguistics at the University of Sydney and a co-director of the Sydney Centre for Language Research.

Eryn Newman is Associate Professor in Psychology at the Australian National University School of Medicine and Psychology in Canberra.

Technology Didn't Give Rise to Misinformation—We Did

Ben Decker, Founder and CEO of Memetica, United States

WHILE MANY EXPERTS might try to point to a singular moment in time when disinformation became a driving force of global chaos, they would be wrong. Trust in institutions, the media and facts has always been eroding. The issue is less about the fact that it is happening and more about how quickly it continues to evolve.

We could liken the decay in trust to the rapidly escalating coastal erosion around the world. Coastal erosion is not a new phenomenon. However, human behaviour, be it coastal urbanisation or fossil fuel consumption, has accelerated sea-level rises and disrupted coastal ecosystems, contributing to one of the most worrying existential threats of our lifetime.

But it's not like we didn't see this coming.

The global scientific community has watched the average global sea level rise every year since at least 1880. It was over a century later that Daniel Pauly, a Canadian biologist, published research highlighting how incremental sea-level rises often go unrecognised until they start causing major environmental issues.[1] Pauly's publication created frameworks for measuring various elements of climate change that are still used today. Even more important was his perspective on human bias and the ways in which our personal experiences prevent us from seeing the proverbial forest for the trees.

Much like climate scientists, who have been warning about these issues for decades now, national security experts, academics, historians and journalists have been warning us about our current information ecosystem crisis for more than a half-century. In 1970, Marshall McLuhan, one of the twentieth century's pre-eminent media scholars, who predicted the internet yet did not envisage Google, Facebook, X or TikTok, suggested that World War III would be 'a guerrilla information war with no division between military and civilian participation'.

Sound familiar?

In 1995, Richard Szafranski, a retired Air Force officer, published the journal article 'Theory of Information Warfare: Preparing for 2020,' in which he laid out the various ways in which military adversaries would use technology to attack the knowledge and belief systems of enemy populations. The concept would later evolve into what we know today as fifth-generation warfare, described by David Axe in a 2009 *Wired* article as 'what happens when the world's disaffected direct their desperation at the most obvious symbol of everything they lack'.[2]

While Axe's article was published on a website, and maybe even promoted on social media (although I couldn't find any historical tweets), Szafranski relied on dial-up internet to send emails in 1995, and McLuhan certainly did not have an email address or a Twitch podcast, let alone a verified X account in 1970.

So how could they have known that we would arrive at this crisis without technology?

Disinformation Existed Long before the Internet

Let's take a quick journey back to nineteenth-century India, when the country was still under British rule. It was there, in the small garrison town of Meerut, that a disinformation campaign sparked the embers of the Sepoy Rebellion, the country's ostensible first war of independence.

In 1857, Indians were growing concerned about British rule, particularly after catching wind of a rumour that Christianity was going to be imposed across the entire subcontinent. When a network of clandestine overnight delivery men began doling out chapatti across the country, some thought it was a warning, likening the bread to a Christian wafer, while others, assuming the British had distributed the bread, suspected that it was coated in pork or cow fat as a means of forcing the conversion of the local population. The chapatti deliveries took on a new meaning after the British Army began using a new type of cartridge for its Enfield rifles that required tallow grease made of beef and pork fat—ammunition that was never given to the local Hindu and Muslim conscripts, who were known as Sepoys. The rumour, what we would today call a 'disinformation narrative', sparked a year-long rebellion among the Sepoys, ostensibly the first major challenge to the British Empire in India.

While most historians would probably not categorise a piece of bread as a form of media, it is hard not to view the chapatti as a pre-digital meme. Since there are no photos of the bread in question, I cannot confirm whether or not there were stick figures and snarky phrases carved into each savoury bit of gluten. It turns out that I'm not alone in that search: British military officers, who believed secret notes were hidden in the bread, also came up empty.

But if we look towards a slightly more academic definition of memes as pieces of 'cultural information that pass along from person to person, gradually scaling into a shared social phenomena', as Limor Shifman aptly put it, then the bread meme metaphor makes a lot more sense.

More than 100 years later, the KGB swapped out flour for wood pulp, using a network of bogus newspapers, alongside radio broadcasts and faulty scientific studies, to undermine American credibility in South-East Asia and Eastern Europe by falsely claiming that the United States invented AIDS.

The Age of Algorithms

So, we have established that there is a historical precedent in the pre-internet era for governments, militaries and local communities to hijack communication networks in an effort to influence behaviour at scale. While I have intentionally limited my discussion of the internet as much as possible, it's time to talk about trolls, algorithmic bias and the gamification of our extremely limited attention spans.

Trolling is almost as old as the internet itself. *New York Times* journalist Mattathias Schwartz first coined the term in the late 1980s to describe someone who 'intentionally disrupts online communities'. Without getting into an ethics debate about the difference between good trolls and bad trolls, at their core, trolls exploit the network dynamics of digital media platforms to influence human behaviour.

Bill Wasik, known as the godfather of the flash mob, wrote extensively about the ways in which he leveraged email, blogs and text message chains to encourage mass participation in his stunts. Years later, Wasik noted how his project had highlighted the unintended consequences of technology promoting the ephemerality of mob participation, harnessing what he dubbed the 'joining urge'. Technology did not create flash mobs, but it certainly helped them to grow, and in many ways the rise of the social media algorithm helped disinformation to flourish online.

The expansion of the internet and social media has given users across the world an unprecedented degree of choice about which sources of information to trust. Trolls of all shapes and morals constantly exploit these choices, pushing content and narratives that reinforce existing worldviews and foster connections with like-minded people. To tip the scales a bit further in their favour, they often employ a wide range of tactics to artificially increase the popularity of any given idea, including the use of incendiary claims, fake websites, bot networks and synthetic media, among others. More often than not, trolls take great pains to bypass content moderation systems by operating just below the threshold of enforceable platform violations.

So the same technology that helped fuel the Arab Spring in 2010–11 also facilitated the rise of QAnon, COVID-19 denial, the popularity of global far-right political parties, and racist conspiracies that have inspired far-right mass shooters from South Carolina to New Zealand and beyond.

My existential dread about the steady rise of disinformation in 2016 led me into journalism, a field that I both love and hate. While I will forever love my colleagues at *The New York Times*, I hated the constant burnout and lingering sense of failure. Reporting on disinformation became a constant game of Whac-A-Mole, a Sisyphean task in the most painfully pure sense. Every story became cannon fodder for the left, and another reason to harass me on the right.

It became clear after the 6 January 2021 US Capitol insurrection that there was simply nothing I could do to win the hearts and minds of people who might disagree with me. The same can be said of many talented journalists all over the world, particularly in repressive political contexts and in the Global South, where there is far less global media attention and support for civil society. Unfortunately, my experiences have led me to believe that future attempts to overthrow governments, forcefully move borders and influence enemy populations will not be slowed down by fact-checks and investigative reports about their flaws, corrupt facilitators or ideological inconsistencies.

I don't tell this story to declare that journalism is dead or that the war is lost. It's more about the fact that traditional efforts to counter disinformation don't seem to be working very well.

So How Can We Push Back?

Technology, as I have demonstrated, is a double-edged sword, so regulatory measures might help with our Whac-A-Mole problem, but nothing here is going to get us anywhere near the finish line. Disinformation has become so over-politicised that we cannot and should not expect any government or collection of governments to achieve any level of meaningful consensus. That is not to say adjacent multilateral efforts like the Christchurch Call to Eliminate Terrorist & Violent Extremist Content Online, or legislative agendas like the European Union's Digital Services Act and the UK Online Harms Act, are not worth it. They are. But global, regional and national policy initiatives rarely address the day-to-day happenings affecting everyday people.

The same, unfortunately, can be said about the disinformation industrial complex, where tens (if not hundreds) of millions of dollars have been invested into research and media campaigns intent on countering disinformation. While the efforts are noble, they have come out of a small cluster of elite institutions (some of whom have employed me and/or funded my research), and as Joe Bernstein describes in a piece for *Harpers Magazine*, they represent an 'unofficial partnership between Big Tech, corporate media, elite universities, and cash-rich foundations'.[3] Even worse, there have been sparingly few attempts to monitor and evaluate the impact of any one given program, let alone the entire cottage industry that has emerged in recent years. Until this industry encourages its own Pauly-like equivalent to implement evaluation frameworks, we will simply never know how much or little has been achieved.

At this juncture, we must urgently return to our central thesis: that disinformation is a human problem that requires human solutions. So how can we measure the extent to which we are winning or losing the Great Information War of the twenty-first century?

We need to start thinking about bottom-up, whole-of-society approaches to building more resilient communities online and offline. We need to focus more on people, and on metrics that reflect the rising or falling sea-level equivalent of our social wellbeing, our sense of community.

Last year, Dr Vivek Murthy, the US Surgeon General, declared loneliness the latest public health epidemic, posing health risks as deadly as smoking fifteen cigarettes a day. Murthy linked the loneliness epidemic, which reached a fever pitch during the COVID-19 pandemic, to the impact of social media on youth mental health.

Research shows that over the past twenty years, people aged 15–24 have experienced a whopping 70 per cent drop in time spent with friends,[4] while other studies have shown that people who use social media for two or more hours every day are more than twice as likely to report feeling socially isolated. It's hard not to acknowledge the correlating, if not causal, relationship with the global rise of disinformation, but there is just no tangible way to measure this.

It is in these very moments of social isolation that we are all prone to Reddit rabbit holes and Google deep dives. Seen through a utopian lens (and some of my own personal experiences), the content can range from DIY home repair to basketball trick-shot compilations and cooking recipes. Unfortunately, that's not the reality for many people on today's internet, where loneliness drives individuals deep into fringe communities with different beliefs and norms, some of which include directing hostility at anyone not deemed part of the in-group. This version of the internet is where extremism flourishes, coups are planned and mass shooters are radicalised.

The anonymity offered by the internet can make users feel safe to act in ways that they wouldn't offline for social accountability reasons, creating an online disinhibition effect that allows users to feel more comfortable promoting falsehoods and spewing hate. It is very much as David Axe described in 2009, 'when the world's disaffected direct their desperation at the most obvious symbol of everything they lack'.

If loneliness is at the root of the problem, and the internet is accelerating loneliness, we need to start reinforcing our community bonds in the real world. We need to rid ourselves of the concept of 'the other' and start focusing on 'contributory autonomy', a concept coined by anthropology expert Christopher Kelty, and referring to people's capacity to contribute meaningfully to collective endeavours. When people feel that they are valued and viewed as contributing members of a community, they are less prone to loneliness and more likely to exhibit empathy for others. And empathy is often all it takes to get someone to consider an alternative point of view.

So how do we support programs that increase empathy at scale? Maybe we should start spending more time learning from 'formers', people who have since left extremist groups and online conspiracy communities, to learn how to communicate better with 'the other'.

Several years ago, I was sitting at a bar in Toronto and got into a lengthy discussion with some gen Z flat-earthers. It wasn't really intentional; in fact, I generally try to avoid random social encounters with strangers. They asked if I had a lighter, which I didn't, yet they sat down, eager to share their YouTube findings in an attempt to sell me on the age-old falsehood. With a few beers in me and time to kill, I figured I'd hear them out, never outing myself as a journalist or tipping them off to my suspicions. After a lengthy 45-minute diatribe that felt like hours, I respectfully used their logic to ask a few questions, kindly poking a few holes in the more absurd elements of their case. We shared a few jovial laughs together and ultimately said our goodbyes over a farewell shot of tequila.

Why? Because 'Question Everything' is a two-way street, and it works really well when we're all nice to each other.

Discourse Collapse: How Disinformation Erodes Public Trust

Layla Mashkoor, the Atlantic Council's Digital Forensic Research Lab, Canada

THE INTERNET IS full of fallacies. Online disinformation can sometimes feel like the web's underlying web—woven throughout its corners and dark spaces, often unsophisticated, sometimes complex and absorbing, and, at its worst, dangerous. Disinformation spreads in a multitude of ways across the globe, crossing subject matter, demographic, language, and platform. It adapts to meet the user, identifying the right tone to maximise gullibility. The purveyors of disinformation are countless and sustain a system that influences and shapes our discourse. Disinformation is on display in many digital offerings, whether as a service offered by marketing firms, as a political tool used to shape conversations, or as a strategy deployed in wars to feign justifications for violence. Like its subject matter, the business of disinformation is vast, and it has been quietly normalised across industries and governments.

The impact of this is detrimental to our shared information spaces, and the threat is heightened around high-stakes events like elections, wars and mass demonstrations. Disinformation erodes the public's ability to earnestly navigate the web.

Access to verified, evidence-based information is vital for making well-informed decisions or determining one's own position on an issue.

During breaking news scenarios, like severe weather events or conflicts, access to good information can be lifesaving. Unfortunately, in such scenarios, which are notorious information black holes, false narratives often begin spreading minutes after an incident, as malicious actors seek to quickly draft a version of reality that suits their interests—political or otherwise—and amplify it using deceptive methods, such as inauthentic accounts, fictitious statements, forged documents or AI-generated synthetic media. This results in an information disorder that leaves the truth in an unfortunate position: often late to arrive and competing against scores of well-circulated, well-worn narratives that seek to craft an alternative storyline. This is why social media can sometimes feel like a landscape of competing realities.

The preservation of democratic norms and institutions is greatly benefited by healthy information systems, underscoring the need to protect our online spaces. Allowing disinformation to balloon threatens the integrity of our information, institutions and democracies.

Foreign Influence Operations

Forty years ago, it would have seemed nonsensical to suggest an investigation into foreign actors creating fake social media accounts to impersonate people in other countries in order to infiltrate local discussions and influence politics. Today, this is an activity that takes place around the globe and is a commonplace line of investigation. Russia, Iran and China are among the most well-documented actors utilising foreign influence operations to achieve political and strategic gains. Over the years, we've observed these threat actors apply various degrees of sophistication and effectiveness in their online disinformation campaigns. In authoritarian states, governments are often the largest and most well-resourced bad actors on social media, deploying domestic influence operations to target human rights defenders, opponents and journalists, and foreign influence operations to achieve policy aims.

It can sometimes be difficult to ascertain the motives of those initiating disinformation operations. Some operations are heavy-handed, pursuing a clear and specific goal; for example, smearing an opponent during an election. At other times, these operations do not follow a specific agenda and instead deploy competing narratives, a strategy in which malicious actors flood discussions around a specific topic with opposing perspectives, often ranging from mild to extreme. This tactic serves to drown out authentic voices, rendering it more difficult to access genuine information and, ultimately, adds confusion to the conversation—feeding the adage, 'If you can't convince them, confuse them'.

For example, ahead of the 2016 US elections, a troll farm operating from Saint Petersburg in Russia created social media accounts impersonating Americans in order to stoke racial divisions amid the Black Lives Matter (BLM) movement. Research from the University of Washington in 2017 examined online conversations around US shooting events in 2016, focusing on groupings of pro- and anti-BLM discussions.[1] Russian trolls were found to have contributed divisive content to both sides of the conversation, sharing highly inflammatory posts using inauthentic accounts designed to reinforce stereotypes. For example, the fictitious pro-BLM accounts used photos of burning police cars and black power flags on their profiles, while the fictitious anti-BLM accounts used photos of cowboy hats and guns.

Eight years later, in the lead-up to the 2024 US election, the tactic persisted. In November 2023, Meta announced that it had removed nearly 5000 China-based accounts that impersonated Americans to debate political issues. The accounts shared criticisms of both sides of the political spectrum, not favouring one party over the other.

This tactic pollutes online conversations by taking a maximalist approach. It floods social media with competing narratives in order to distort the information landscape, compromising the integrity of online discussions. Consequently, it becomes challenging for the public to retrieve information or draw a conclusion about a subject.

It appears that the goal of some disinformation operations may be to make the online space so chaotic, frustrating and contradictory that users are compelled to disengage from the topic altogether.

Another common feature of many foreign influence campaigns is the identification and exploitation of authentically divisive domestic issues. In another example from the 2020 US election, Iranian actors impersonated the US white supremacy group Proud Boys in an influence campaign targeting US officials. Two Iran-based actors hacked at least one US state's elections website to obtain confidential voter data, which was used to send threatening pro–Donald Trump emails to various US political and campaign officials from accounts that impersonated the Proud Boys. In response, the United States charged two men associated with the Iranian cyber-group Emennet Pasargad.

Russia is particularly adept at using this polarisation tactic and frequently applies it to influence operations across the world. Russia's global influence strategy is to position itself as an alternative to Western powers, and it seeks to win allies and popular support by exploiting complex histories and geopolitical dynamics. In the Middle East, for example, Russia promotes anti-US narratives, hoping to widen the schism between Arab countries and the United States in order to position itself as a more beneficial ally to these nations. To justify its actions in Ukraine, Russia will cite the Iraq War and spread narratives regarding Western hypocrisy. Russia behaves similarly in West Africa, where it works to amplify anti-France narratives in order to promote itself as an alternative security guarantor.

These influence operations seek to deepen existing fissures within the target's domestic landscape. They are particularly dangerous because they prey on feelings of injustice and exploit real grievances. They manipulate real emotions to spread falsehoods, and they weave threads of truth throughout the disinformation to maximise impact. Some of the most effective disinformation campaigns are those that elicit emotional responses because counter-disinformation measures can struggle to break through an emotional response.

Countering these types of operations requires navigating complex local dynamics and acknowledging genuine grievances.

Allied Influence Operations

In the spring of 2024, during the war between Israel and Hamas, the Digital Forensic Research Lab (DFRLab) identified an online influence operation targeting US politicians and Canadian media that *The New York Times* later attributed to the Israeli Government. This is significant as it exemplifies a country launching a foreign influence campaign against its own allies—a further entrenching and normalisation of state-sponsored disinformation.

In February 2024, independent researcher Marc Owen Jones first reported on an inauthentic X network spreading messages in support of Israel and critical of the United Nations Relief and Works Agency for Palestine Refugees (UNRWA). This occurred as several countries were ceasing funding to UNRWA over allegations from Israel that staff members had participated in the 7 October 2023 terrorist attack. Further investigation by the DFRLab revealed how this network of inauthentic accounts impersonated Americans and targeted US politicians in an effort to influence policy, including then president Joe Biden, vice-president Kamala Harris and various members of Congress. The network was unsophisticated in its creation. For example, the DFRLab reported that

> one account identified as 'a middle-aged African American woman' while using a male name and an avatar of a Black man, another identified as a 'Jewish man' while using a female display name and avatar, another identified as a 'white American man' yet had an avatar of a Black man.[2]

The DFRLab also uncovered a sister network using AI-generated images to promote Islamophobic content. The network promoted a fake Canadian non-profit organisation, United Citizens for Canada

(UCC), that claimed to have been created by citizens concerned about 'violent Islamic movements and organizations in Canada'.[3] The inauthentic network promoted UCC's content and amplified it to Canadian media figures, presumably seeking further amplification, with comments suggesting there was a risk of sharia law being applied in Canada. The network also falsified social media engagement for the organisation in an attempt to forge credibility.

Meta and OpenAI attributed these disinformation campaigns to the Israeli political consulting firm STOIC. Meta also took the unique step of issuing the company a cease-and-desist letter to halt activities that violated the platform's policies. *The New York Times* found that Israel's Ministry of Diaspora Affairs hired Tel Aviv–based STOIC to foster online support for its war in Gaza.[4] The ministry allocated a budget of $2 million for the operation.

As social media increasingly becomes part of domestic and foreign policy toolkits, democratic states must set norms around acceptable behaviours and condemn the use of state-sponsored disinformation. Worryingly, recent examples suggest things may be trending in the other direction. In June 2024, Reuters reported that during the height of COVID-19, the US military launched an influence operation aimed at discrediting Chinese-made vaccines. The campaign used inauthentic accounts to impersonate individuals in the Philippines and spread anti-vaccine content during the global pandemic.[5] As the United States publicly advocated for vaccines, it was operating a covert influence campaign that spread anti-vaccine content.

AI-Accelerated Disinformation

Artificial intelligence acts as a catalyst for disinformation, whether it's a deepfake video, robocall audio or a fake image generated to closely match a real one. Increasingly, AI is being used to advance and accelerate disinformation. The growing accessibility of AI tools and synthetic image generators provides the capacity for disinformation to be created at scale. Whereas efforts to deceive once relied on manual tactics, like image editing in Photoshop, AI lowers the technical barrier for entry and offers the ability to automate several elements of deceptive campaigns. That said, while AI plays a critical role in advancing the threats associated with disinformation, its integration into the disinformation ecosystem has not been as rapid as was initially forecast.

Tracking deepfake videos released over the course of the war in Ukraine offers a window into the evolution of the technology and its improvements. One month after Russia's invasion of Ukraine, pro-Russia sources spread a poorly made deepfake video in which Ukrainian President Volodymyr Zelenskyy was alleged to have resigned and fled Ukraine. At the time, the video was mocked for its rudimentary quality. Since then, deepfake technology has made significant improvements, with later releases becoming increasingly realistic.

AI brings risks and advancements, and, as it continues to integrate into our systems, detection and transparency functions must be prioritised when building and deploying tools like image generators. Currently, AI detection tools are imperfect, meaning that manual review continues to be the most effective mechanism for identifying AI content. The uncanny valley effect of synthetic media typically makes it possible to determine whether an image is AI, but as the technology develops, this is becoming an unreliable method for detection. As noted by Sam Gregory, Executive Director of human rights organisation WITNESS, the disclosure and provenance of AI-generated media must be prioritised, with a responsibility pipeline that integrates developers and platforms into solutions, rather than placing the burden of responsibility for detection on real-world users.[6]

Preserving Information Integrity

There are no easy answers when it comes to resolving the threat of disinformation. The first step is to accept a degree of imperfection.

Many have envisioned the internet as a digital public square and, if we think of our online spaces like our offline spaces, we should strive for prevention and control with the understanding that perfection is impossible. Just as public offences are impossible to eliminate entirely from the public square, disinformation may be impossible to eliminate from the online square. Expectation-setting is a helpful starting point.

Efforts to identify, expose and remove online disinformation are both Sisyphean and Herculean. A community of open-source researchers, fact-checkers, journalists, academics, programmers and many others dedicate an immeasurable degree of effort to controlling the spread of online harms. However, this objective can often feel like a moving target. Only half of the puzzle is visible to us, and other stakeholders must also be involved in crafting solutions.

Social media platforms play a critical role in fencing in the spread of disinformation. Through transparency reports, whether mandated by policy or offered voluntarily, platforms can begin to offer insights into their operations and decision-making structures that will better inform future recommendations. Co-designing solutions with civil society organisations also allows for local nuances to be considered. But to continue to investigate online harms, researchers require access to data. Unfortunately, platforms are shifting away from providing the data and access they once did. From X's prohibitively expensive application programming interface (API) to Meta sunsetting its CrowdTangle tool, the research community has been forced to do more with less. This is chiefly concerning because, as the threat of disinformation is being accelerated by AI, the loss of research tools puts us at a disadvantage in efforts to identify and expose falsehoods.

The pendulum must swing away from the normalisation of disinformation and influence tactics. The standardisation of online disinformation as a strategy used by states in geopolitical rifts accelerates a phenomenon that we at the DFRLab have referred to as 'discourse collapse'. This happens when our interpretation of reality is not just malleable but preyed on for deception; when bad actors attempt to draft our realities before they unfold; when institutions held to higher standards engage in the same malicious behaviours they publicly condemn; when information is hardly tethered to reality, when it's malleable, can bend in any direction, whiplash back against its own intended message, and take on new meaning depending on the speaker.

Discourse collapse emerges from the cracks in public trust. The threat of discourse collapse reminds us why it is imperative to protect our democratic institutions and norms from those who seek to use the online space to undermine them.

Agree to Disagree: Trust and Civic Debate

Tracey Kirkland, Continuous News Editor, ABC, Australia

A FEW DECADES AGO I was walking along a beach in Spain with a friend and we were having a philosophical discussion about absolute truth. I, with youthful zeal, was arguing for its existence and he, against.

'Take this ocean, for example,' he said, gesturing expansively towards the horizon. 'I might say it's warm and you might say it's cold. The truth is relative.'

'We can argue all we want about our experience of it,' I said. 'The truth is, this water is 23.6 degrees Celsius.'

Enjoying a robust debate, we discussed the merits of science (water temperature) and fairly reliable information (the handwritten sign at the beach), then agreed to disagree, changing the conversation to something we both agreed on: the merits of good tapas.

I compare this with my experience at a dinner party a few months ago when a philosophical debate with someone turned both hostile and personal when we disagreed. You might argue it's just individual circumstance and the company I keep, but I've noticed that the temperature on topics of community concern has been turned up to the point where people are not only definitively taking sides, they are also becoming openly antagonistic, even towards friends.

'I've done my research,' my dinner companion argued, which, I soon realised, meant they'd read something on Facebook. In fact, that wasn't the only time this year I have been cornered at what would normally be a mundane event and then lectured about one conspiracy or another. One close friend has cut off all contact with me because of my position in the mainstream media, believing I'm involved in covert, government-aligned, COVID propaganda.

Without getting too nostalgic, that Spanish conversation, which is significant enough to have stayed with me for thirty years, took place pre-internet, pre–social media, pre-COVID, pre–mobile phone. It was a time of widespread trust in public institutions, government agencies, media and science, which—despite all their faults and biases—were seen as essentially trustworthy.

In my experience, and in the experience of many others who work in the public sphere, since then something has fundamentally shifted. The public has grown increasingly sceptical of our institutions, which has caused a cataclysmic shift in the way we discuss important public matters. Civic debate has fractured. You only have to look at X (formerly Twitter) to get a taste of what's changed. On social media platforms, what was once civil debate is now vile public brawling and name calling.

British philosopher AC Grayling blames, in part, our online platforms. 'There is a significant difference in kind now, not just in degree, of scepticism and doubt in political processes and institutions,' he says, 'and the difference in kind is the result of the universal opportunity to publish one's opinions on social media where people can rally support in their social media silo. The resultant anger and frustration will result in conspiracy theories and the pushing of misinformation, false facts and distortions in order to score a point. The result is a kind of mess, and we are in that mess now.'

You could argue it is too simple to blame social media for the deterioration of civility in public debate. But something in this current age is different, sometimes dangerously so.

The high-level discourse that flowed after the attempted assassination of then presidential candidate Donald Trump at a rally outside Butler, Pennsylvania on 13 July 2024 is a great example. World leaders were quick to point to the polarisation and incivility in public conversations as a major cause.

Then US president Joe Biden called for calm: 'Our politics has gotten too heated ... we all have responsibilities to lower the temperature.'

Former US president Barack Obama called for reflection: 'We should ... use this moment to recommit ourselves to civility and respect in our politics.'

Australian Prime Minister Anthony Albanese called for wisdom: 'We all need to be on guard against those seeking to use misinformation to create division.'

But as far-right politics creeps its way across Europe, we can see this is not an isolated example. On 15 May 2024, Slovakian Prime Minister Robert Fico, himself blamed for inciting divisive debate, was shot several times in an assassination attempt. Here, too, world leaders pointed the finger at public hostility.

'I am horrified by where the hatred towards another political option can lead,' said Fico's close ally and president-elect Peter Pellegrini. 'We don't have to agree on everything, but there are plenty of ways to express our disagreement democratically and legally.'

'It should be a warning to us about where deepening spite and aggressiveness in society can lead,' said Czech President Petr Pavel.

Slovakia's outgoing president Zuzana Čaputová let loose a rallying cry: 'The hateful rhetoric we've been witnessing in society leads to hateful actions. Please, let's stop it.'

More than a year earlier, in a speech at the second Summit for Democracy, UN Secretary-General António Guterres gave the same warning: 'The walls are closing in on civic spaces. Freedom of expression is in freefall. Dissenting voices are silenced. Engulfed in crises, people are being easily seduced by promises of simple solutions.

Polarisation is being supercharged by social media. Irrationality is running rampant.'[1]

The UN leader said the world was suffering from a bad case of 'Trust Deficit Disorder'. 'People are losing faith in political establishments, polarisation is on the rise and populism is on the march,' said Guterres. 'Mis- and disinformation is poisoning public discourse, polarising communities, and eroding trust in institutions.'

Australia is not immune from the ills of this increasing polarisation in civic debate. According to ASIO Director-General of Security Mike Burgess, 'politically motived violence now joins espionage and foreign interference as our principal security concerns'.[2]

Sadly, along with failing trust in institutions and the erosion of civil debate has come a distrust of 'facts'. Science has become an obvious target, taking a particularly hard hit during COVID. But even before the pandemic, personal experience, heightened by social media algorithms, had taken on new significance. In an interview with the *Washington Post* in 2018, US president Trump succinctly summed up the change: 'I have a gut, and my gut tells me more sometimes than anybody else's brain can ever tell me.'

For half of US citizens, this seems a preposterous statement. For the other half, though, it makes perfect sense. And that division is indicative of this new era where personal experience outguns facts for millions of people. What's more, Trump and leaders like him are simultaneously highly distrusted and highly trusted—it just depends on which side of the political divide a person sits.

Despite Trump being a poster boy for intuitive facts—'alternative facts'—the trend is global. This new world of 'gut feeling' is marked by an unsettling decline in respect for objective truth, leaving citizens to question the motives of their leaders and organisations, especially in the public sphere. According to the Reuters Institute's *Journalism, Media and Technology Trends and Predictions 2024* report, that change in trust is prompting people to look for answers in new, less trustworthy places: 'The toxic nature of many conversations about news and politics [has] pushed many people towards private spaces such as messaging apps. This has led to even more unrepresentative and problematic content for the more open platforms to deal with.'[3]

Add to this the rise of artificial intelligence (AI), which can distort the truth with barely a trace of manipulation, plus the fact that social media is rife with misinformation and disinformation, and extreme political polarisation, and we have the perfect recipe for ugly and dangerous civic debate.

The problem seems to be terrifyingly circular. As trust in public institutions diminishes, civic conversations are poisoned; and as civic conversations are poisoned, trust in public institutions diminishes. The only way out is to break the cycle, which is difficult when social media companies allow alternative facts, gut truths, mistruths and outright lies to be shared and amplified. It means citizens are left feeling like there are only two sides to any debate, with little nuance or grey areas, and that they need to pick a side and defend it with their lives. Dissenting voices are ignored, or worse, silenced.

It also leaves large parts of the community feeling confused and alienated. Those who choose not to rely on intuition are left to wonder who they can trust and where the truth actually lies. How can we have strong public debate if those who speak up are regularly vilified or cancelled?

What Has Happened to Good Public Discourse?

We have the Greek philosopher Socrates to thank for introducing the ancient world to the craft of public debate as a way of solving pressing civic issues. It's well documented that, in ancient Greece, men skilled in the art of argument gathered in town squares and amphitheatres to eyeball each other and work through the moral and political issues of the day. Plato and Aristotle brought a formality to the proceedings, introducing more structured debating practices that included the trading of questions and answers between opponents—or, in modern day debating terms, argument and rebuttal. In Aristotle's mind at least, this kind of interaction between people with competing views or interests was a means of calming dissent and fostering better relations.

Humans being human, as the practice developed it became clear that public debates were not always about finding the best solutions. For some, it became a sport. Dodgy showmen, trained in the art of performance, began debating for the sake of winning alone. So by the time civic debates were thriving across ancient Rome, the philosophers Cicero and Quintilian were kept busy trying to convince the public that good debaters must demonstrate both the art of persuasion *and* be of sound character.

Ancient India and China also developed cultures that encouraged lively public debates, and by the Middle Ages civic debating was a distinctive feature of Christian medieval intellectual gatherings, further enhanced by the advent and growth of universities. By the seventh century, Islam had initiated its own cultural debating traditions with a focus on theological questioning.

Setting aside debating as a sport, the common thread running through this rich history is the clear purpose of considering and questioning the views of others *for a shared outcome that benefits society*. There is also a focus on the arts of both critical thinking and persuasion.

But as democracies grew larger, so did party politics, laying the groundwork for divisive debate based on toeing the party line and electioneering. According to AC Grayling, this ushered in something about which US founding father James Madison had expressed fear at the end of the eighteenth century. In Madison's Federal Paper No. 10, says Grayling, 'he points out that the big danger in democracy is factionalism, meaning parties, political parties, forming and competing with each other to get their hands on the levers of power so that they can run their agenda. And this has become entrenched in the political processes of democracies or so-called democracies, and this is where the poison flows from'.

This goes some way towards explaining the present time where, globally, politics is more polarised than ever. The place we now air our public grievances is no longer a small, face-to-face marketplace hosting debates between like-minded people with civic intent, but rather a global, virtual marketplace of hidden corners and anonymous speakers who can spout whatever they like with little restriction or oversight.

There's no question the internet and social media have incredible upsides. Most of us know at least one couple who met online. We have all likely used the internet in the past twenty-four hours to search for information. A girlfriend going through breast cancer treatment told me recently of the incredible support she has received within online communities. Fellow survivors helped her choose surgeons and tattooists, and assisted her in navigating an incredibly emotional and difficult path forward. The impact literally has been life-changing.

But this same public space is where algorithms rule, where lies and conspiracy theories can be amplified within silos and echo chambers, where misinformation and disinformation are threatening public conversation to the point where polarisation has gained a dangerous foothold, and cries of 'If you're not with me, you're against me' ring loud. In this murky arena, civility is absent as people pick a corner, erect barricades of 'alternative facts' based on their 'research', and throw missiles of bile and contempt, not willing to even imagine a metaphorical bridge crossing the gulf of opinion. In this environment, scepticism sizzles, doubts are magnified and fear takes hold.

Shouldn't we therefore be asking ourselves where to find reputable sources of information, and questioning whether social media is really offering us 'facts'? What are we liking? What are we forwarding?

A study from Yale shows that the reward system set up by the social media platforms, which encourages likes and comments, means users often don't take much notice of *what* they are sharing, greatly expanding the amount of misinformation being circulated. 'This was kind of a shocker for the misinformation research community,' says research co-author Gizem Ceylan. 'What we showed is that, if people are habitual sharers, they'll share any type of information, because they don't care [about the content]. All they care about is likes and attention.'[4]

While social media is an amazing tool for connection and sharing information, we need to understand its limitations and its dangers. There is so much room for distortion and falsehoods, and what we see is often not real at all. Some people get their information from social media without ever interacting with facts. If their 'research' is flawed, their arguments become flimsy, ill-informed and unbalanced—and sometimes dangerous. Uncivil debates then erupt that are based on false evidence and lies. We need to see this for what it is.

It's especially difficult for women, people with a culturally diverse or Indigenous heritage, and those from the LGBTQIA+ communities to find their voice in this fraught online space, as they have become relentlessly targeted. Some have become too scared to speak out lest they are publicly shamed for their views, become the target of vicious pile-ons or, at the other extreme, are cancelled. Online hate has become so bad that many media companies have turned off their comments sections. In an interview with *ABC News*, American author and social commentator Roxanne Gay lamented the state of our civic square. 'The older I get, the less tolerance I have for being treated badly,' says Gay. 'And I wish that we had a better calibre of public discourse. I wish we could disagree without it reverting to name calling. I wish that I could have an opinion without someone telling me I'm ugly ... What does that have to do with what I said?'[5]

Julie Inman Grant, Australia's eSafety Commissioner, who has pitted herself against some of the world's biggest, most powerful companies for their lax attitude towards online safety, says sexualised abuse towards women is rife online: 'When women come to us, they can be dealing with death threats, doxing, threats of rape and explicit content of them shared without consent. The tactics might vary but the agenda is often the same: to intimidate them into silence and submission. If we don't want women's voices hounded out of online spaces, we need to protect them.'

Research into online safety has shown that one in three women surveyed in Australia experienced online abuse in a work context and frequently lowered their public profiles because of that abuse.[6] If women stop speaking, they lose their advocacy, their agency, their voice.

Natalie Harvey, CEO of women's media and lifestyle website *Mamamia*, also worries about the direction in which the social media sphere is headed. 'When Meta turned off news content in Canada, it was replaced by politics that was not fact-checked. Instead, we got politics from influencers. What does that do to our town square?' says Harvey.

'What is becoming commonplace unfortunately across social media platforms is that what people are seeing or being served as news, is just uninformed opinion,' says Network 10 President and Paramount Australia Head of Streaming Beverley McGarvey. 'It is more important, now than ever before, to maintain trusted and regulated news sources on platforms, because without this, the avalanche of misinformation will continue to propagate.'

There is also so much content available online, a firehose of yelling and provocation, that it is hard to figure out who to believe. And the institutions once trusted to sort through the noise, to inform us of the facts, have become diminished in this fragmented civic square.

Research done by the Pew Research Center in the United States shows that Americans expect distrust in others to grow even more in the years ahead and trust in institutions to keep falling,[7] setting up a future where divisions widen, cynicism skyrockets, people are more disconnected and distracted from what politicians are actually doing, and there's a significant withdrawal of voices from vital discourse. That should have us all concerned about the consequences for democracy and social cohesion.

How to Have Strong Public Discourse without Compromising What We Stand for

Our civic debate *can* be different, but we need to be deliberate about it. Firstly, we need to ask ourselves what kind of society we want to build? A certain level of distrust is a healthy thing. Scepticism alone is not a bad thing. Debate, by its very nature, advocates for more than one outlook. But if people can't agree on basic facts or find a place to put their trust, how can we find a community-centred way forward to deal with the pressing issues of the day? The whole purpose of debate is to understand each other better and find an outcome that benefits society. In fact, after a good debate, the listeners should have learnt something or heard a different perspective that may inform their own opinion.

Debating, publicly or formally, should be a healthy and respectful way of hearing the views of others while airing our own concerns or opinions. It should help to *resolve* conflict, not *create* it. We don't need to all agree—that is not the point—but we must be able to discuss issues without humiliation or personal attack. When I was growing up, if someone in my household resorted to name calling, that meant they had lost the argument.

We all trust what we already know, and algorithms serve us up more of the same. It seems safe enough, but we need to recognise that it can actually be unhealthy to only read what we agree with. Instead of existing in our own digital bubbles, we need to consciously seek out and consume information that challenges our opinions and helps us empathise with others who think differently. We need to be willing to see the other side. We also need a vibrant civic space that has room for nuance and opposing views. Bridges can then be built on shared values of honesty, goodwill and openness, rather than rifts being caused by narrow individual opinions. And we need strong education campaigns that teach citizens to think critically, to question what they read, to search for facts, and to exchange ideas in a way that is civil and open minded, with a focus on good research and debate.

I am the editor of a national, continuous news channel, and every day my team and I try to facilitate discussions about the major issues of the day in a way that informs, illuminates and educates. Sure, we hear high-pitched accusations of bias, stupidity and incompetence all the time from people on one side of the debate—sometimes both—who don't like what we discuss, but we don't let that distract us from the important job at hand. We have a crucial role to play in our democracy, ensuring the voiceless are given a voice, the powerful are held to account, and the facts are elevated above the noisy melee that now constitutes 'news'.

Likewise, the expectation—of experts, politicians, in fact all of us—should be that we won't resort to personal attacks in public conversations but will instead debate with rigour, drawing on our expertise and experience. How else can we expect consensus on the major issues of our time? Climate change policy, for example, is being stymied by mudslinging and mis/disinformation. Climate wars have dominated Australian politics over the past decade, even as the country has been burned by massive bushfires and towns were wiped out by the worst floods in a century. Throughout, civil debate has been largely absent and polarisation rife. The only viable way forward, regarding climate change and the myriad other issues impacting us right now, is for us all to rise above party politics, identify the stakeholders and their hold on the debate, make clear the facts, and talk to each other with respect and a desire for solutions.

An additional step would be to consider the creation of citizens' assemblies, where informed citizens gather to discuss, talk, listen and then advise government, as a way to help strengthen civic debate and democracy. The assembly's main goal is to *learn*, then thoroughly debate a chosen issue and present a set of recommendations. There are great examples in Belgium, Canada, Iceland and the United Kingdom. According to AC Grayling: 'The astonishing thing that comes out of deliberative democracy exercises is that people's minds do come to be changed and they do come to understand the interests and motivations of other people.'

Could we take this one step further and develop an online citizens' assembly? It could be a digital space where well prepared citizens could set out their thoughts and enjoy robust debate (read: listen and learn), and where the audience could read and interact with the result. In some ways, it is what X used to be. Could we deliberately and purposely recreate that with the shared goal of strengthening democracy?

Government institutions and media certainly have roles to play in improving civic debate. They need to be transparent and inclusive, honest about their bias and willing to admit mistakes. And they need to listen carefully to all sectors of the public. What is the point of the media exposing greed and corruption, calling the powerful to account, 'following the money', if no-one believes them?

'To harness the power of democracy, we must strengthen its defences,' says António Guterres. 'This means investing in a new social contract between government and their people to rebuild trust and social cohesion; bolstering the system of checks and balances; tackling inequalities, combating corruption, prioritising education and expanding opportunities; setting up guardrails in the digital world to protect against its perils while realising its promise; and realising the universality of all human rights—civil, cultural, economic, political and social.'[8]

We need a civic space, firm ground, a marketplace, where ideas can be aired, shared, and allowed to rub against each other to be tested, without fear of ridicule—like what happened during my walk on that Spanish beach three decades ago. This space needs to be saturated by a minimum level of trust, truth and civility, by basic decency, so that fake news, influencers and misinformation don't become our accepted norms. The safety in a space like that doesn't exclude hard discussions and differing opinions, but it does encourage the crucial bubbling up of ideas and innovation. Such a space will help us leave this Age of Doubt behind and embrace a future that, while still complex, nuanced and ever-changing, will also be vibrant, cohesive and democratic.

Right now, a whole lot more debate is needed.

PART II
TRUST AND DEMOCRACY

Trust in Government and Radical Impartiality

Patricia Karvelas, journalist and broadcaster, ABC, Australia

A 'CRISIS' IN DEMOCRACY is the framing we've come to continually hear—often from the media, which has a tendency to escalate our legitimate fears at times when we most need a sober, reflective and constructive approach to grappling with what are very real threats to our social and democratic compact. In Western democracies around the world, the liberal democratic project is under serious strain, exacerbated by social media algorithms that are fuelling dissent and polarising people further, rather than bringing citizens together on what unites us. We have already witnessed very real risks to our social cohesion, and the disturbing emergence of bad actors—both domestic and foreign—who are sowing dissent on contentious issues in our community.

We are at a genuine crossroads, with trust in politics and institutions fast eroding. We need real solutions to raise the democratic literacy levels of all Australians. We need to equip the public with the tools to identify misinformation and disinformation, and we need to place obligations on tech giants to stem the rise of deliberate lies that feed distrust in our democratic institutions.

In July 2024, the Albanese government's Strengthening Democracy Taskforce released a report based on wide consultation and research.

It positioned Australia as a 'global leader' and 'innovator' in democracy and argued we need to recognise and safeguard against our own vulnerability to anti-democratic headwinds, and look at defending democracy as an issue of international importance. The paper declared that Australia shouldn't become 'an island of democracy in a sea of autocracy'. It found that Australia is in a stronger position than many other countries, but there are worrying signs of polarisation and distrust in our democratic system that we need to reckon with. It also rightly identified the problems—but we need more action to arrest the decline.[1]

A recent analysis by local cyber-security company CyberCX reveals just how serious this is. A network of at least 5000 AI-run accounts has been exposed in a suspected Chinese information warfare campaign to spread divisive political discourse on the social media platform X. CyberCX has uncovered an operation linked to a Chinese university and AI company that appears to mainly target contentious American narratives but has sometimes also engaged with Australian content. 'While the information operation capability is currently relatively ineffective, we assess it could be leveraged to conduct harmful activities in future,' the company warns in the report.[2]

Researchers also warn that the cluster of unauthentic accounts, dubbed the Green Cicada Network, is almost certainly controlled and coordinated by an AI large language model (LLM)–based system. They also found that while the network predominantly engages with US political and cultural issues, it has also been observed amplifying and intervening in hot-button political issues in Australia, the United Kingdom, India, Japan and other democratic countries. 'We observed limited amplification of Australia-specific issues and posting from purportedly Australian personas. Amplified issues include support or opposition to political candidates, nuclear energy, economics, housing, migration, protests and foreign policy,' says the CyberCX report.

'Here we have a fake network that is infiltrating our democratic discourse and trying not necessarily to support one side or the other of these debates, but trying to drive a wedge [between] sides of this debate, trying to deepen division and deepen polarisation,' says CyberCX spokesperson Katherine Manste. At this point, the AI is apparently not very good at what it is trying to do, but it will inevitably get better and will become harder for experts to even identify. This disruption will happen without our knowledge and could manipulate our debates to create further distrust.

Let's reflect on the assertion that the network is trying to 'drive a wedge' between different sides of democratic debates. That idea alone should send chills up the spines of all Australians. It demonstrates that division is the aim here, and that will have deleterious impacts on our democracy.

The Joint Select Committee on Social Media and Australian Society has been hearing about how social media companies operate in Australia, including the impact they have, particularly on young people. The committee is considering what changes the parliament needs to introduce to deal with what has become a collective crisis. It has been contemplating the big question of what kind of regulation may be effective in Australia to reduce harm.

Specifically, the committee has been exploring the decision of Meta to abandon deals under the News Media Bargaining Code, the important role of Australian news and public interest journalism in countering misinformation and disinformation on digital platforms, and broader issues relating to the influences and impacts of what Australians see on social media. The reality is that social media blew up so fast and accelerated so hard that the consequences were barely debated. We gave away our privacy—we overshared and allowed algorithms to tell us what we wanted and what we liked without really reckoning with what it meant and how we wanted to use it. We only started having deeper ethical deliberations after we were already addicts and mugged by the pace of change. Now we are immersed in a debate about whether we should ban platforms like TikTok because of its data vulnerability in China, but the horse has in many ways already bolted. Millions of young people are not only obsessed with the platform, many have also monetised it, making it a brave government that stands in the way of that basic economic reality.

In Australia, democracy will be significantly further challenged by AI, which has moved from sci-fi fantasy to everyday use—from facial recognition apps on our phones to the $100 billion ChatGPT platform that generates human-like responses to every possible instruction; from deepfakes with the potential to swing elections and damage democracy, to the uncontested inevitability of workers being made redundant. All of it is happening in real time, and it is having a big impact on trust. It has the potential to disrupt democracy further without intervention and reform.

What Does the Research Say?

Australia has relatively high levels of satisfaction with its democracy. In a recent survey by the non-partisan Pew Research Center in the United States, out of twenty-four high- and middle-income democracies, Australia had the third-highest level of satisfaction with the way its democracy was working, behind India and Sweden. Additionally, Australia had the largest increase in satisfaction between 2022 and 2023.[3]

The head of the School of Politics and International Relations at the Australian National University (ANU), Professor Nicholas Biddle, told me that dissatisfaction with democracy is concentrated in a number of groups: those with low levels of education, those in the middle part of the age distribution (particularly 25–34 years), those with low incomes, those who think rising prices are a problem, and those who think the income distribution in Australia is unfair. Biddle also said satisfaction with democracy declined after the Indigenous Voice to Parliament referendum. While those who voted 'Yes' and those who voted 'No' were less satisfied, the decline in satisfaction was much larger for 'Yes' voters.[4]

Biddle explained that satisfaction with democracy in Australia by January 2024 varied across three main dimensions—age, education, and income. Younger Australians were the most likely to say that they were fairly or very satisfied with democracy (76.7 per cent for those aged 18–24). Older Australians were also relatively satisfied, with a value of 73.3 per cent for those aged 65–74 years and 73.6 per cent for those aged seventy-five years and older. All other age groups, however, had values below seven-in-ten, with the lowest level of satisfaction among those aged 25–34 years (63.4 per cent satisfied or very satisfied).

For those who had not completed Year 12, satisfaction with democracy was quite low, with only 61.1 per cent fairly or very satisfied. Those with a degree or higher qualification were the most satisfied, with 78.2 per cent of those with an undergraduate degree reporting that they were satisfied or very satisfied, and 76.7 per cent of those with a postgraduate degree doing the same. In the middle were those who had completed Year 12 but had no post-school qualifications (72 per cent) and those with a certificate or diploma but no degree (64.6 per cent).

Biddle said there were equally large differences in satisfaction by income. Under two-thirds of those in the lowest income quintile were satisfied with democracy (64.7 per cent). This rose to 79 per cent for those in the highest income quintile, with a reasonably consistent gradient in-between. The professor added that those Australians who have more negative attitudes towards, and experiences of, the housing market are much less likely to be satisfied with democracy than those with a more positive attitude or a better experience.

'The biggest difference ... is for those that are currently having difficulty with housing payments. Only 51.9 per cent of those in payment stress were satisfied or very satisfied with democracy, compared to 72.8 per cent of those who were not under payment stress,' he said.

Views on income inequality correlate highly with satisfaction with democracy. In early 2023, Australians were asked, 'How fair do you think income distribution is in Australia?' More Australians thought that the income distribution was unfair or very unfair (60.5 per cent)—far fewer thought it was fair or very fair (39.5 per cent). And only 51.2 per cent of Australians who thought the distribution of income was very unfair were satisfied or very satisfied with democracy in Australia. This increased to 77.8 per cent of those who thought it was unfair, 87.1 per cent of those who thought it was fair, and 95.8 per cent of the very small proportion of Australians who thought the distribution of income was very fair.[5]

This data demonstrates significant demographic vulnerabilities—groups that are struggling in our economy are less trusting of our democracy. It also demonstrates that good social policy that lifts people up and tackles inequity could entrench trust that the system is in fact working in the best interests of people.

The data is crystal-clear: a reduction in economic security is leading to a reduction in trust. We've seen this all over the world, including the rise of disaffected white, working-class voters in America that enabled Donald Trump to successfully call for the 'swamp' to be drained. Biddle argues there is a nexus in his research between economic inequality and trust in democracy that should alarm all politicians and which flags the need to address the most acute issues.

The Role of Government and Politicians

Politicians across the political spectrum are ultimately responsible for building trust with voters and engaging with emerging and sometimes challenging issues without reverting to spin and obscuration. Every day on my television program at the ABC, and often on the weekly panel show I host, my job is to interview and talk to politicians and use my interactions with them to be the public's advocate for answers on key policy issues that are in the public interest. Yet politicians increasingly revert to talking points, even though I can report with absolute certainty, from the audience feedback I receive, that the public is offended by it and it increases cynicism in politics. Politics is becoming more negative, the language is hardening, the rhetoric is inflamed. Why can't we return to what the research says? Voters say they want to hear honesty, vision, empathy, hope, strength and shared values.

Counterintuitively, however, we also know that negative campaigning can work. The question is what damage will it do in the long term. Biddle argues that political parties should be very careful about exploiting divisions over income, housing and economic inequality, because 'low education and housing difficulties are highly predictive of dissatisfaction with democracy, which can negatively impact on the system as a whole, not just one party'.

And that's the catch. The erosion of trust in democracy means that our elections will become more volatile, and politicians who can communicate effectively with voters and address their material needs can and will build support—economic security is key. But those politicians must resist the temptation to go for the quick political sugar hit of negativity, because it creates long-term damage.

The Role of Journalism and Journalists

Objectivity and impartiality have always been central tenets of journalism, particularly in political reporting, where it has been essential to maintain trust with audiences. But the acceleration of social media and of hyper—and in my view dangerous—polarisation has made the intersection of reporting and politics more troubled, with hyper-partisan actors and active trolling at work harassing those journalists who pursue objectivity and are equally robust with all politicians. The power of social media has been in how it gives citizens a voice, and that voice is powerful and important. But it has also allowed those most biased and invested in one political perspective the opportunity to engage in damaging and sometimes highly gendered pile-ons on journalists who have had the temerity to ask difficult questions of favoured politicians. The ability of social media to distort the truth, and the speed with which it can do this, has meant that some reporters have faced a barrage of harassment. I worry that it could have a chilling effect, discouraging people from taking roles on the front line, given how febrile and divided the environment is.

I have started to use the term 'radical impartiality' to describe what I believe we need to be doing more of across the media to rebuild trust with audiences. At a time of great fragmentation, we must lean into our roles as frank and fearless navigators of our country and our world. We also need to be pushing for more civics education at all levels, because we live in a world of dangerous disinformation where democracy is being deliberately eroded by those who want to disrupt the system.

What does radical impartiality look like? I call it 'radical' because to choose to pursue everyone in the political class equally means journalists will continue to annoy partisans, and it is partisans who are the noisiest in the debates both on the left and the right. But in-between is the silent majority who are increasingly not rusted onto political parties or particular media outlets, and who deserve a media that is not driven by political biases, but rather by journalists who are prepared to be unpopular at times in the pursuit of the truth. This is a conversation journalists must be having more prominently, because trust in the media is essential in a robust democratic country. It is our obligation to ensure this is front and centre in our work.

Data collected by the ANU in January 2024 suggests there is a strong relationship between trust in media institutions and satisfaction with democracy, but that the relationship depends on the type of institution. Just after the Voice to Parliament referendum, the ANU asked people how much trust they had in 'traditional news media, such as newspapers, television or radio'. They found that only 1.4 per cent of Australians trusted it completely, but 44.7 per cent trusted it somewhat. This left 36.7 per cent who do not trust traditional news media very much, and 17.1 per cent who do not trust it at all.[6]

While trust levels regarding the news media are lower than we would like, there is even less trust in social media, which includes X, Facebook and WhatsApp. According to the ANU, only 0.4 per cent of Australians trusted social media completely, and only 17.3 per cent trusted it somewhat. This left almost half of Australians (49.5 per cent) saying they did not trust social media very much, with almost one-third (32.8 per cent) not trusting it at all. Clearly, a lot of distrust is directed towards social media in Australia, providing some backing for a government that is able to regulate it effectively.

What is particularly interesting about this data, though, is that trust in traditional news media was much more closely related with satisfaction with democracy than trust in social media. According to the ANU survey, 78.9 per cent of those who trusted traditional news media (completely or somewhat) were satisfied with democracy, compared with 54.7 per cent of those who did not trust traditional news media (not very much or not at all) and who were satisfied with democracy. When we look at social media, however, those who trusted social media were slightly more likely to be satisfied with democracy than those who did not trust social media (72.1 per cent compared with 64.5 per cent), but the difference was much smaller.

Professor Biddle argues that if our aim is to increase the level of satisfaction with democracy in Australia, then steps that enhance trust in traditional media might receive a higher return than steps that enhance trust in social media. 'Putting this another way,' he says, 'political leaders that undermine trust in traditional news media are taking a big risk with satisfaction with democracy in Australia.'

Lifting the Level of Trust

At a time when false information is spreading more than ever before, public institutions and the media must do more to build public trust and tackle the loss of it. The aforementioned statistics show us the public is looking for places to put their trust and that, given the right response, there is an opportunity here that can be seized.

Let's return to the role of politicians in our liberal democracy. To have real impact on trust levels, they must allow themselves to be fully held to account by the media and the public. We must build the resources of our institutions to be places where citizens can turn for the truth—where politicians can be rigorously challenged when they trade in misinformation. Likewise, engaging with the issues that matter to voters means they can reinvigorate trust in the democratic system.

Australia is in a unique position. Polarisation here, while no doubt growing, is not hard-baked. It still operates at the fringes. With compulsory voting, we have a system that does not actively disenfranchise voters. It is time to double down on elevating facts and demanding of our leaders that they use proportionate and truthful political rhetoric.

Trust in Science: Strengthening Peer Review to Build Resilience

Cathy Foley, Chief Scientist, Australia

IN AUSTRALIA TODAY, we can expect to live for just over eighty-four years.[1] This is amazing considering the human predictive life span from genetic markers is thirty-eight years.[2] So why is this? It's because science and technology have enabled society to adopt medical interventions, improve nutrition, provide the potential for access to enough food, and create economic prosperity thanks to materials extraction and technological development. Humans, through science and technology, can now control their lives and livelihoods more than ever before.

One of the first technological disruptions to contribute to our increased longevity was the fifteenth-century invention of the printing press. It democratised information, enabled alternative perspectives to be shared, lifted education, and so changed societies—think the Reformation, the beginning of democracy and industrialisation. It demonstrated clearly how access to knowledge provides the power to change our world.

Since then, civil societies and liberal democracies have developed with a dependence on trust in fair elections contesting distinct political perspectives, the separation of powers between different branches of government, adherence to the rule of law in everyday life, a market economy with private property, universal suffrage, protection of human and civil rights, and adherence to a constitution. The public has traditionally expected that their leaders will be held to high moral and ethical standards, earning trust through honesty and motivations based on national benefit.

The printing press also enabled the development of the scientific method credited to Francis Bacon in the 1600s. With the ability to print and distribute documents, science moved on from being a solitary pursuit involving handwritten copies of scientific papers and collected data, which were hard to access and often contained human transcription errors. Scientific publication in journals began in 1665 through the Royal Society in London, initially with editors publishing work submitted from members of learned societies. An article was accepted based on the assumption the author was an expert.

Jump ahead several centuries to the 1970s, and the contemporary peer-review process began its own evolution, with recognised expert reviewers being tasked with reviewing manuscripts, providing comments that would eventually lead to authors revising their submissions until they were deemed acceptable.[3] This development further contributed to public trust in the scientific process and method.

Fast-forward to today and we are experiencing a new digital information revolution. In the science and research sector, this has coincided with massive growth in the number of papers submitted to journals, and in sophisticated digital tools that manage the peer-review process. This is how research now self-corrects, as bodies of knowledge grow with the contributions of researchers from all corners of the globe.

Access to all sorts of information has rapidly increased with the advent of the World Wide Web, search engines, social media and, most recently, generative AI that uses LLMs to interface with this technology. AI is the new generation of technology that has further democratised access to information, in the same way the printing press did. But there's a catch. AI does so without any discrimination between what information is correct and trustable and what is not. Social media and access to web-based information does not provide a vehicle to discern whether you are reading disinformation or misinformation intended for mischief-making, or to elevate and promote individual perspectives that are not motivated by honesty and broader benefit. And with this, we are seeing a shift in public trust of public institutions, and of science.

In early 2023, soon after the release of ChatGPT, I undertook a national conversation on behalf of the government to gather information to inform the refresh of the National Science and Research Priorities. I asked a cross-section of about 700 Australians from all parts of the country what science and research are needed to make Australia the country we want it to be. The overwhelming response was that Australians want to preserve our liberal democracy and to maintain our national values in the light of new technologies.

During the COVID-19 pandemic, we witnessed how scientific research was central to the political debate and how different governments responded to the evidence. Surprisingly, it was not a case of either trusting science or not. Why was this the case?

At the time, research prioritising health over the economy was highly trusted, but public health initiatives during the pandemic were not.[4] Climate change, Great Barrier Reef water-quality research and the adoption of genetically modified organisms are other examples of where there has been a divide in trust of the science.[5] In Europe, 'populist' citizens voiced how 'anti-elitists', not 'elites', should make decisions and so were more sceptical about science than non-popularists.[6]

Since the pandemic, there has been an acceleration in the development of new digital tools, and with that has come rapid growth in misinformation and disinformation, creating more confusion and distrust. In liberal democracies, the conventional wisdom is that governments operate with a level of honesty even if they provide a 'peculiar, messy version of truth'.[7] But 'alternative facts', bending of the truth and the promotion of conspiracy theories have made it difficult to know what can be trusted when we are surrounded by so much fake information sold as 'trustable'. The strategies used include cherry-picking evidence, using illogical reasoning, relying on supposed experts who are not true experts, and requiring impossible standards to prove these 'experts' are wrong.[8]

Why should we worry about misinformation and disinformation when it comes to trust in science? Since the printing press, humanity has been exposed to broad views, so shouldn't such a breadth of information be seen as healthy dialogue?

New digital technologies and the dissemination platforms of social media are amplifying information at volume and without discrimination, which makes it hard to know what is evidence-based and what is not. For example, many times I have read news from mainstream media outlets that includes information I know to be incorrect presented as fact. Over the years, we have seen some political leaders openly flouting the truth for their own political expediency. Some might say that this is the 'new normal', all part of the mix of our digital world, but what are the consequences?

An individual's vulnerability or resilience to misinformation is influenced by a complex interplay of biological, psychological and social factors.[9] Research shows that psychological stress can alter brain function, impacting cognitive processing and emotional regulation. There is research evidence that, on hearing false and potentially false information en masse, our brains change.[10]

For example, imaging of the magnetic fields created by the electrical currents that fire nerve synapses in our brains has shown significantly bigger responses to hearing good grammar in the left posterior temporal region.[11] What we hear and what it means to us affects the brain's activity. And there is now evidence of a reduction in the signal from the amygdala on extended exposure to dishonesty.[12] The amygdala is the almond-shaped structure that lies in the temporal lobe and which is a major processing centre for emotions and links to memories, learning and our senses.

Today's easy access to digital information certainly provides the stimulus for this effect. So are there interventions that can reduce susceptibility to misinformation and disinformation and enhance societal resilience?

Science provides a source of trusted knowledge. It is important to remind ourselves how trustable science is done. Canadian scientist David Suzuki has said:

> Science does not progress in an easy, linear fashion. It's not like you have an idea, set up an experiment, prove your theory and then cure cancer. In science, you learn as much from your failures as you do from your successes. Every paper, every theory and every experiment build on those that came before. As Sir Isaac Newton and other scientists have said, we're all standing on the shoulders of giants.[13]

People not engaged in the scientific professions can be confused seeing the popularisation of a scientific breakthrough contradicting another report that has different conclusions. What they need to understand is that the basis for the scientific method is that if scientists' research is undertaken in a trustable way, collectively the 'self-correcting' of the body of knowledge created and published via the peer-review process should then be trusted.

As in any relationship, trust is earned. We scientists must earn the trust of the public and hold up our side of the social contract, as most Australian research is publicly funded. Our first role is to build the evidence with integrity using the best-quality research practices, aiming for research excellence that will have impact.[14] Doing quality research is not easy, however. The classic steps require securing the research funds, planning and designing the project, accessing the equipment and infrastructure needed, undertaking literature reviews to draw on the research that has gone ahead, and noting where our work fits into building up the evidence base. Once the research is complete, the next steps include analysis of the results and writing up our research as a paper to submit for peer review to an academic journal. It is the peer-review process that provides the quality assurance. The process is: authors submit their research paper to a journal; the journal editor sends this paper out to expert peer reviewers who assess it; after some back and forth for revisions and academic discussion, the manuscript is accepted and the paper is published.

Researchers use a peer-review process to check their research is valid at the time of publication. Once published, the research is viewed by other researchers. This process has greatly benefited humanity, from the discovery of vaccines through to technology development that has helped us understand the universe at the largest and smallest scales.

The fruits of researchers' labour, humanity's knowledge, which is published in academic journals, has developed over the decades and is now a profitable industry. There are thousands of academic publishers, but today about 75 per cent of papers are published by about fifteen international publishers. Globally, about four million research papers are published each year. To access these journals, originally academic libraries bought subscriptions and housed the hardcopies. But around 2007, the publishing system shifted from hardcopies to digital access. In this way, the holders of knowledge shifted from the librarian to the publisher.

The business model for academic publishing is a good deal for publishers. They obtain the content for free as the authors sign over copyright at no charge. The peer reviewers are not paid. The academic editors are either volunteers or paid a small honorarium. Saying that, the publishers do have significant costs associated with critical services like providing the software for the upstream manuscript management for the peer-review process, paid staff, the downstream published digital journals, and the creation and management of metadata.

To pay for that, articles are held behind a paywall. Libraries buy subscriptions to these digital journals. Individuals who are not members of an academic library can access journal articles by paying a charge to read a single paper at a time. Authors can also choose to pay an extra fee, which can range between $3000 and $15,000 per paper, for their paper to be free to read for anyone—this is called an 'open access' paper.

Here is what concerns me. Today, most people are not members of an academic library: teachers, students, public servants, parliamentarians, professionals, industry, the public—all must pay a charge to read the publicly funded research if it is not open access. Recent roundtable consultations by an Australian Government department found that, when a member of the public clicks through a web portal looking to find the original research document and comes up against a paywall, it creates mistrust of the 'hidden' information—as though there is something to hide!

In the role of Australia's Chief Scientist, I studied open access for nearly three years. From this work, I proposed a model I call the 'Public Model'. The model would involve creating a centralised digital academic library with a single national relationship with each publisher (much like we do with pharmaceutical companies). As compensation for our contributions of content—Australia provides a bit under 4 per cent of the research published globally—and untold hours of peer review and editing, the publishers' 'in-kind' payment would be providing people residing in Australia with access to research literature via appropriate authentication if they are not part of an academic library link. This extra market is untappable for the publishers. Such an arrangement could lift the publishers' social licence that was challenged due to making significant profits from free labour and content. Additionally, Australia would benefit from better access to research literature, which could lead to improved social cohesion.

Enabling access to information that is known to be trusted allows a reader to know what information is evidence-based or not in a sea of fakes. Could this be one pathway to preserving the liberal democracy Australians say is most important to them in a world of growing misinformation and disinformation? If so, it could help us create a more resilient Australia.

Better industry access to research literature could also increase our new-to-the-world products and potentially contribute to lifting Australia's economic complexity and enable more globally competitive businesses. Such a model could lead to better evidence-based policymaking by government, noting that the public service and parliamentarians have very limited access to research literature.

Researchers are keen for their research to have impact. They do not want to be the 'monks of old' in the monastic libraries keeping their research to themselves. The public, meanwhile, is hungry for access to trusted information, and industry needs to innovate more. A pathway to available, accredited, evidence-based information is there for the forging if we rethink the model to engage with academic publishers to enable more access to research literature in much the same way that the printing press did in the 1600s.

We know the peer-review process provides a trusted information tick of approval. And Australia's peer-reviewed published research is overwhelmingly trustable, considering that papers retracted for research misconduct such as plagiarism, data fabrication and manipulation amount to about 0.003 per cent of the one million or so papers published by Australian authors in the past ten years.[15]

The public has never had broad, easy access to research literature. Moving research literature onto digital platforms creates a new opportunity. But this also means that we researchers must be clear to our stakeholders on when we are providing the evidence, when we are providing our opinion, and when we are advocating for something. We must not add to the confusion.

We live in an exciting time, with rapid change accelerated by the digital information revolution. Due to this, humanity is at a juncture where our brains could be physically changed by misinformation and disinformation due to their sheer volume, intensity and easy access. As preserving our Australian values and liberal democracy is a priority and potentially under threat because of this access, trusted science and research that is easily accessible via open access is one pathway for Australia to be the resilient and prosperous country we want it to be—to maintain our values and enable wellbeing for all. Let's find a way to achieve this.

Trust in Religion:
We Are Like Cut Flowers

Michael Stead, Anglican Bishop of South Sydney, Australia

TEN YEARS AGO, I was lamenting the collapse of trust in religion to a friend, and in religious institutions in particular. The conversation took place during the Royal Commission into Institutional Responses to Child Abuse, and I suggested that this was a primary cause. The sins and systemic failures of my (Anglican) denomination and others had—rightly—eroded public confidence.

My friend, a senior lawyer, both agreed and disagreed. In his view, public confidence was collapsing across many institutions: government, the legal system, financial institutions—and religious institutions along with it. While the exposure of the Church's failures through the royal commission had exacerbated a decline in trust, what the Church was experiencing was a specific manifestation of a much wider societal turn towards distrust of institutions.

The decade since seems to have proved my friend correct. And my reflection is that to fully understand the decline in trust in religion, we need to understand both the specific issues at play as well as the context of wider societal change. And, also, to recognise that a loss of faith more broadly—particularly in Christianity—has eroded the foundations of the values our society is built on.

Australian data shows relatively low trust in religious institutions, compared with other bodies. The Australian Leadership Index is an ongoing online survey that measures community perceptions of a range of leadership attributes. One of the attributes measured is trustworthiness. Over the past three years, religious institutions have consistently scored at the lower end of the scale for trustworthiness, at similar levels to the federal government and media companies, but 10 per cent below law-enforcement agencies, almost 20 per cent below public health institutions and 30 per cent below emergency services. It is cold comfort that we are not dead last—religious institutions, media and the government are still perceived as more trustworthy than casino operators.[1]

Furthermore, confidence in religious institutions has been on the decline for the past two decades. The Australian Survey of Social Attitudes (AuSSA) asked the question 'How much confidence do you have in churches and religious institutions?' in 2005, 2011, 2014 and 2018. The percentage of people answering 'No confidence at all' rose steadily (2005: 20 per cent; 2011: 22 per cent; 2014: 23 per cent), then jumped to 29 per cent in 2018.[2]

However, it is not just religious institutions that have a trust problem. There has been a widespread decline in trust in institutions in Australia in general over the past decade and a half. For example, in the fifteen-year period from 2007 to 2022, the Australian Election Study asked voters whether those in government could be trusted to do the right thing nearly all the time, or whether they were too often interested in looking after themselves.[3] In 2007, the split was 57 per cent (look after themselves) to 43 per cent (trusted to do the right thing). By 2022, the trust deficit had widened considerably to 70 per cent to 30 per cent—that is, only 30 per cent of people trusted those in government to do the right thing.[4]

This collapse in trust is not isolated to Australia. Gallup has been polling Americans about their confidence in US institutions for decades. In the most recent results from 2023, shown in the graph, the confidence score for most institutions was at or near an all-time low. Over the past fifteen years, there has been a dramatic 24 per cent slump in public confidence overall.[5] Confidence in the Church or organised religion dropped from 52 per cent to 32 per cent (a 20 per cent drop).[6] It is even worse when the political polarisation in America is taken into account. Among those who vote Democrat, confidence in organised religion has slumped to 25 per cent.[7]

Confidence in US Institutions

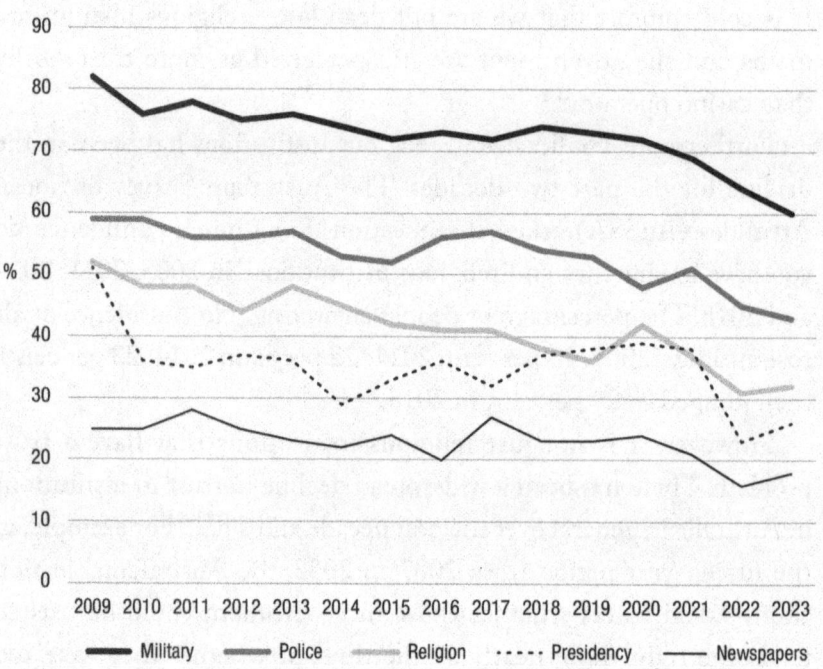

Source: Gallup

In light of this, it is reasonable to assume the decline in trust in religious institutions in Australia is the product of two factors: the contextual reasons why trust has been eroded in religious institutions in particular, and the decline in institutional trust in general.

Two recent reports suggest similar reasons for the first factor. The NCLS 2021 Australian Community Survey (ACS) reported that the percentage of people who agreed or strongly agreed that 'Religion is good for society' dipped significantly from 39 per cent in 2016 to 33 per cent in 2018, returned to similar levels in 2019 and 2020, and rose to 44 per cent in 2021. The report suggested a possible explanation for the drop in 2018:

> The 2018 ACS was run at a time when the outcomes and responses to the Royal Commission into Institutional Responses to Child Sexual Abuse were attracting significant attention. The Marriage Equality plebiscite was also conducted in late 2017 and while Christian leaders and institutions were vocal on both sides of the debate, they were more strongly identified with the 'No' campaign.[8]

Similarly, a report analysing the 2022 Australian Cooperative Election Study, surveyed just prior to the 2022 federal election, concluded: 'Religious child abuse scandals have affected trust. Women are sceptical about the capacity of religious leaders to protect the children in their care ... and to respond to the Australian Royal Commission into Institutional Responses to Child Sexual Abuse.' The report noted that the survey was conducted in the midst of 'a contentious debate over the rights of religious organisations, such as schools, to discriminate against LGBTIQ+ people', in the wake of 'the high-profile campaign against marriage-equality ... prosecuted by mainstream churches, such as the Anglican Archdiocese of Sydney and the Catholic Archdiocese of Sydney, in 2017'.[9] The report concluded: 'Organised religion is facing a crisis of trust throughout Australia, with women experiencing this acutely. Approximately one third of all Australian voting women state they have "no trust at all" in organised religion and religious leaders.'[10]

This report provides a fascinating insight into the impact of religious practice on trust. It revealed that 11 per cent of women 'Practice regularly', 16 per cent 'Practice sometimes', 26 per cent are 'Religion, no practice' and 47 per cent are 'No religion'. Of those women who practised their religion regularly, only 2 per cent reported 'No trust at all' in organised religion, and 64 per cent reported 'A great deal / quite a lot' of trust. For women with no religion, 59 per cent reported 'No trust at all', and only 5 per cent reported 'A great deal / quite a lot'.[11]

Among those who identified as Christian, women outnumbered men by 55 per cent to 45 per cent. As the report notes, 'women are not abandoning their religious affiliation at quite the same rate as men. In the 14-year period to 2018, according to HILDA [the Household, Income and Labour Dynamics in Australia survey], 11 percent of women left their religion, while 14 percent of men left theirs'.[12] A reasonable inference is that those women who are actively involved in the life of their church/synagogue/mosque make a positive assessment of religious institutions and their leaders (and remain 'in'), while those with little or no contact with religious life have no reason to change their negative views (and so remain 'out').

In relation to child sexual abuse, those inside the Church are acutely aware how much our practices have been transformed over the last fifteen years. Like other denominations and religions, the Anglican Church of Australia has acknowledged with deep shame our past failures and willingly embraced stringent child-safe procedures, minister screening, safe ministry training and mandatory reporting. But for those on the outside, with no visibility of this, it is not surprising that a deep distrust and suspicion remains. I recognise that we have a long way to go to restore public trust, and it is not clear how to do this, given the in/out polarisation.

The decline in rates of religious affiliation also feeds directly into the decline in trust in religious institutions/leaders. Those who report 'No religion' also report very high levels of distrust of religious institutions and religious leaders, so as the proportion of 'No religion' increases in the population (as older generations, who are more religious, are replaced by younger generations who are less religious), the overall rate of distrust increases. It is arguable that this demographic shift alone accounts for the majority of the collapse in trust in recent years.

To illustrate this, let us assume that the rates of distrust reported by women in the 2022 Australian Cooperative Election (ACE) survey are similar for men, and that 'distrust rates' have been constant over time—simplistically, 59 per cent of those who select 'No religion' report 'No trust at all', and 9 per cent of everyone else reports 'No trust at all' (9 per cent is the weighted average of the distrust score for Protestant, Catholic and 'Other Religions' in ACE 2022). The table shows a calculated 'No trust' percentage based on these assumptions.

	No religion	Calculated 'No trust'
2006 Census	19.3%	19%
2011 Census	23.1%	21%
2016 Census	30.1%	24%
2021 Census	38.9%	28%
2022 ACEs	47.0%	33%

Calculated 'No trust' compared to AuSSA

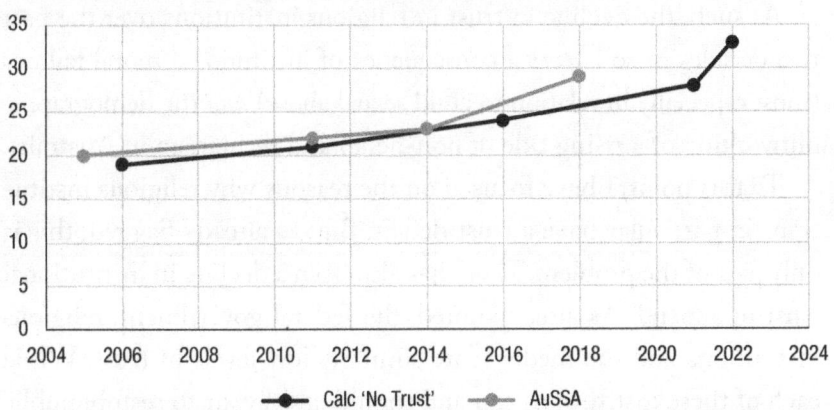

Sources: Census, ACE survey and AuSSA data

Undoubtedly, the interplay between (no) religious belief and distrust of religion is more complex than is represented in this model. Nevertheless, it illustrates what we intuitively would expect: there appears to be a high correlation between 'No religion' on the census and 'No trust at all' in religious institutions and religious leaders.

There is a similar correlation between trust and religious attendance, as shown in the table. Those who attend regularly have low distrust, and those who never attend have high distrust. The distrust rates did not change significantly between the AuSSA conducted in 2014 and the one held in 2018.

	Attends monthly or more	Attends less than monthly	Never attends
2014—'No confidence at all'	2%	15%	40%
2018—'No confidence at all'	2%	14%	41%

What did change between 2014 and 2018 was the proportion of people who said 'Never attends', which rose from 43 per cent to 60 per cent. Those attending less than yearly dropped from 18.4 per cent to 10.8 per cent. This (mathematically) is the reason why the overall 'No confidence' number rose from 23 per cent to 29 per cent.

As such, the decline in trust in religious institutions over the past two decades or so is *both* a consequence of institutional moral failures (most especially in relation to child sexual abuse) *and* the demographic outworking of a rising tide of non-belief and secularism in Australia.

To this point, I have focused on the reasons why religious institutions in particular have a trust deficit. But, as already flagged, this is only part of the problem. There has also been a decline in institutional trust in general. As already noted, the federal government, religious institutions and the media score similarly low levels of trust. While each of these institutions can and should endeavour to restore public confidence, doing so without also addressing the overall decline in trust is like passengers scrambling over each other to get to the stern of the sinking *Titanic*. Or, to use a different aquatic metaphor, if we can reverse the current falling tide of institutional trust, then trust in all institutions will tend upwards with the rising tide.

So why is the trust tide ebbing and what can be done about it?

Here is my thesis. Religion in general—and the Christian faith in particular—provides the necessary conditions for societal trust to flourish. Western liberal democracies are built on foundations inherited from Christianity. For a long time, we have not been a Christian society, but we have nonetheless continued to operate on, and benefit from, these Christian foundations—we have been like cut flowers in a vase that continue to have the appearance of vitality even though they must eventually wither. The collapse of trust in recent decades is because our society has now largely abandoned these foundational principles.

Let me unpack this. First, the connection between faith and trust.

In English, the connection is not so obvious, but both Greek (*pistis/pisteuo*) and Latin (*fides/fiducia*) demonstrate the close connection—to have faith is to put trust in. Christian faith is trust in the promises and character of God as he has revealed himself in the person of Jesus Christ. There is an element of uncertainty to faith. Hebrews 11:1 says that 'faith is the assurance of things hoped for, the conviction of things not seen' (English Standard Version). Christians believe that God is a loving, gracious and forgiving heavenly Father *not* because this is self-evidently true from our experience of this world, but because we believe in / put trust in / have faith in what Jesus said about his father. At its heart, the Christian faith is based on trust in a trustworthy God, rather than having to prove things for ourselves. Whether or not it is reasonable to do so depends entirely on whether or not you think Jesus is trustworthy.

A religious faith—a willingness to trust in things we cannot prove for ourselves—encourages a disposition of trust towards others, unless and until we assess them as untrustworthy.

This is borne out by the results of the 2018 AuSSA survey. On all confidence measures apart from the last, the rate of those who indicated 'Complete / a great deal / some' confidence among those who attend religious services regularly (monthly or more) is significantly higher than those who never attend.

'Complete / a great deal / some ...'	Regular attender	Never attends
Confidence in parliament	59%	36%
Confidence in business and industry	80%	69%
Confidence in churches / religious organisations	85%	24%
Confidence in courts and the legal system	75%	63%
Confidence in schools and the educational system	81%	82%

Similarly, 76 per cent of regular attenders said that people can 'Almost always' or 'Usually' be trusted, compared to only 60 per cent of those who never attend. Religious people are more likely to trust societal institutions and people—they are predisposed to trust.

This societal dynamic ('I'll trust you unless you are untrustworthy') has progressively been replaced with a different dynamic, which is not based on trust but proof ('I'll only trust you if you are proved trustworthy'). That is, the starting disposition is not one of trust, but suspicion. We assume that politicians are self-interested, unless they prove otherwise. We assume that the media are manipulating the truth, unless we can independently verify. We assume that children are not safe from sexual abuse in religious institutions, unless we have proof to the contrary. We withhold trust until we have personal experience or evidence of trustworthiness.

For example, according to the 2024 Edelman Trust Barometer, only 51 per cent of people trusted CEOs to do what is right, but 69 per cent of people trusted 'my CEO' to do what is right—that is, the personal experience of a trustworthy CEO did not flow into a trust in CEOs in general.[13] When it comes to putting trust in media sources, the standout winner was search engines—our own research on Google is more reliable than digital, print and social media.[14]

But why have we only fallen off the trust cliff in recent decades? It is because three of the foundational trust assumptions inherited from Christianity have finally collapsed.

First, we have moved from truth to post-truth. Objective truth was an inheritance from Christianity. From its outset, scientific endeavour assumed there was objective truth to be discovered, premised on a consistent and orderly God who had made a consistent and orderly universe. The first shift away from this occurred centuries ago, when science dispensed with the God who gives order to creation, but nonetheless still sought 'the truth' through a combination of rationalism and empiricism. Trust in God's order was replaced by a trust in human reason, human observation and experimentation. Fast-forward to today and that shift has left us with profound uncertainties, because we can find scientists and other experts on both sides of every contentious debate, all claiming to speak the 'truth'. Now, each individual has to decide for themselves which 'truth' they will believe. This is made increasingly difficult in an age of misinformation, deepfakes and social media algorithms that create echo chambers where the only voices I hear are those that agree with and reinforce my point of view. In 2016, the *Oxford Dictionary* selected 'post-truth' as its 'Word of the Year', recognising that we now live in a world that permits 'alternative facts'. The individual is the final arbiter of what is true for them.

Second, we have moved from justice to social justice. Our justice system originated in notions of right and wrong inherited from Christianity. Murder, theft, lying and adultery were wrong because the God of the Bible said so, and we accepted that God had authorised human systems (police, judges, gaols and so on) to restrain and punish wrongdoing. We have long since moved away from this foundation, replacing God as the arbiter of right and wrong with the anthropocentric notion of 'harm done to victims'—an act is wrong if it harms another human being. Nonetheless, for a time there was a broad societal consensus on the harms the justice system ought to restrain. But that consensus has now collapsed, as justice has morphed into social justice. Social justice requires that every individual has equal human rights and opportunities, and any impairment to an individual's exercise of these rights is harmful and warrants the intervention of the state. The problem is that we do not agree on what to do when human rights are (potentially) in conflict with each other. God is no longer the final arbiter of this question. The individual is the final arbiter of what is 'just' in their eyes.

Third, we are in danger of abandoning democracy in favour of ochlocracy (mob rule).[15] Western liberal democracy is founded on a Christian view of human fallibility—we are all flawed, but redeemable. Because of our inherent human flaws, a system of government needs checks and balances, to call people to account and correct them when they make mistakes and do the wrong thing. But failure is not necessarily fatal. A government might be voted out at the next election, but there is always the possibility of restoration in a future election. This assumption of human fallibility and the possibility of restoration used to be deeply embedded in many of our social institutions. People could make mistakes, spend a season on the backbenches, and then be restored. But, largely due to the internet, these foundations of democracy with institutional corrective mechanisms are being undermined by ochlocracy. We are sadly all too familiar with the phenomenon of the social media pile-on and cancel culture, when any error of judgement or indiscretion, or even just an unpopular opinion, leads to calls for boycott or erasure. For fear of being 'cancelled', politicians, business leaders and, sadly, religious leaders hide their mistakes rather than acknowledge them, and the resultant secrecy and deception feeds into a culture of distrust and strident calls to step down. The shouty individual—empowered by the grassroots collective—dominates our social and political discourse.

If this is the diagnosis of the decline in trust in our society, then what is the solution?

It will not surprise you that I think that the fundamental way to rebuild societal trust would be a widespread reawakening of trust in God as he is revealed to us in Jesus. However, I recognise that this essay alone is not going to bring this about (though I do hope that it may have piqued your interest enough to consider this option, especially if the reason why you have rejected the God of the Bible is because of lack of 'proof').

But if considering Christian faith is not (yet!) an option for you, there is still a way forward. Our current trust crisis is a consequence of the rise of extreme individualism, where the individual chooses their own truth, their own justice and their own form of democracy. This kind of autonomous individualism corrodes society. Even if we don't have a shared belief in God as the final arbiter in these matters, surely we can agree that every single individual cannot be the final arbiter for themselves.

The first step is accepting that there is *something* beyond ourselves that establishes ideals and boundaries, even if that 'something' is nothing more than some kind of societal compact, in which we have just agreed to live according to these principles because they seem to work.

And we don't necessarily have to agree what that *something* is. Just acknowledging something beyond ourselves relativises the absolutes of our own individualism, and encourages us to engage in humility with those who look to a different *something*. And since we would no longer need to regard others' views as a direct challenge to our own autonomy, it would then become possible to move from a disposition of suspicion to a disposition of trust.

Trust in Policing: Force and Our Freedom

Graham Ashton, former chief commissioner of Victoria Police, Australia

No society can ever be completely free. Human nature has too many flaws to allow that to succeed. The question is, what are the fewest freedoms a society must sacrifice to achieve a fully functioning community? And who will be trusted to enforce those sacrifices?

In Australia we have had, for at least 200 years, the benefits of the Westminster system of government, with an independent judiciary and a standing force to police society's rules. Traditionally, policing has enjoyed high levels of public trust, which has been essential in delivering this service. Police rely on their community's active support in generally following society's rules, and its trust and confidence in reporting crimes. Police are granted the right to use force, when necessary, to protect the community from harm, giving the police force both great power and great responsibility.

Trust in policing is critical to a strong, functioning society. Policing is done with the consent of the community and, if trust is eroded, that consent is put at risk and can become a flashpoint for community discontent. When things go wrong, a community sometimes lashes out at what it can see, and police officers, who are a very visible presence, can become targets. The George Floyd riots in the United States are a good example. These riots were, in many cases, directed at police who were accused of racism, in this case the murder of African Americans. While people were within their rights to take that view, police quickly became a lightning rod for public discontent. This risked masking the broader structural disadvantage and racism that contributed to George Floyd being in police custody in the first place. Rather than 'Let's seriously address social disadvantage and causal factors' the cry became 'Defund the police', without serious thought being given to what the consequences of such a policy might be for broader community cohesion.

Over many decades, community trust in Australian policing remained high. In fact, even during periods when police failures were heavily publicised, trust levels were largely unaffected. The general community understood that policing was a 'tough job' and they trusted that if things 'went bump in the night', the police would be the ones who came to their aid. In some ways, they had no choice but to trust police. Who else could they call for assistance? It was in their interests to blindly trust that the police could be relied upon. Therefore, when police did fulfil their potential by saving a life or going above and beyond to help their community, these things were celebrated because they fulfilled that narrative.

But things have changed, and they are continuing to change. The national, annual *Report on Government Services* (ROGS) is the only report that seeks to measure public trust in policing in Australia. Over many years, ROGS has reflected how policing has enjoyed among the highest levels of public trust in society. Regularly, the satisfaction levels of community members who received policing services were in the 80 per cent range and remained very resilient. Similarly, overall satisfaction in policing was also strong. But the most recent ROGS suggests cracks are appearing in public trust in policing. The measure of whether police treat people fairly and equally was at 63.6 per cent. That is a ten-year low compared with a high of

77.7 per cent in 2014–15. And, disappointingly, people agreeing or strongly agreeing that police were honest was just 66.5 per cent. That is another ten-year low compared with 75.9 per cent in 2014–15.

There is no one reason why community trust in police is dropping. It is clearly an amalgam of a range of factors that have created a perfect storm which is eroding public trust and creating cynicism. This set of circumstances is not just restricted to policing but is appearing in almost every societal function that people rely on.

Leaders in the police force have been examining various methods of improving public trust. Most Australian agencies have trust issues in common and are collaborating to find solutions. In the past year, for example, two Australian police commissioners have issued formal apologies for police interactions with Indigenous communities. This follows earlier work by the former West Australian police commissioner in this area and has been crucial in rebuilding trust.

The 2024 apology by the Northern Territory police commissioner for 'hurt inflicted upon Aboriginal people' was a sincere attempt to acknowledge the past and build trust for the future. Apologies such as these can positively impact those affected and receive broad community support. But it's worth noting that they are not without controversy within police ranks. Internally, statements like this can actually make some police members feel unsupported. This is critical because it is future police actions that will determine trust and show that the commitment to such an apology is meaningful. Police must walk the talk. It is therefore essential that any police commissioner communicates effectively internally when considering a trust-building apology of any type. This communication must ensure police members are able to understand the rationale for the apology.

More in the Spotlight than Ever Before

We live in a time when the internet and social media dominate public communication and when legacy media are left vying for an audience. In this context, there are four significant changes that have turbocharged the decline in trust in policing.

Firstly, everybody who is 'connected' has the opportunity to speak globally within moments. This has seen a rise in citizen journalism which, with respect to trust in policing, means any police misdeed garners immediate public attention. In Australia, police will have hundreds of thousands of interactions with the community every day, which in almost all cases positively reflect on policing. However, it takes just one case of police acting badly to kick off viral internet attention. This can lead to an aggregation of negativity and, consequently, a distorted view of police behaviour that affects public trust.

Police are a reflection of the community they serve, and every sizeable barrel has its bad apples. In my experience, those officers shown performing badly on the internet by citizen journalists are a very small percentage of the total policing population. Yet, those behaving badly, now more than ever, affect communities' opinion of the whole.

Secondly, the introduction into mainstream policing of body-worn cameras has also had an impact on public trust. This was foreseeable. Body-worn cameras were introduced to provide courts with a real-time visual account of police engagement with the community and also as a safety measure for police officers. Footage, when released to the community, provides a raw account of what are often very tense and dangerous situations. But while it does benefit police for the community to see what they are dealing with close-up, it can also set up the police for judgement if their conduct is not perceived as appropriate. In our contemporary community, we are quick to judge the actions of others and want to attribute immediate blame to any individual we judge responsible for a negative outcome. Body-worn camera footage enables this as never before and can lead to the community judging police actions without knowing the full circumstances. This can have a very negative impact on police trust. There have also been examples where body-worn camera footage has been selectively edited to portray police actions in a negative light, again further impacting trust levels.

Of course, the converse can be true when it comes to this footage. We have seen examples where exemplary police actions, or circumstances that have led to police fatalities, have shown the community how difficult policing can be and earned trust that police will go to great lengths to protect them.

Thirdly, the role of opinion in legacy media has contributed to a degradation of public trust in many institutions, including policing. Opinion dominates the landscape of today's mainstream media— opinion all too often formed along political lines, with left-wing and right-wing views influencing understandings of all public issues, almost without exception. If one wing criticises police over a law-enforcement issue, the other wing will seemingly always line up to take the opposing view. Either way, law enforcement gets criticised. With the exception of emergency management, it is hard for me to think of a policing-related event in the past decade that has attracted wholesale praise of the police.

This politically motivated criticism also has the effect of unwillingly dragging police into the political narrative, where they become criticised, wrongly in many cases, as being the 'lap dogs' of politicians. This erodes public trust in policing as the community rightly desires that police act independently of the political class.

A further product of opinion-led journalism has been a readiness to give a voice to outspoken individuals from inside the policing industry who are critical of policing decisions or actions, when in fact these people often have no or little real understanding of how or why those decisions or actions were taken. All too often, these individuals are actually held in low regard by their industry peers but are given prominence and credibility by the media, because their comments fit the prevailing or preferred narrative.

It is difficult to imagine this situation improving anytime soon. Opinion-led journalism is not going anywhere because it speaks to the bases of some news outlets and is cheap to produce when compared with quality investigative journalism at a time when media companies are financially stretched.

Finally, one of the strengths of policing in Australia over more than 150 years has been its connectivity with, and responsiveness to, its local community. This local bond has long built trust between the police and the community. In our modern society, however, the speed of communications has led to a much stronger sense of a global community. That means poor policing actions in some faraway land can be seen with immediacy here in Australia and have the potential to become conflated with local policing. In these circumstances, it is not hard for the community to form a homogenous view of policing that diminishes hard-won local trust.

The manner in which some of these local issues are portrayed can also exacerbate these issues. On many occasions I have read disturbing accounts of police actions, only to almost reach the end of the story before I am informed that the incident occurred on the other side of the planet. If a reader just consumes the headline, or even the first part of the article, they will no doubt believe the poor police behaviour was local.

Some PR is needed here. It is important for police leadership to do all it can to ensure that, as much as possible, the community understands that the standards of policing in Australia are among the best in the world, and also that they are often not consistent with what is seen internationally.

COVID-19 and Policing

The recent global pandemic also had a profound impact on trust in policing. During the pandemic, police were required to do some things that were intended to protect community health, but which they hated doing and were anathema to why they joined the police. One of the prime examples of this involved the police directing law-abiding citizens to leave public spaces. This, for one of the few times in our history, placed the police in an adversarial relationship with the majority of the community. There may have been sound reasons for doing this, as every police action may have prevented the spread of a serious disease among an unvaccinated community, but the impact on public trust was profound and will take many years to recover.

It has been many decades since the general community in Australia has had its general movement restricted. We have to go back around eighty years to see this occurring at significant levels. During the world wars, the community could fully understand the threat and why restrictions and rationing were necessary in this context. In the COVID-19 context, however, the threat was more difficult to comprehend, at least early on. What people could see, however, was uniformed police restricting their movements. It is hard when, for generations, times have been so good that people do not easily remember that our freedoms have been achieved through sacrifice, and that even today, sacrificing some freedoms is sometimes necessary to preserve those freedoms into the future. In order to maintain public trust during these times, it is essential that great effort is put into communicating this fact. It is equally important that these sacrifices are commensurate with the threat and that they are as brief as possible.

Police and the Community

In today's fast-moving society, there is little community appetite to look deeply into issues. Increasingly, this leads to the community forming an opinion based on whatever is presented as the first sound bite, with little opportunity for the other side to be heard. This exacerbates trust in Australia's institutions as they often require a more detailed issue analysis than is readily forthcoming.

Policing is always trying to play catch-up as media issues emerge—it is usually the second rather than first mover. This leads to greater consumption of negative policing news rather than positive stories. For this reason, policing has, over recent years, focused on communicating directly with its audience through its own social media platforms, and it is continually expanding this first-mover remit.

Because policing has reflected the community for a long time, it is important our police appear approachable and friendly towards the public. This bond of trust stems from the community understanding that the police are drawn into service from that community and understand their issues.

The onset of modern terrorism and the need for harder-edged policing responses to events such as sieges, kidnappings and gang activity has led to the formation of specialist squads of highly skilled officers, often wearing military-like uniforms or all-black apparel and armed with highly visible long-arm (shouldered) weapons. While this response capability is necessary in today's society, it can have the effect of making our police indistinguishable from overseas counterparts who may serve in countries with substantially less oversight and accountability than occurs in Australia. To many Australians, this look is militaristic in nature and makes our police look less approachable.

When going back to first principles of public trust in policing, policing ranks must draw from the community they serve. Police must reflect the community. This is central to their approachability and has been a mainstay pillar of public trust over one-and-a-half centuries, but it is being put at risk through the aforementioned militarisation. Again, this is not to say these specialist approaches aren't crucial—they are. But they must be mitigated when considering approachability strategies.

The benefits of an approachable and trustworthy police are best illustrated in rural communities. In these locations, police are often operating alone, with backup many kilometres away. They simply cannot do their job if they are not fully supported by the community. In order to achieve this, effective country police embed themselves in the community. For example, they run the football or netball club, volunteer at community events and become essential local cogs. Obviously, this considerably elevates public trust. It is a shame that the sheer transactional volume of police engagement in our cities makes this sort of engagement almost impossible.

Law and Order

Structurally, it is important to understand that the police only form part of our justice system, but that a loss of trust in one part of the justice system can affect the other components. When you hear a community member say they have experienced a loss of trust in our justice system, they rarely differentiate which part of the system they are referring to. Is it the police? The courts? Our laws? Our legal community? Loss of trust in one sector can affect the whole.

When setting policy and practice, all justice sectors must understand this threat to trust. It is important that all sectors realise they are part of our justice ecosystem and think of themselves in this context. This is very difficult to achieve in practice, but it is nonetheless worth aspiring to.

Given these increasing threats to public trust, policing must take care to actively curate its reputation through its actions, and continually ensure that its own conduct is as professional and fault-free as possible.

An Indigenous Perspective on Community Trust

A Q&A with Yalmay Yunupingu, Yolŋu Elder, teacher and Senior Australian of the Year 2024, Australia

The Yolŋu people are the traditional owners of North-East Arnhem Land, Australia.

A note from Yalmay: 'This is not directly pointing at anyone or talking about them. This is just a general conversation to open up trust-building. We want people to live in a safe environment and workplace.'

Q [Tracey Kirkland]: The Indigenous people of Australia are made up of hundreds of groups, all with their own customs, languages and cultures. Can you tell me about the concept of trust in Indigenous communities, the concept of trust between communities and within communities?

A: Trust is very interesting and an important word to use. It's about being reliable and trust-building. Faith is another word; faith needs trust. Truth is the foundation of truth-telling that will allow better relationships to be safe and free.

The people we trust are those we work closely with, those that walk beside us, understand the cultural things that we do in the community, those that have an understanding of our language and culture. We trust those people. But sometimes we meet people and work with people we don't trust at all. They can be very friendly at first, but behind our back they can criticise us or talk about us. And there's no trust.

There are people that we know, that we have worked with for a long time, that we can trust, and people that we do know [but] that we are unsure whether they are trustworthy or not. We also adopt *balanda* people [non-Indigenous people] into our Yolŋu family. Sometimes there is trust and, in some ways, they are not trustworthy.

At school we use a metaphor of the cycad nut. The nuts in the cycad palm [*ngathu*] are very poisonous. The women collect the *ngathu*, they take them back to the camp, they open the nuts, they classify them into different categories. They break the seed open, they then put the nuts into fresh water and leech the poison. Then, in a couple of days, the women collect them and pound them to make a bread. They use paperbark on both sides and put them on hot coals. Once they are cooked, we think about the important people in the family that are related to *ngathu* and they eat the *ngathu* first, then the rest are shared among other family members. It is a living Yolŋu bread that people in the past ate as they walked from place to place.

The metaphor symbolises that if people want to work with us, there should be trust. It also indicates that it's a time of healing, understanding and respect. It indicates people that we don't trust are poisonous.

This story indicates people coming into our communities who don't really know what they're doing, they do things in their own way. They don't follow the community rules. These people might be bringing poison into the community.

At school or any workplaces, they are the kind of people that we don't like to trust. It makes Yolŋu people feel uncomfortable, people can feel it. They are like the poison from the cycad nut. It's hidden at first and needs to be brought out. Trusting new people is sometimes hard for us because new people in the community can hide their true personality; it shows in their actions. Through their behaviour, it shows that they are untrustworthy people.

In the end, the way we build trust is by watching their actions. Once we see their actions, what they're doing, hear what they are saying, the criticism they make about other Indigenous people, then we know if we can really trust them or not.

Q: How important is it for you to have a system of trust like that so that you can recognise those people who are, as you say, 'the poison'?
A: *Gurrutu* [kinship system] relationship is a foundational truth that aims to bring people together. We need to follow this system in the correct way, in a way that this land has placed. In the Yolŋu community, there's about twenty or twenty-two kinship names that connect everyone to their family lines and their ancestors. With *gurrutu*, we respect that. When there's a fight in the community, politics can come into play. To defend politics, we talk about the kinship relationships, where the person comes from, whether it's through their mother, grandmother, great-great-grandfather and so on.

Our kinship system talks about intergenerational kinship. This will help people understand *gurrutu* patterns. It means that a Yolŋu person knows and understands where this person comes from, which kinship line they come from. This is creating unity to connect and come together.

Unfortunately, some people don't trust or value the *gurrutu* system. They don't believe in it. They can make things harder or more difficult for people.

One thing that helps when a new person comes into our community, especially if they are working with people, they need to have a proper cultural induction. It means they will know what the expectations are. They need to understand us to build trust with the community, in our workplaces and schools and in other organisations. When we do have new people come into the community, they get adopted into a Yolŋu family. The adopted Yolŋu family teaches them about our language, culture and protocols, the right and wrong.

We do exactly the same at school. We run cultural inductions, we run orientation, to help them fully understand and integrate into our community. By understanding the cultural sensitivities of the community, there will be more trust between Yolŋu and *balanda* and they will fit in better.

Q: You are a highly experienced educator and a community leader. What role do you think teachers have in teaching and building trust?
A: We, as teachers, want the children to be able to abide by the rules inside the school and outside in the community. Together we develop shared rules. That way they should be able to abide by those rules because we have agreed on them. It sets up a responsibility and there's a shared goal. One of the things that we've also been using is *raypirri* [a process of sharing customs to encourage discipline]. *Raypirri* might be a smoking ceremony or storytelling. This is a holistic approach about Yolŋu children to bring them up as better children. It's a way of explaining to them the protocols of the community.

The teaching of trust is really the responsibility of the wider community, because it's their role to teach kids who they can trust and how they do it. So, when they come to the classroom or go to work, they should know how to behave and what the community expects. But we do still teach them to behave and not to fight. The school teaches them social and emotional wellbeing. They also have consequences for them.

Q: And when you give the example of 'the poison', how do you explain to the children who could potentially be poison and who is trustworthy within the community?
A: Most of the older kids have seen the process of *ngathu* in one of the workshops we do, but it can take a while for them to process what the metaphor really means. We want to make them understand the meaning of *ngathu* because it indicates to children who they can and can't trust.

AN INDIGENOUS PERSPECTIVE ON COMMUNITY TRUST

We have another metaphor in our community. *Worrk* is our burning off season, it's something we do once a year. The process of *worrk* involves burning off all the dead, fallen trees and grass to make the land clean, just like we clean our own houses. Then new shoots appear after a couple of weeks. *Worrk* talks about regeneration, it talks about rejuvenation, it talks about revitalisation. It indicates people and environment, how we can look after each other and have trust in each other.

I'm on the board of an organisation called Djalkiri Foundation, which means feet or footsteps. We run workshops for people building the foundation of trust. We run workshops for workplaces and organisations using *gurrutu* or kinship concept. We use *gurrutu* to help people fit in because the trust has already been built, it's already there. Having natural trust through *gurrutu* makes such a difference for young people who are trying to find work.

It's an honour to be Senior Australian of the Year, but I also have other titles to make me who I am. Some people in Indigenous communities don't trust me because they think, being in a position like this, I'm behaving like a non-Indigenous person. I'm for any race. I don't like politics. I don't want to be a politician. I just want to be Yalmay, just ordinary Yalmay. That's what I want to be. And I would like to help my community. I would like to help my people. I would like to help Australians build trust with us.

Q: So, as someone who is now a recognised leader in Australia, being a valued voice for Indigenous communities, would you say that you trust politicians?
A: Yes and no. There are people that I know from the past that I trust, who have been fighting for us for many years, for funding. I was in an Australian teacher's union for a long time. The unions have been fighting for funding for public schools and other funding for resources for remote schools. We are not very well resourced out here. When you go into an urban school, they are better resourced there,

but we are not. Yolŋu communities don't get good resources to help us with things like computers, books, papers and all the stuff we need to teach. And this is one of the things that I've been fighting for in collaboration with the union and school.

It seems like a lot of funding has been given to private schools and we are left thinking, 'What about us?' So, I trust those politicians that have helped us, but when they don't follow through and do what they say they will do, they are some of the indicators that there is no trust.

I think about our national anthem, 'Advance Australia Fair'. What does that mean? Who does that represent? That song line represents to me the trust we all share. It's something we can build on.

Q: You speak three Indigenous languages as well as English, and a lot of your life's work has been connecting children with their language. What is the importance of that when it comes to trust?
A: Language is really important. We've got thirteen languages in our community and the language that we teach at the school is the children's first language, Yolŋu *Matha* [Yolŋu tongue]. It's the language that children first learn in the community, called *dhuwaya*.

It is really important we educate them about concepts like *gurrutu* and *worrk* while they're very young. Because as they're growing up, they will pick up and understand who they belong to, who they are, where they come from, what their language is, how their community works, their kinship mark, kin name and all that other identity that comes with those. And so, when they grow up, they know who they are. That way, they build trust. Trust in themselves and who they are, and trust in the community, trust in what they can be.

PART III
TRUST AND THE MESSENGERS

Trust in the News Media: A Global and Audience Perspective

Nic Newman and Amy Ross Arguedas, Reuters Institute
for the Study of Journalism, United Kingdom

TRUST IS AT the heart of the contract between journalists and the public. At least in most free and democratic countries, journalists believe they are in the business of creating trustworthy content, whether they are reporting from a war zone, running an investigation into corruption, doing a timely analysis of political events, or writing something lighter or more entertaining. Journalists at reputable news organisations go through often rigorous processes to check that what they publish is true, that quotes are an accurate and fair reflection of what was said, and that stories are selected in good faith—in the service of readers, and more widely in the service of democracy itself.

But this is not always how things are seen by the public. According to *Digital News Report* data, just 40 per cent of our global survey sample across forty-seven markets say they trust 'most news most of the time'.[1] In around a third of countries, more people say they *dis*trust the news than trust it, and the same applies to many popular news brands with a long heritage. Polls show that journalists can be among the least trusted of all professionals, only slightly more than politicians and estate agents.[2] Some of this is self-inflicted, with well-documented violations of ethical or professional practices (for example, phone hacking);[3] biased, self-serving or sensationalist coverage; and systematic under-representation of marginalised groups. But there are structural factors too. As news organisations have lost much of their power and influence in the internet age, trust itself has become more distributed and increasingly contested. Traditional media reporting is widely discussed and argued about in social media, with individual journalists often vilified and, in some cases, physically attacked. So-called 'alternative facts' are often promoted *above* those that have been journalistically verified, leading to many ordinary people understandably being confused about where to turn in today's increasingly complex information space. All of this matters because if people can't agree on basic facts, how can they debate and make progress together on the complex issues facing our democracies and the world?

It also matters to journalists and media organisations because high trust is closely linked to the ability to generate revenue, which in turn provides protection from undue influence by advertisers or other powerful interests. There are other, more principled reasons to care about trust, too. Years of research has shown how people who trust the news less are less likely to believe in the information it presents and learn from it.[4] In an era of AI-driven synthetic content, where it is likely to be even harder to tell what is real from what is false, many experts expect trust to become an even more important currency.

So what do we know about trust, and what could we do to improve public perceptions of journalists and the media?

What Does the Data Show about Trust?

For almost a decade, our surveys have tracked trust at a general level by asking people whether they feel they can trust most news most of the time. The graph here shows significant variation in the proportions across countries. In the Nordic region, Finland (69 per cent), Denmark (57 per cent) and Norway (55 per cent), which have relatively low levels of political polarisation and high trust in political institutions,[5] have consistently topped the trust charts, along with Portugal, which has a strong tradition of journalistic independence enshrined in its constitution. Some African countries where the media has also had a strong reputation for robust scrutiny of those in power also perform well in overall trust. Greece and Hungary (23 per cent) have

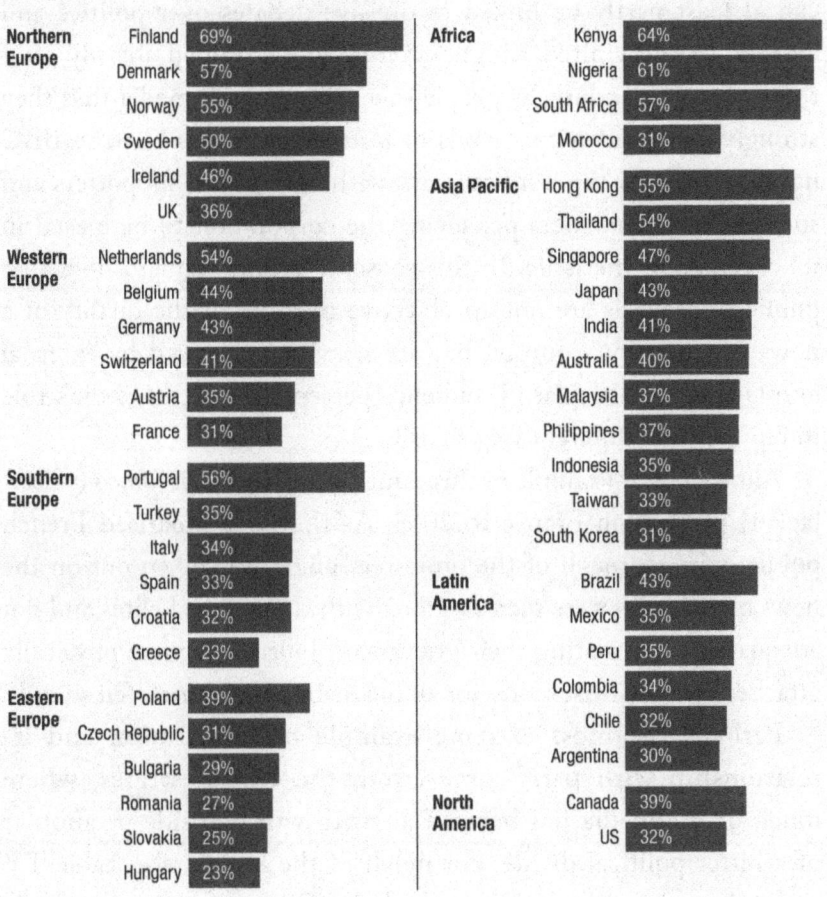

Proportion that Trusts Most News Most of the Time

Region	Country	%		Region	Country	%
Northern Europe	Finland	69%		Africa	Kenya	64%
	Denmark	57%			Nigeria	61%
	Norway	55%			South Africa	57%
	Sweden	50%			Morocco	31%
	Ireland	46%		Asia Pacific	Hong Kong	55%
	UK	36%			Thailand	54%
Western Europe	Netherlands	54%			Singapore	47%
	Belgium	44%			Japan	43%
	Germany	43%			India	41%
	Switzerland	41%			Australia	40%
	Austria	35%			Malaysia	37%
	France	31%			Philippines	37%
Southern Europe	Portugal	56%			Indonesia	35%
	Turkey	35%			Taiwan	33%
	Italy	34%			South Korea	31%
	Spain	33%		Latin America	Brazil	43%
	Croatia	32%			Mexico	35%
	Greece	23%			Peru	35%
Eastern Europe	Poland	39%			Colombia	34%
	Czech Republic	31%			Chile	32%
	Bulgaria	29%			Argentina	30%
	Romania	27%		North America	Canada	39%
	Slovakia	25%			US	32%
	Hungary	23%				

Q6_2016_1. Thinking about news in general, do you agree or disagree with the following statement? 'I think you can trust most news most of the time.'

Base: total sample in each country (n ≈ 2000).

Source: Reuters Institute Digital News Report 2024

the lowest levels of trust amid perceptions that the news media is subject to undue influence by powerful business or political interests. But while we do see declining trust in many countries, this is not the case everywhere. In some countries, we have seen stability and even slight increases, especially during and after the peak of the COVID-19 pandemic.

Low trust levels in the United Kingdom (36 per cent), United States (32 per cent), Argentina (30 per cent) and France (31 per cent) can at least partly be linked to divisive debates over politics and culture. In the United Kingdom, trust levels dipped sharply after the Brexit referendum, as people saw things in the media that they strongly disagreed with. Levels of *dis*trust in brands like the BBC has doubled over the last few years, with both Brexit supporters and some ardent Remainers perceiving the corporation to be biased in its coverage of the issue. In this sense, it is important to note that public trust levels are not an objective measure of the quality of a news organisation's output, but are heavily influenced by external events and in particular by audience perceptions of the media's role in representing different views fairly.

Another clear example of this came during the *gilets jaunes* (yellow jacket) protests in France in 2018. As the issue polarised French public opinion, much of the protesters' anger was taken out on the news media, who were seen as siding with the political elites and not adequately representing their grievances. Journalists were physically attacked and the trust scores for all the main TV channels fell sharply.

Perhaps the most extreme example of polarisation and its relationship with trust comes from the United States, where much of the media has become aligned with one side or another of a bitter political divide. For much of the last decade, cable TV channels such as Fox, CNN and MSNBC have taken increasingly partisan perspectives on a range of political and social issues, with each talking to a largely sympathetic crowd. *Fox News*, for example, is highly trusted by supporters of Donald Trump, according to our

Digital News Report data, but deeply distrusted by those who identify as progressives. The reverse is true for CNN and MSNBC as well as *The New York Times* and *The Washington Post*. With Donald Trump accusing those titles of spreading 'fake news', it is not surprising that by 2019 only 9 per cent of those that self-identified on the right said they trusted most news. It is also not surprising, then, that so many people believed just a year later that the 2020 election result was stolen from them, despite clear evidence to the contrary.

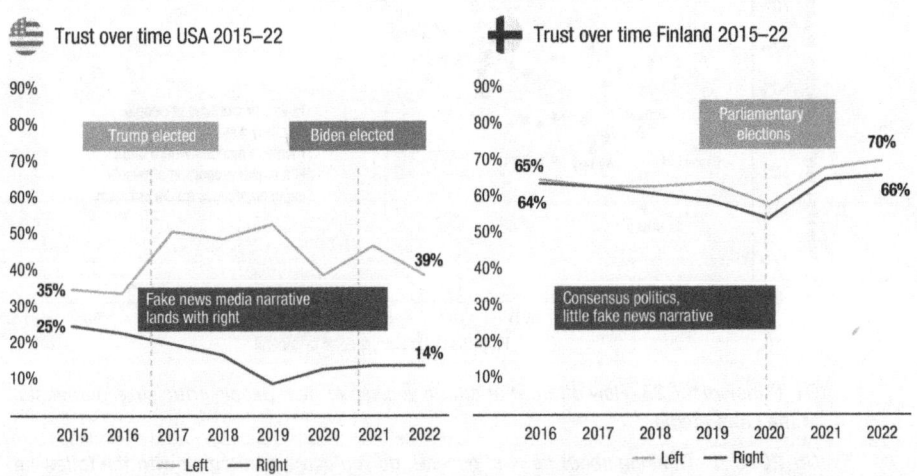

Q6_2016_1. Thinking about news in general, do you agree or disagree with the following statement? 'I think you can trust most news most of the time.'
Base: all respondents, 2015–22 (n ≈ 2000).
Source: *Reuters Institute Digital News Report 2024*

Across the world, populist politicians such as Viktor Orbán in Hungary, Jair Bolsonaro in Brazil, Andrés Manuel López Obrador in Mexico, and Rodrigo Duterte in the Philippines have taken a leaf out of Donald Trump's playbook, accusing the media of 'fake news' as a way of deflecting criticism and rallying supporters. Activists aligned with these politicians have amplified these messages on social media, which may have contributed to further undermining overall trust. In our data, we see a correlation between countries where people see widespread media criticism in social media and other channels and where trust in the news is low, though it is important to note that our data does not allow us to determine a causal relationship.

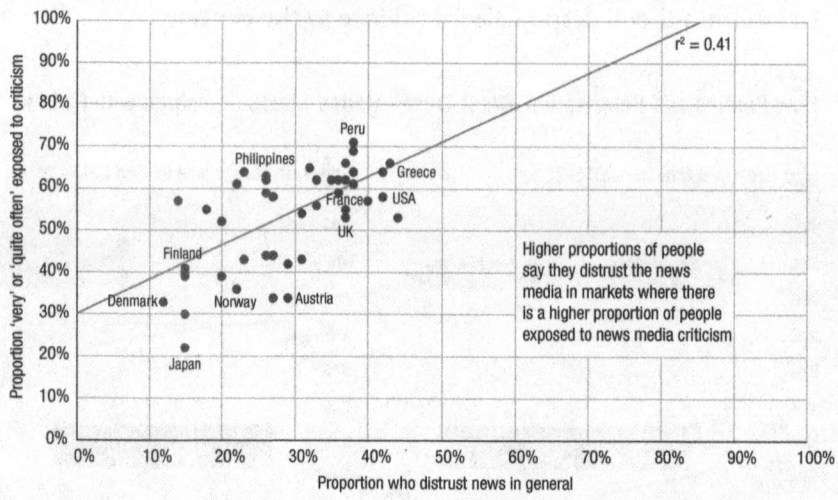

Correlation between Exposure to News Media Criticism and Distrust in News

Q1_Criticism_2023. How often, if at all, do you see or hear people criticising journalists or the news media?

Q6_2016_1. Thinking about news in general, do you agree or disagree with the following statement? 'I think you can trust most news most of the time.'

Base: total sample in each market ≈ 2000.

Source: Reuters Institute Digital News Report 2023

More widely, research also shows that people trust the news they find in social media much less than what they source via traditional news media, and some academics argue this is an important contributing factor to a decline in overall trust.[6] *Digital News Report* data shows that social media has now become the primary experience of news for many younger and hard-to-reach news users, but news in these networks tends to be encountered incidentally, from a variety of sources, not all of which are trustworthy or even familiar to people.

Research shows that this can lead to people, especially those with lower knowledge, writing off all news as untrustworthy or to rely on potentially misleading heuristics.[7]

A Problem of Representation and Relevance

While it is easy to blame politicians and social media for low trust, the news media itself has much to answer for. Generally, younger people, people with low income, and people with lower levels of formal education tend to trust the news less. Studies also show that marginalised audiences—for example, along lines of race and class—are often less well served by the news media, and less likely to think the media cover people like them fairly.[8]

Traditional media companies have spent much of their time over the last decade chasing clicks or super-serving elites, who are interested in news and most prepared to pay for it, and this has left many ordinary people out in the cold. Interest in 'the news', which audiences tend to define in a relatively narrow way around politics and other serious subjects, has been declining in almost all countries for the last decade. Across most countries in our survey, almost four in ten (39 per cent) say they often or sometimes avoid the news, with many people from these underserved groups seeing traditional media as boring, depressing, and in many cases irrelevant to their lives. Many young people say traditional news is formulaic, agenda-filled and often too hard to understand, and they prefer more engaging and positive formats in social media. Our data shows that in newer social networks such as TikTok, Snapchat and Instagram, younger groups are more likely to pay attention to celebrities and social media influencers than they are to journalists, even when it comes to news. But the lack of regular use or familiarity with trusted news brands may leave them vulnerable to less reliable perspectives, and this in turn may be making them increasingly sceptical of *all* information, taking very little on trust.[9]

'There's too much news nowadays. Some are fake and some are real but I get confused and get a headache.'—Male, twenty-seven, United States

'You can't really trust anywhere, can you? Everyone's got some kind of agenda.'—Female, thirty-three, United Kingdom

Sources: Reuters Institute research, including the
Digital News Report and Trust in News Project.

Rebuilding Trust in the News Media

Given the decline in engagement with mainstream media and the rise of scepticism or even cynicism towards the news media outlined in this chapter, news leaders, platforms, and policymakers are more than keen to find ways to reverse the trend. In doing so, it is worth reflecting on the different factors that audiences say are most important to them in deciding whether or not to trust a news outlet. We find that high standards, a transparent approach, lack of bias, and fairness in terms of media representation are the four primary factors they say influence trust. The top responses are strongly linked and are consistent across countries, ages and political viewpoints. An overly negative or critical approach, which is much discussed by politicians when critiquing the media, is seen as the least important reason in our list, suggesting that audiences still expect journalists to ask the difficult questions.

While evidence about which specific interventions help move the trust needle in practice is very limited, these results provide an important starting point for how media companies might build greater trust. Most of the public want news to be accurate and fair, avoid sensationalism, be open about any agendas and biases including lack of diversity, own up to mistakes, and not pull punches when investigating the rich and powerful. People do not necessarily agree on what this looks like in practice, or which individual brands deliver on it. But what they hope news will offer is remarkably similar across many different groups and closely aligned with what many journalists themselves at least set out to deliver.

Proportion That Say Each Is Very or Somewhat Important When Deciding What News Outlets to Trust

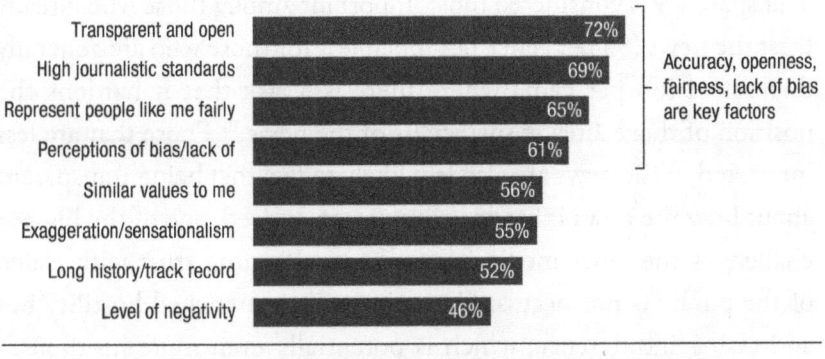

Q1_Trust_reason_2024. Still thinking about trust in news ... how important or unimportant are the following to you when it comes to deciding which news outlets to trust?

Net: very/somewhat important. Base: total sample in all markets = 94,943.

Source: *Reuters Institute Digital News Report 2024*

Audience interest in transparency and openness seems to chime with some of the ideas behind recent industry initiatives, such as the Trust Project, a non-profit initiative that encourages publishers to reveal more of their workings using so-called 'trust indicators'; the Journalism Trust Initiative, orchestrated by Reporters without Borders; and others. Some large news organisations, such as the BBC, have gone further, creating units or sub-brands that answer audience questions or aim to explain how the news is checked. BBC Verify, launched in May 2023, aims to show and share the work done behind the scenes to check and verify information, especially images and video content, in an era where misinformation has been growing. 'People want to know not just what we know [and don't know], but how we know it,' says BBC News CEO Deborah Turness.

Leaving aside the risk that journalists and members of the public often mean different things when talking about transparency, with the former focusing on reporting practices, and the latter often on their suspicion that ulterior commercial and/or political motives are in play, our data suggest that these initiatives may not work for all audiences. Transparency is considered most important among those who already trust the news (84 per cent), but much less for those who are generally distrustful (68 per cent) where there is a risk that it hardens the position of those already suspicious of the news.[10] Those that are less interested in the news are also less likely to feel that being transparent about how the news is made is important. Indeed, one of the biggest challenges the news media faces when cultivating trust with much of the public is not necessarily overcoming entrenched hostility but addressing indifference, which is potentially even more insidious.[11] How does one build trust when there is no relationship on which this trust can exist? This is potentially where news literacy and other forms of outreach or engagement may be needed, especially if conducted in partnership with government and other civil society groups.

BBC Verify

Source: BBC

But publishers could also do more to directly address the problems of low interest and news avoidance.[12] These include simplifying language in news stories, explaining the context more clearly, rethinking political coverage to make it more accessible and relevant, developing more engaging storytelling formats such as short-form video and podcasts, and developing more positive and constructive approaches to journalism.

What Next for Trust?

With trust in news already at historically low levels in some countries, many worry about the potential negative impact of generative AI technologies over the next few years. Public concern about misinformation and disinformation has been rising for the last few years, with the majority (59 per cent) of those polled in forty-seven countries already worried that they find it hard to distinguish what is true and what is false on the internet.[13] Election campaigns around the world are increasingly being affected by AI deepfakes, designed to discredit opposing candidates or undermine the democratic process. These have included an audio recording falsely purporting to be Joe Biden when he was running in the 2024 US election, asking supporters not to vote in a primary, and a campaign video containing manipulated photos of Donald Trump. The conflict in the Middle East has been accompanied by an information war in which artificially generated pictures have been posted by supporters of both the Palestinian and Israeli sides, aimed at winning sympathy for their cause. The impact of these cases so far appears to have been limited, but ordinary people are increasingly coming across synthetic images or videos in their feeds and worry about where this is heading.

'Thankfully, they are still pretty easy to detect, but within five years they will be indistinguishable,' said one twenty-year-old participant in recent research on AI and the news.[14]

While most ordinary people have become accustomed to parsing text for bias and agendas, pictures and moving video have largely been taken on trust, but in an era of AI, that can no longer be taken for granted. It is possible that this change, combined with a proliferation of low-quality synthetic content, will further undermine people's trust in *all* information over time. On the other hand, it could provide an opportunity for the news media and journalists to re-establish themselves as beacons of trust in an ever more complex information space. But to make that a reality, they will also need to address the many and complex reasons why so many people have lost faith in the news, reinforcing a positive vision of what journalism at its best aims to be: accurate, fair, transparent, free from biases, as well as relevant and useful to groups across society, not just to those who are already interested in news.

Fact-Checking and the Golden Age of Journalism

Fergus McIntosh, Head Research Editor, *The New Yorker*, United States

> *Facts are simple and facts are straight.*
> *Facts are lazy and facts are late.*
> *Facts all come with points of view.*
> *Facts don't do what I want them to.*
>
> 'Crosseyed and Painless', Talking Heads

EVERY TRIBE HAS its myths, and journalists are no exception. In America, one common story goes like this. Once, in the prelapsarian era before social media—or, perhaps, before smartphones, or Ronald Reagan—there was a time when journalists were trusted. Back then, everybody, or at least everybody who mattered, read muscular daily newspapers and watched straight-down-the-line TV reporting. When citizens had to make political decisions, a robust social contract with the media ensured that they were well informed, and even if they couldn't always agree on what to do or who to vote for, they could rely on the facts. But then something changed: people stopped paying attention to the news, or decided that they didn't believe it anymore. They got distracted by cable TV, Facebook and TikTok. They became ill-informed, and started to make decisions that went against their best interests. The media decayed and fragmented, along with the nation. Opinion and news became indistinguishable, misinformation ran amok, and that is how we came to live in the post-truth world.

This story is not unsupported. Polls have long shown declining levels of trust in the media. Trust in many other institutions has fallen too, but in journalism it has plummeted. Since 1972, Gallup has been asking people in the United States, 'How much trust and confidence do you have in the mass media?' The numbers used to be highly favourable, but in 2024 (and previously only in 2016 and 2023), more people said they had none (36 per cent) than said they had a lot (31 per cent).[1] At the same time, a survey of how highly Americans rated the ethics of various professions found that only a fifth believed journalists' ethical standards were 'high or very high': a better ranking than car salespeople and senators, but worse than bankers and chiropractors. Almost half said that journalists' standards were 'low or very low'.[2] Increasing numbers of Americans say they do not follow the news,[3] and when they do, it is increasingly via factually unreliable social or alternative media.[4] In some places, the picture looks rosier—the Nordic states, outliers as ever, have far higher levels of media trust[5]—but one recent survey showed the balance of media trust and distrust across twenty-eight countries to be neutral at best, and negative among the most developed.[6]

At the same time, large swathes of the news business have been on the retreat, stricken by dwindling advertising revenue, hostile governments and declining audiences. In the United States, the number of working journalists dropped by more than a quarter between 2008 and 2020.[7] Meanwhile, in 2022–23, the Committee to Protect Journalists recorded more journalists jailed worldwide than ever before.[8] Technological change—most recently and acutely the mainstreaming of generative artificial intelligence—and political polarisation present their own challenges. In the United States, for example, the fall in trust of journalists has been sharper and more consistent among Republican voters,[9] and the conclusion that many people turn to the news more for affirmation than for information can be hard to resist.[10] What passes for truth often depends on where one falls on the political spectrum: it's no coincidence that Donald Trump's venture into social media has 'truth' in its name.

It's a grim picture, but buried in the statistics is another story. People still worry about misinformation, even if they can't agree on what to call it. 'Fake news', aptly defined as 'information divorced from reality',[11] is not a new concept, but more Americans than used to now register displeasure with inaccurate or unverified information on social media,[12] and a majority now think that somebody, perhaps even the federal government, should do something about it.[13] There seems to be widespread recognition that bad facts are bad news—globally, fears of an 'information war' are rising[14]—and, despite endemic scepticism and distraction, there is an enduring thirst for reliable information. The question is, where can it be found, and how can its purveyors make themselves heard amid the noise?

One answer has been to lionise accuracy. For some, this represents a business opportunity. NBC, CBS and the BBC have all launched fact-checking units,[15] and for the first presidential debate of 2024, *The New York Times* tasked twenty-nine staffers with fact-checking the candidates' statements in real time.[16] Not every entrant in the emergent accuracy economy is as large or well resourced: over the past decade, hundreds of small fact-checking websites have sprung up around the world,[17] including many in countries, such as India, where press freedom is far from a guarantee. Whether rooted in service or aimed towards revenue, though, this sort of 'political fact-checking',[18] which spotlights specific claims and seeks to prove or disprove them, is not as neutral as some might like to imagine. Setting out to counter and correct inaccuracies, it often takes the form of rebuttal, and necessarily entails editorial decisions over what to cover[19] (no outfit can scrutinise every statement by every politician, and none of them wants to). Its reach is limited, and it is unclear whether it is always helpful: as one journalism professor puts it, 'Disinformation itself has become kind of a toxic term for a lot of people.'[20] An insistent focus on misinformation or disinformation may even inflate the scale of the problem, to the benefit of what the writer Joseph Bernstein has labelled 'Big Disinfo',[21] and to the detriment of a publication's appeal to uncommitted readers. The provision of accurate facts does not, in itself, necessarily engender trust: 'notions of news and truth are linked to what people do with information rather than what journalism unilaterally decides are accurate portrayals of reality', says Silvio Waisbord.[22]

What is more certain is that from time to time, every journalist, no matter how well meaning, gets something wrong, or misses the point. If journalists want to be trusted, they need to not only police the accuracy of others, but also to ensure that their own work is careful and considered. One way to achieve this is to practise the traditional (or 'primary') variety of fact-checking, which, whether carried out by someone called a Fact Checker or by reporters themselves, aims at verification in advance of publication.

Today, anyone who wants it can find reporting that is, as Michael Schudson puts it, 'deeper, more analytical … less fully focused on what happened in the past twenty-four hours, more investigative, and more likely to take "holding government accountable" or "speaking truth to power" as an essential goal' than was the case fifty years ago.[23] If there ever was a golden age of journalism, we may still be living in it. The trouble is, much of the public—turned off, bored, or riled into disbelief—has ceased to listen. Pointing out the mistakes of others is not enough. If people are to trust journalists, we need to earn it.

∼

The New Yorker has a reputation for accuracy. At least, that's what the magazine tells itself. In reality, whether or not it is to be believed depends on whom you ask.

A prospectus announcing the first issue of *The New Yorker* in 1925 promised that,

> As compared to the newspaper, *The New Yorker* will be interpretative rather than stenographic. It will print facts that it will have to go behind the scenes to get, but it will not deal in scandal for the sake of scandal nor sensation for the sake of sensation. Its integrity will be above suspicion.[24]

(The same document was also where Harold Ross, the founding editor, was first rude enough to say that his new publication would 'not be edited for the old lady in Dubuque'. The past hundred years have brought remarkably little change to some aspects of the magazine's attitude, which remains equal parts tongue-in-cheek, earnest and supercilious. But today, such subscribers are highly desirable.)

True to Ross's mandate, *The New Yorker* maintains an obsessive interest in facts, one that can sometimes seem to go beyond any obvious practical advantage. It didn't take long for the early editors to recognise the usefulness of at least basic stenography. In 1927, the magazine published a profile of the poet Edna St Vincent Millay, 'America's first starlet',[25] claiming, among other fanciful details, that her father had been a stevedore (he was a schoolteacher).[26] The embarrassment inspired Ross to install a fact-checking department, and since then, checkers have left their marks all over the magazine. John McPhee, in an essay published in 2009, depicted fact-checking as a pursuit bordering on mania. To shore up one important but rickety anecdote of his concerning wartime nuclear reactors, a checker placed calls that 'ricocheted all over the United States: from Brookhaven to Bethesda, from La Jolla to Los Alamos'. The chase culminated, moments before the press deadline, in a call to a Florida police department, which the checker enlisted to track down a crucial witness. (He turned out to have gone to a mall.)[27]

Not many pieces require such heroics: the reality is that fact-checkers are busy people, who traffic only infrequently in the dark arts of deep research. Most facts can be checked far more easily, especially with the benefit of the internet, and since there are so many, a checker has to prioritise. When a particular fact turns out to be especially sticky, persistence and attention, rather than any kind of special knowledge, are generally what's needed. Checkers, of course, are not infallible, and their successes are mostly attributable to hard work and creativity. What is truly extraordinary about having a fact-checking department is that it exists at all. At the time of writing, thirty people work in fact-checking at *The New Yorker*, almost all of them full-time. It is labour, at scale, that produces accuracy.

Today, with a few pragmatic exceptions, fact-checkers go over everything published by *The New Yorker*,[28] editing for accuracy, balance, fairness and context. Writers are asked to share their sourcing; checkers review both research materials (books, articles, emails, documents) and original reporting. For complex topics, and as needed for corroboration, they do their own independent research, perhaps conferring with relevant experts. And unless there's a good reason not to, they get in touch with every person and entity mentioned in the story, and comb through what's attributed to or said about them.

This fulfils a few functions. If the person cooperates, as they typically do, the checker can verify factual details, including those that appear within quotes. If they disagree with something, they get a chance to comment or correct the record.[29] And if they are angry, well, it's better to know. (This step is also important in libel-proofing a piece: under US law, a good-faith and thorough effort to discover the truth is a solid defence should you accidentally publish an actionable inaccuracy. No matter how solid your standards are, it doesn't look great if you didn't bother trying to contact the person involved.) Checkers may discover hidden holes in a story, or garner perspectives that ought to be included. Most importantly, perhaps, this process, which is a kind of re-reporting, gives a fact-checker an opportunity to find out the basis of each statement of fact or opinion: is it personal experience, the pages of a half-remembered book, a third-hand rumour, or years of study? The value of a source, whether a person or a document, comes down mostly to their access to information, and to its quality.

Depending on the stakes—are we talking about what I ate for breakfast, or the location at which I saw the crime occur?—and on what other sources are available, a checker may then need to seek corroboration or to do some reporting of their own. Finally, based on all this, they can decide what to say, and how: after a fashion, they decide what the magazine believes to be true.[30] Truth, in this sense, is sought and rendered, something produced by rigorous inquiry and informed consideration rather than something discovered. Many points, tweaked where necessary, can be stated as fact, but often a checker will want to insert a citation ('according to ...') or present conflicting accounts. Tone matters, and may be used to indicate the level of confidence: a well-judged assertion may be one that leaves room for doubt. Falsehoods which reveal something about the speaker may have enough value to keep, so long as they are rebutted, but statements that are truly unverifiable, or clearly and unfixably specious, will typically be cut: deciding what not to publish is sometimes just as important as deciding what to keep in. In the landscape of a story, fact-checkers' trails can often be followed along a path of hedges and denials, but an elegant fix may render the footwork behind it invisible. (Dispiritingly, checking tends to be at its most visible when it goes wrong, as when, despite *Der Spiegel*'s dozens-strong research department, a star reporter there recently turned out to have fabricated many of his stories.)[31]

Subscribers to *The New Yorker*, of whom there were roughly 1.3 million at last count, seem to place a good deal of trust in this process. We know that they do because they're so upset when we get something wrong. (Letter writers' snide tendency to complain about failures of '*The New Yorker*'s vaunted fact-checking department' is surely a form of flattery.) Because *The New Yorker*, like many other publications,[32] trades on its reputation for accuracy,[33] readers can easily feel cheated, even betrayed, when an error slips in. This is not simply a commercial problem. 'Trust,' as the philosopher Annette Baier once wrote, 'is a fragile plant,'[34] one that can easily be damaged by the kind of increased scrutiny or scepticism that a flaw, once noticed, tends to induce. Once the roots have withered, they can be hard to restore.

Trust is something that journalists ask for. It's also something that they give. Just as readers learn about the world from the news, so journalists learn from their sources. Another philosopher, Neil Levy, points out that 'much—perhaps most—of what we know, we know on the basis of testimony, and (except in some unusual cases) we acquire knowledge through testimony only when we trust speakers'.[35] Most information comes to us from other people, whom we choose, deliberately or without thinking, to believe. As journalists, how and why we make those choices is particularly important. In the same essay, Levy writes that 'trust makes us vulnerable', and if this is the case for a writer, it's doubly so for their reader. No reporter can avoid that vulnerability, but mediating it is essential to earning and keeping the trust of a reader. Journalists choose whom to trust on their readers' behalf.

For journalists, as for anyone, there are certain shortcuts to trustworthiness, including reputation, expertise and transparency—the sharing of sources, for example, or the prompt correction of errors. Some of these shortcuts are more perilous than others. Various outfits, positioning themselves as neutral guides to the marketplace of ideas, now tout evaluations of news organisations' trustworthiness,[36] but relying on these requires trusting in the quality and objectivity of the evaluation. Official data is often taken at face value, but numbers can conceal motives: think of the disputes over how to count casualties in recent conflicts. Governments, meanwhile, may use their powers over information to suppress unfavourable narratives: in Hong Kong, 'fake news' laws ostensibly aimed at misinformation threaten free expression; some see the same spectre in America.

While certain categories of information may come to be considered inherently trustworthy, these, too, are in flux. For decades, the technical difficulty of editing photographs and videos allowed them to be treated, by most people, as essentially incontrovertible. With the advent of AI-based editing tools, footage and imagery have swiftly become much harder to credit. Similar tools are already being used to spoof voices based on only seconds of recorded audio. For the average person, this might manifest in scams,[37] but for a journalist, it puts source calls in question. Technologies of deception tend to be accompanied by ones of detection or verification—cryptographic keys, for example, have long been used to verify identity online, and a battery of companies already promise that they can spot AI-manipulated imagery—but especially at a moment of rapid change, these remain deeply fallible. Though chatbots and AI-enabled search engines promise to help us with research (when a colleague at *The New Yorker* 'interviewed' ChatGPT, it told him 'I aim to provide information that is as neutral and unbiased as possible'[38]), their inability to provide sourcing, and their tendency to hallucinate, look more like a shortcut to nowhere, at least for now. The consequent problems extend far beyond journalism: election campaigns, where subtle impressions can lead to big differences in voting behaviour, seem increasingly vulnerable to deepfakes and inscrutable algorithms.[39] Like everyone else, fact-checkers have only just begun to grapple with the consequences.

In such a landscape, it becomes difficult to know what is true, and, consequently, to make decisions. Trust and naivety can feel uncomfortably close. We live in complex societies, where the media often functions as 'the expert system helping people navigate the social and political world'.[40] If this system fails, and nothing takes its place, the consequences look dire. But failure—the endpoint of the story of generational decay, of gold exchanged for dross—is not inevitable. Fact-checking of the sort practised at *The New Yorker* is only one potential, highly specific and resource-intensive solution, but its relationship to the basic tenets of editorial good practice make it worth examining. It acknowledges the messiness of truth, the requirements of attention, the way we squint to see more clearly. It tells you to say what you mean, and know that you mean it.

How Constructive Journalism Can Restore Trust in Democracy

Ulrik Haagerup, founder and CEO of Constructive Institute, Denmark

For once I was a bit early, and as I was waiting in the vast reception of the News Corp. headquarters next to London Bridge to do a workshop for editors at *The Times* on constructive journalism, I could read the writing on the wall. Literally. The letters were enormous, but hardly any of the staff from *The Times*, *Sky News* and *The Sun*, rushing in and out on deadlines, seemed to notice. It was a shame because they are good. Since the News Building was opened in September 2014 by then London mayor and future prime minister Boris Johnson, who was once fired from *The Times* for lying in his reporting, the writing on the wall has read: 'Because the time is now to see things differently and to do things differently to reconnect with our past in order to redefine our future. To rethink continuously the business of storytelling.'

As any of us half-fat middle-aged men know, if we do not dare take off our clothes even behind closed doors and take in the consequences of what we see, we will never change. As a consequence, we will continue to drink too much beer, eat too many French fries and end up with tight pants and an early stroke. The point is, I thought to myself as I looked at those letters, if we are not self-critical, we, as an industry and as a profession, might *talk about* change, but it may never come because we are too busy, really, *to* change. And if we do as we have always done, we probably will get the same results we always have. It is time to change the diet, so to speak. Because, as an industry, we are not in good shape—our results are not great.

So, the writing on the wall, visible at New Corp. since 2014. That was twenty-seven years after the birth of the internet, which would eventually digitally connect the world at the speed of light, vastly outperforming newsprint working at the speed of trucks and paperboys on bicycles.

It was sixteen years after two students from Stanford started Google with the idea that all information should be made accessible to everybody. And that the collection of personal data about each user's life and preferences was the hidden price for 'free' access. This allowed advertisers to suddenly target their services and products to individuals, outperforming the classifieds, which for centuries had financed independent journalism and made commercial newspaper publishing one of the most profitable businesses on the planet.

It was ten years after the launch of Facebook, which made it possible for anybody to be able to tell any story to anyone else, and only seven years after Apple's iPhone not only put the internet into the pocket of everyone, everywhere, but also made every user a publisher through text, sound or video—breaking the monopoly of journalists on being the only professionals able to mass communicate.

So we have had time to understand what was coming: cutbacks, lay-offs, shutdowns of century-old news organisations, the spread of news deserts, and the rise of mistrust.

Polarisation Is the Next Pandemic

In 2006, the total advertising revenue for newspapers was approximately $126 billion globally. By 2016, this figure had dropped to around $60 billion, less than half of what it had been a decade earlier. The estimated advertising revenue for newspapers in 2024 is projected to be about $28 billion, indicating a dramatic decline of approximately 78 per cent over the full eighteen-year period. But, like the frog in a pot of slowly heating water, we didn't really move, and now we are being boiled.

The non-commercial news market is also affected: in the summer of 2024, the BBC announced another round of lay-offs, as more and more Brits stopped paying their licence fees for public service content. Netflix and other entertainment streaming services are taking the family's focus and its budget.

Even more worrisome, it has become socially acceptable for people, especially in Europe, the United States and Australia, to tell each other they don't need news. News avoidance has spread beyond young people and women, who were the first to turn their backs on traditional news media. When asked why by the Reuters Institute for the Studies of Journalism at Oxford University, they explained that news makes them feel depressed and overwhelmed, and they increasingly do not trust it.

One of the many consequences of this is that many of us don't know anything about people who are not like us and who do not share our views on social media. As a result, we are more divided than ever—polarisation has become the next pandemic. The virus of division spreads among us, not only via misinformation from Russia and the algorithms behind social media, but also through the culture of politics and the news media.

My brave colleague Maria Ressa, founder of Rappler Media in the Philippines and winner of the Nobel Peace Prize in 2021, summed up the challenges better than anyone when she opened our fourth Global Constructive Journalism Conference in Bonn in June 2022: 'Without facts, you cannot have truth. Without truth, you cannot have trust. Without trust, we have no shared reality, and government, journalism and democracy cannot work. That's the given today.'

She then asked the right question of me and her other journalism peers in the room, 'So, what do we do? How does journalism evolve?', before answering her own questions: 'Constructive journalism is the way journalism should always have been. And I think we are forced to think this way: to define the problems very clearly so we can help our societies find the right solutions. And the critical word there is "help".'

The New Constructive Mindset

The idea of journalism as a helper of society, a facilitator of dialogue, a good friend that helps people navigate a complex world, has, for many in the news industry, been provocative and revolutionary. We call it constructive news because, more than ever, our societies need trustworthy journalism—by which I do not mean lightweight, happy-go-lucky nor activistic reporting.

As a newly appointed news director at the Danish Broadcasting Corporation, or DR, in 2007, I found my own news programs too negative, built on the journalistic mantra 'If it bleeds, it leads'—the first words I learned at journalism school back in the early 1980s. 'A good story is a bad story. If nobody gets mad, it's not journalism, but advertising.' That mindset was proven by tabloid media to work. And that logic travelled first to local TV and then to the mainstream media. Algorithms on social media sped up this culture-build, which said the extreme, the dramas and the conflicts always won the war of attention.

The consequence was a news service from a serious public provider that did not have to make people buy their stories, as they were forced to pay for them already. It also meant that DR painted a picture of the world as terrible, fearful and depressing, leaving out stories about progress and people, cities and countries, that we might learn from. And politicians, who wanted access to the voters through the news media, learnt from day one in public office that no political journalist wanted to hear about their own ideas, but a harsh attack on their opponent's point of view would create a conflict that opened the gates to the front pages and studios, infusing the democratic conversation with a toxic culture.

I decided in 2008 to go public with criticism of myself and the sense of the world we gave Danes with our news mix and our journalistic culture. And I advocated for a new kind of journalism that was 'constructive', a word that means 'having a beneficial purpose'. I thought nobody could be against that. Boy, was I wrong.

Former CEOs of DR demanded my resignation, most reporters thought I had a brain tumour, and the commissioning editors shut down the idea, insisting that the purpose of journalism was to be critical. I replied that the purpose was to enlighten people and, in order to do so, we needed to be critical. But it was a tool, not the goal itself, and one of our biggest mistakes was that we had mixed up the two concepts. Nonetheless, when I was interviewed on my own main news show, the first question from the popular anchor was: 'Shouldn't you have been a priest instead?'

But journalism won out, and we began to experiment with new stories on potential solutions to the problems we continued to uncover. Old Danes in rural districts were dying because of a lack of doctors, so we looked at what they had done in Norway, where young doctors from the university in Oslo were travelling 2000 kilometres to the hospitals north of the Arctic Circle. Because we could document that they had solved their problem with a different strategy, with lower interest rates on study loans, jobs for spouses, nice kindergartens, fancy commercials with polar bears, clean air and northern lightning, we could offer a viable and tested solution—the trick being that the unavoidable stalling of politicians over such an issue now looked unacceptable.

The shift in focus from only covering the *what* and the *why* to also ask about the *now what* and the *how* produced great stories. It moved our coverage from only looking at today, and sometimes yesterday, to include stories about tomorrow—which ought to be the essence of politics, but rarely is.

In the lead-up to a national election, our commercial competitor invited the party leaders to a boxing ring, complete with spectators in either red or blue T-shirts, disco music, smoke machines, and half-naked girls with pompoms. Our top management then asked us to do the same thing to win viewers back. Instead, we created a new format called 'Night of Democracy' in our own concert hall, which was so beautiful (the event did go more than slightly over budget) that you had to refrain from artistic impulses on stage. We asked the party leaders to come up with ideas to solve the challenges Danes faced. We then asked the audience to applaud if they heard a good idea, and told them that it was okay to praise nasty attacks on a political opponent, but not afterwards to complain about the harsh tone in the debate. We also asked them to consider applauding politicians who dared to say they were in doubt or who even adjusted their point of view after hearing an argument from another leader. Our debate took twice as long as the boxing match—and attracted twice as many viewers.

Doubt as a Conversation Starter

We also introduced new formats for our political debates, which for years had carried names from warfare—'Duel' or 'Crossfire'—and where we had mostly invited politicians with viewpoints as far from each other as possible in order for the conflict and entertainment to grow. But too often these had turned into shouting contests, leaving viewers to choose winners and losers instead of the best argument—assuming they did not switch channels in frustration over the tone in politics.

One of the formats we called 'Far from Borgen'—Borgen being the nickname of the national parliament. We took two politicians with different views on a certain political issue, and took them out in public so they could talk to real people. One program was about windmills at sea close to the coastline. Another was about the never-ending conflict over Danish policy on prostitution: should we make it illegal, like in neighbouring Sweden, or make prostitutes pay tax, like in Germany? In that program, we made two politicians from different parties with opposing views on the issue visit a brothel. Viewers saw them pick up the phone and talk to clients, and talk to the women working there. One of the women explained that she liked her job, was independent, felt that society should respect her choice, and that she was mature and bright enough to decide what to do with her own body. It was clear that she made an impression, with the politician who'd wanted to make her services illegal obviously noting her arguments. Then another woman explained that she needed to do eleven anal intercourses a week to pay for her drugs, and suddenly the other politician, the one who'd wanted to make prostitution legal, was not so sure anymore.

The driver of this political format was doubt. Doubt is a conversation starter. Viewers sitting at home ask each other: what do we actually think about this?

Doubt creates drama: will meeting reality change anyone's mind?

Doubt leads to new questions and new answers: what surprised them the most? What was the best argument they heard against their original point of view?

Doubt creates empathy: it's human not to be completely sure, and the programs showed politicians getting out of their comfort zone and allowing themselves to be human beings like the rest of us. And viewers got to see two political opponents on a joint mission—they even saw how these politicians respected and sometimes even liked each other.

Doubt allows nuance: in media and politics, we are used to portraying reality in either black or white. Crooks or victims. Either, or. Here, viewers were presented with the dilemmas of life and politics.

A Global Megatrend

The constructive content strategy—offering potential solutions and nuanced engagement—added something valuable to our breaking news and investigative reporting model that paid off for DR, as it later did for so many more national, regional and local newsrooms. Soon we were the most trusted and biggest news provider, and when I quit after ten years to launch the Constructive Institute as an NGO at the great Danish university in Aarhus, most of the DR reporters and editors had incorporated constructive journalism into their daily routine.

Today, constructive journalism is called 'a global megatrend' and endorsed by the biggest global media organisations. We were keynote speakers at the WAN-IFRA Global Congress in Copenhagen in 2024. The head of all communications at UN institutions, Under-Secretary-General Melissa Flemming, opened the conference with these words: 'Despite fundamental challenges for the global news industry, we see hope. Solutions and constructive journalism sweeps worldwide into more and more newsrooms. And constructive journalism has started right here in Denmark.'

The Reuters Institute *Digital News Report* asked publishers around the world how they would counter news avoidance. The top three answers were elements of constructive journalism: explainers, Q&As and inspiration. Number four was constructive/solutions journalism itself.

The International News Media Association sent out a report in 2024 recommending their global members implement constructive strategies, such as more and more newsrooms around the world.

Our Constructive News Mirror, an algorithm which can scan and find constructive articles on any news site, documents that there is a demand for this new journalistic approach. The Norwegian Public Broadcaster, NRK, which has made a board decision to implement constructive journalism across all content—children's programs, fiction, documentaries and news—now finds that people read constructive stories more than traditional stories. They spend significantly more time on them. And they are more satisfied with their news provider after reading constructive stories.

One of the many clever changes NRK has made is to its approach to political debates on its main news show. Before, they'd invite two politicians with views as far away from each other as possible—far left or far right. Rarely would the debates end up in anything more than a loud argument. Now, they do not cast for the extreme but ask politicians closer to each other to debate—sometimes politicians from the left parties, sometimes from the right, sometimes from the middle. 'The results are far more interesting debates, higher trust and better ratings,' explains debate editor at NRK, Anne Kartine Førli.

One of the most successful online startups in Denmark, Zetland, bases its content on constructive journalism. They constantly experiment to rethink news publishing. They call their subscribers members, and serve them not more but better stories—often only two major pieces a day. They read aloud their written stories. They have no advertising, no editorials, and their seventy newspeople reach twice as many digital subscribers as the biggest traditional news providers, with an average age around forty-two.

One of Zetland's senior reporters, Nanna Schelde, was one of the first of so far close to 100 fellows at Constructive Institute since 2017. Therefore, we are even more proud to see that her approach to journalism does not have personal bias, clickbait or sensation as driving forces, but rather doubt and genuine curiosity. One story in her series started with a question to her readers. She had promised her daughter a smartphone when she turned ten. But now she had doubts: was it a good idea to give a child a smartphone, even though she was the only one in her class without one? It turned out she was not alone with that doubt. And the dialogue with her readers guided her to experts, science, facts and cases. Her findings not only led to massive feedback, but also to the biggest U-turn in the history of Danish educational policy—a ban on smartphones in Danish public schools, the reintroduction of books, and widespread discussion at dinner tables all over the country on not only digital habits among children and teenagers but also among their parents.

One of the many questions for the new Constructive Institute Asia Pacific, which will open in 2025 at Monash University in Melbourne, will be whether constructive experiments like these also can win back trust and profits on the other side of the globe at a time when robots make it impossible to tell true from false. AI could be the end of journalism—or a new beginning. Remembering that Martin Luther King did not mobilise by shouting, 'I have a nightmare,' I believe in the latter.

As John Whiterow, the then editor-in-chief of *The Times* of London, expressed publicly after my second workshop for his editors: 'Constructive journalism can be misunderstood as reporting "good news", an idea most journalists turn their noses up at. But let me explain how I understand it. We are all familiar with Kipling's six honest serving men: the *"What"*, *"Where"*, *"When"*, *"Who"*, *"Why"* and *"How"*. And we are all familiar with the fact that our trade has come under pressure from fake news and from an American president who derides the lying "mainstream media" as untrustworthy. Constructive journalism is one way in which the trust in the mainstream press can be restored. How? By adding one more element to the mix. *"What Now?"'*

Many of us have become immune to the relentlessly negative slant of much of our news coverage. Recalling the old adage that news should be 'something that someone, somewhere wants to suppress', we can easily commission stories digging up dirt and crime and exposing evils. And of course we should do this. But constructive news aims to empower the reader by spending more time on the 'What Now?'. Without any doubt, the writing is on the wall.

There Is No Middle Ground: Reclaiming the Public Square

Catherine Tait, former president and CEO, CBC/Radio-Canada, Canada, and Eli Pariser, co-founder of New_ Public, United States

> Social trust is a measure of the moral quality of a society ...
> When people in a society lose faith or trust in their institutions
> and in each other, the nation collapses.
>
> David Brooks, 'America Is Having a Moral Convulsion',
> *The Atlantic*, 5 October 2020

WE KNOW THAT, as a species, humans love to gather, to exchange ideas and, eventually, to try to persuade others of the rightness of their positions. From Speakers' Corner in London's Hyde Park to Facebook, we are a social species, engaged in discourse, yes, but also in speechifying and ranting. The explosion of social media as the twenty-first century's dominant means of communication is evidence of this irrepressible human instinct.

But that instinct hasn't led us where we hoped. Facebook was welcomed as the harbinger of wider democracy and greater freedom of expression and yet, ten years later, we are all grappling with how to contain it and the harms it propagates against our children, against women and against myriad under-represented or marginalised groups. Disinformation, fake news and deepfakes are the new enemy of democracy, and artificial intelligence may become technology's Trojan Horse.

As public broadcasters—or public service media—with many of us born from both world wars, our proximity to local audiences has been our secret sauce for decades. In Canada, who else but the public broadcaster will serve the vast north of the country in eight indigenous languages? Who else will deliver news and cultural programming to minority French-language communities outside of Quebec? Who else will serve as the emergency broadcaster in climate change disasters? And who else can connect a nation so geographically and demographically broad and diverse?

Only recently have we realised that, anchored in traditional linear television and radio services, we might have lost our public to the more interactive, immersive and engaging social media platforms. These platforms 'know us' through data tracking and collection in ways that the linear one-to-many model never could hope to do, or even imagine.

As online hate became the norm on so many social platforms, many of us turned off the 'comments sections' on our own—de facto disinviting our audiences from any conversation—in order to protect against the crashing waves of misogyny, racism and other forms of vile communication. We moved away from X in an effort to distance ourselves from a platform which had moved from a public good to a gladiator's amphitheatre.

And then Meta turned us off. During the summer of 2023, when devastating wildfires threatened vast swathes of Canada, Meta shut down access to CBC/Radio-Canada news on its platforms. Its argument was 'lack of sufficient interest in news' among its users. Despite our pleas to maintain our news during the crisis, for humanitarian reasons—the evacuation of Yellowknife in the Northwest Territories and many remote communities mostly inhabited by indigenous peoples—Meta did not reverse its decision.

Many of us in public service media have built audience reach across Meta's platforms, leveraging the low-bandwidth-optimised

Facebook to provide important access and connectivity in isolated areas of the country, and Instagram to provide critical access to hard-to-reach younger audiences. In fact, we all use third-party platforms like Spotify, YouTube and TikTok to connect with those younger audiences. But those platforms do not necessarily share critical audience data generated by our content and so we risk losing that direct relationship with our viewers.

What now? A public broadcaster without a public faces a serious existential crisis.

There is no middle ground between the Silicon Valley giants and 'old' media models in our current media landscape. We clearly cannot relinquish our audience to social media platforms that do not favour credible, trustworthy news. But the financial models of old media, dependent on advertising and subscription revenues, have been overturned and trampled by the crushing force of global digital powerhouses like Meta and Google. Not satisfied with just hoovering up most of the media revenue available in foreign territories, these giants have resisted—mostly successfully—the regulatory attempts to extract some portion of their commercial returns from the sovereign nations they have pillaged.

There have been small wins along the way—mostly in Europe—but the free-market ideology that has fuelled globalisation has reached its zenith with the digital giants. Australia had its moment, but Canada has largely compromised in its multiple attempts to rein in the voracious appetite of these media marauders.

In 2020, in the middle of the pandemic, a group of idealistic digital activists came to CBC/Radio-Canada with a proposition. What if the public broadcaster were to re-engage with audiences in new ways? What if we were to create a safe place for civil conversations online? Those under the not-for-profit banner New_ Public, many of whom grew up in the blossoming of social media only to be disheartened by its rapid wilting, were motivated to 'save the internet'. With the belief that all existing platforms were designed to fan traffic at any cost in order to generate revenue, New_ Public's co-founders wanted to test their hypothesis: if we remove the revenue imperative and incentives for negative engagement, could healthier, more productive conversations online follow? And importantly, could disenchanted users be coaxed back to participate in safer online conversations?

New_ Public's pitch went like this: you at CBC/Radio-Canada have the audiences, the reach and the scale to test the concept. We can help you design the digital products or solutions to improve or deepen connections online with your public.

A word about present-day public service media. We are all under siege. Growing populism worldwide, the erosion of trust in public institutions and media, and the financial collapse of many private media outlets have contributed to an increase in outright hostility towards perceived left-leaning or biased public media. This is not healthy scepticism or debate about our institutions; it manifests as a direct threat and attack on the very existence of publicly funded independent journalism.

There is no doubt that there is a correlation between growing distrust of media and the rise of social media and the proliferation of disinformation. The European Broadcasting Union has measured higher levels of civic engagement and satisfaction with democratic institutions (electoral processes and so on) of citizens in countries with well-funded public media.[1] And so, when New_ Public proposed a way forward—not only to regain a more intimate connection with our audiences but also, in a small way, to bring back public interest to the promise of greater democracy via the internet—it made sense to explore the opportunity with other public media organisations. A four-way partnership was born: Germany's public broadcaster ZDF, Belgium's French-language service RTBF and Switzerland's SRG SSR joined CBC/Radio-Canada in an historic, first-ever collaboration of its kind. The Public Spaces Incubator (PSI) set out with New_ Public, guiding us on a journey without certainty of outcome but with certainty of purpose.[2]

New_ Public got its start as a research project in 2018 seeking to address a big question: what does 'good' online look like? Its co-founders, Talia Stroud and Eli Pariser, were frustrated by a digital conversation that focused on tweaks, regulations and adjustments to the big platforms—particularly Facebook—rather than starting by asking, 'What kind of digital information environment do we want?' Over several years of research, Stroud and Pariser came to the conclusion that there is a missing element in our digital environments, and that the best way to understand it is by reference to our physical community environments. In physical communities, it's taken for granted that public spaces and institutions—places like parks, libraries and sidewalks—are critical for social cohesion. Bookstores are great, but libraries do something different because they're organised to serve the public, not just their owners and customers. Stroud and Pariser argued that we need analogous 'digital public spaces' online—not to replace privatised spaces like Facebook, but to complement them with spaces truly built around public needs. And they published a comprehensive set of metrics—the 'Civic Signals',[3] validated by surveys of 20,000 people in twenty countries—to define how these public digital spaces can be better measured.

But this left open the question of how to scale access to digital public spaces, and here, Stroud and Pariser, along with Deepti Doshi, a co-director of New_ Public who joined after a stint on Meta's internal incubator and community and groups team, began to think about public service media. Public media, after all, have an aligned mission to safeguard and support the public sphere, plus enormous scale and audience trust, and the means to think big about a new approach to digital conversation.

In June 2022, PSI was born, and the group began to meet. It quickly became clear that building alignment across five institutions, nine time zones and three languages was not going to be easy. Meetings were quiet and interactions were sometimes stilted until the group met in person in Mainz, Germany, where it was unequivocal how similar the problems each of the public media institutions were facing, especially regarding digital innovation, and how excited we all were about building something new together. While Zoom and DeepL-based translation of calls and documents was critical to helping the group communicate and understand each other, it was a shared mission that really bound the group together.

The incubator was structured in three phases. In the Discovery Phase, we would get to know each of the partners and their contexts, conduct desk research, and do interviews with users in each of the countries to understand what their feelings and needs about social media might be in order to identify areas of opportunity. In the Design Phase, we would conduct three virtual 'sprints' to start developing prototype ideas that were responsive to these needs. And in the Development Phase, we would turn these ideas into working code, test them out with users, iterate the designs, and then get them ready for a public debut. At the end of the project, the code for all of these prototypes will be open-sourced so that others can benefit from this work and take it forward as well.

This work resulted in a set of six core 'archetypes',[4] synthesised to represent public service media audience members. Ranging from those who lurk but feel reluctant to engage, to those who love the drama of a fight, these archetypes helped deepen our understanding of end users' behaviours and motivations so that we could be more tactical about how to optimise the design. And after surveying a number of opportunity areas, we identified a centre of gravity around a particular set of ideas that could define a unique lane for the project: 'public conversation'.

As we did our research, it became clear that *public* conversation, of the type you might see in a city hearing or a town meeting, isn't like other types of conversation. It's less about building relationships or understanding between particular people, and more about, as democracy advocate Danielle Allen puts it, helping a community see and shape itself.[5] And one evaluates public conversation not by whether one got to speak but by whether one's needs, experiences and ideas were represented in the conversation. This was an exciting revelation because it suggested a lane for our project that was distinct from the general-purpose lane that social media occupies, and a way to evaluate the many ideas that were popping into our distributed team's heads in countries around the world.

Together, we developed a framework for understanding how public conversation is different.

Public Conversation Model

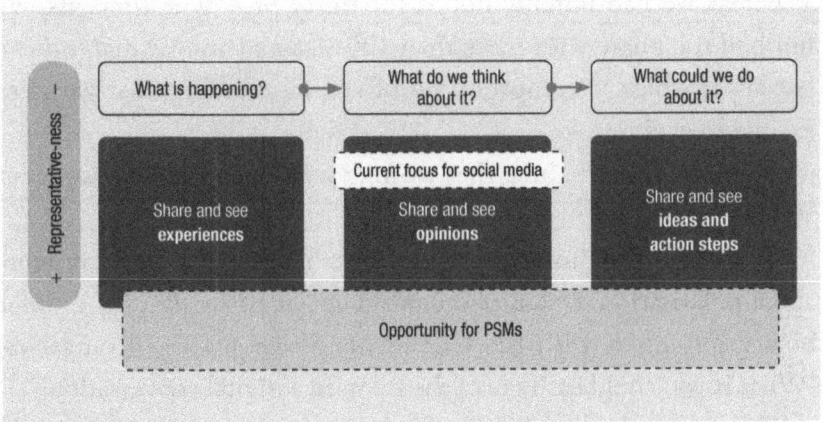

Public Spaces Incubator

Public conversation, we believe, seeks to help a group of people understand what we're experiencing—across all of the diversity in the group—what we think about it, and what we might be able to do about it.

We also came to understand more clearly why the design of standard commenting sections and digital conversations so frequently leads to toxicity. Sociologist Elisabeth Noelle-Neumann observed a social dynamic called 'the spiral of silence'.[6] People, Noelle-Neumann observed, have a deep need to stay part of the in-group, but they don't necessarily know what the in-group believes. When the first person speaks in a group, people tend to infer that their speech is 'in' the in-group, and censor themselves if they disagree so as not to be cast out. Only people who passionately disagree are likely to speak up against this in-group phenomenon, which means that it's very likely that the most passionate voices on both sides are among the first to speak, and immediately get into conflict. Like a bar in which a fistfight has broken out, other people stay silent and clear out, not wanting to get into the middle of the fray.

With these insights in mind, we started developing actual prototypes—and surprised ourselves with a wealth of exciting ideas. Whereas we had initially hoped for thirty prototype concepts, we finished the phase with more than 100—some stronger than others, but all of which were novel ways of communicating what we were excited to explore.

Here, we'll share three that we're moving into the Development Phase.

One of our first prototypes, Comments Slider, builds on the insights about polarisation dynamics described above. In an effort to counter binary responses, with the Comments Slider we asked ourselves, 'What if you could easily read the room in a digital conversation?'

Comments Slider visualises comments along a spectrum, and allows viewers to position themselves and explore the perspectives of others. It pushes people beyond the binary of thumbs up, thumbs down. And, based on answers, the feature offers another layer of active facilitation: encouraging comments where there are few, and identifying common ground.

Like politics, the people who are most likely to speak in digital spaces are not always the best suited to do so. So we also considered how to 'call in' different experiences and perspectives with Missing Perspectives.

This prototype allows journalists to identify what perspectives they'd like to hear from. As commenters contribute, they can self-identify with these perspectives; missing perspectives are encouraged.

Viewers can then interact with a live visualisation that provides some additional analysis of the perspectives.

And we heard the need, especially from younger people, to have a sense of co-presence—this is part of what has driven so many to seek out group chats and other arenas where people feel 'together' in an experience. Out of that prompt came the notion of Public Square View.

By turning on Public Square View during a live stream, users are able to see how many people are watching and interact with them. After the live stream, users can join a topic room based on their interactions to keep the conversation going.

We are excited about all of these ideas, but we also know that they'll likely change a lot as we embark on PSI's next phase: trialling the prototypes with the public in alpha and beta testing, getting feedback, and iterating these.

But the whole experience thus far has made us hopeful. In part, this hope stems from the unlikely fact that we managed to bring together over 200 people from around the world to be creative[7]— and it worked. In part, it stems from seeing how much opportunity there is to invent new ways of being together, if we're not bound by the metrics and commercial models of Silicon Valley. And in part, it's because we're beginning to understand how to make digital public spaces a reality.

Jane Jacobs, an ardent advocate of urban planning and public space, once observed that communities are safest not when they have a large and militarised police force, but when they are filled with families and grandparents and lots of 'eyes on the street'.[8] We aspire to bring this spirit to digital life, marginalising the trolls and welcoming the people who have felt unwelcome in digital spaces for much of the last twenty years.

The Public Space Incubator has shown us that a different kind of public conversation and a different kind of social media are possible. As 'old media' public broadcasters, we can reclaim the public online space for our audiences and foster healthy, open discourse for stronger social cohesion. Our mandate remains the same: supporting engaged citizens in social debate as a cornerstone of democracy. As PSI embarks on a second phase, from development to implementation, we look forward to welcoming new public media partners, including Germany's ARD and Australia's ABC. And, as we scale these digital solutions, we are eager to revitalise our public purpose in a digital future for public service media.

Strengthening Global Trust

Kristian Porter, CEO, Public Media Alliance, United Kingdom

THE YEAR 2024 will be known as a time when close to half the global population had the opportunity to vote,[1] a year that gave us a health check on the status and capacity of the world's democracies, and in turn, a litmus test on the state of free and independent media. It is during these often-volatile events that free and independent journalists and newsrooms should be able to fulfil their most vital mandate: to hold power to account and accurately inform the public without fear or favour. Democracies survive and thrive where there is a free press and where, as part of a healthy and plural media landscape, an informed citizenry has the option to access news and information from a variety of sources, especially viable and independent public service media (PSM).

According to the *Reuters Institute Digital News Report 2024*,[2] public broadcasters in Australia, Canada, the United Kingdom, South Africa and across Europe are still considered the most trusted sources of news in their jurisdictions. This trust stems from PSM's core values of editorial independence, accountability, universal access, transparency and impartiality, as well as the regulatory protections that safeguard them from political interference or censorship. But beyond this, it is also the long-standing trust that audiences have in the brand of PSM, based on the standards they have set over many years.

And while each public media organisation differs in its structure, governance and funding models,[3] based on the sociopolitical, economic and cultural context, this high level of trust is something that is shared across many of the fifty-plus members of the Public Media Alliance (PMA).

Some studies show that where there is strong public media, citizens are more informed, with a reduced knowledge gap between the most advantaged and disadvantaged in society,[4] while other studies indicate that countries with an independent and well-funded public media outfit have a healthy democracy.[5] There are two takeaways here: firstly, that independent public media is an outcome of a healthy democracy; and secondly, that independent public media also perpetuates and manifests the health of a democracy.

Even in the most oppressive authoritarian states, citizens turn to trusted international PSM like the BBC World Service, Deutsche Welle and ABC International in search of reliable sources, while during the height of the COVID-19 pandemic, it was public media that people turned to for lifesaving news and information. However, trust is hard won and easily lost, and trust is in decline. This is especially the case among younger audiences,[6] where news avoidance is on the rise,[7] and the rapid market disruption of streaming platforms and social media has given near-endless alternatives should audiences want to tune out.

The core values of public service media are certainly idealistic, but they are also fragile. And in a year when free and independent news media is needed most, press freedom rankings have tumbled, with the operating conditions for many of these fundamental democratic institutions severely compromised.

Globally, many public service media organisations are confronted by similar challenges. Funding constraints, political interference and the spread of disinformation are, more than ever, shared threats to their viability, and not just in countries with weaker democratic institutions.

Relevance and Bargaining Power

The rise of third-party platforms has caused a fragmentation of audiences and has long been seen as a substantial cause of declining trust in, and relevance of, PSM. To many, these platforms offer new and alternative sources of information, especially to those who feel misrepresented or marginalised by traditional outlets.

Of course, there have been many positives from this proliferation. For example, digital media startups have tapped into groups who historically have been let down by the mainstream press, such as Indigenous people and young audiences. This has led to the mainstream press re-examining their own work. But it is in these online spaces, often owned by multinational organisations that are not bound by their own policies or regulatory pressures to counter misinformation and disinformation, that distrust in PSM grows. Countering these narratives, maintaining visibility in an increasingly crowded space, regaining and maintaining trust, and adapting to rapid technological changes requires major investment in both time and resources.

In some cases, the situation has been compounded by attempts to restore the balance between traditional news media, including PSM, and tech platforms. In Canada, the launch of the Online News Act in 2023, which it was hoped would force the larger tech companies (Google and Meta) to enter negotiations with news media to compensate them for the content published on their platforms, resulted instead in Meta blocking Canadians from viewing, accessing and sharing news article links on its platforms, including viewing news content from international news outlets.[8] And while initially there was relative success for the News Media Bargaining Code (NMBC) in Australia, which brought Google and Meta to the negotiating table in 2021, Meta has since announced that it will not participate in further bargaining rounds and has removed Facebook's news tab in the country.

This lack of accountability for social media giants—also highlighted in X's mislabelling of public media in 2023[9]—paints a grim picture, particularly for public interest media in smaller markets, such as the Caribbean, where bargaining power is far more limited.

The implications of blocking access to reliable sources of news are profound, especially in times of emergency or during elections. It leaves a hole in which misinformation and disinformation can thrive. Many communities, especially in Canada's north, use Facebook as the dominant conduit to find and share news content. The same goes for many Pacific states, where Australia's public broadcaster, the ABC, is a key source of news and information. Recent research by UK regulator Ofcom found that 71 per cent of 16–24-year-olds use social media as their primary source of news.[10] But beyond this, it also demonstrates the imbalances in bargaining power between the platforms and the providers of accurate sources of news and information, let alone the reliance of PSM on these third-party services to reach audiences.

Indeed, effective bargaining codes could be one solution to sourcing additional and alternative financial support for PSM, which is needed more than ever amid the global rise in inflation, the cost-of-living crisis and a significant decline in commercial revenue. After all, the initial round of funding gained from the NMBC helped the ABC to fund sixty much-needed regional news jobs. But the disparity in bargaining power poses a major hurdle to the success of these codes, especially considering the multinational social media giants. And with major cuts to budgets, programming and jobs at PSM such as at the BBC, CBC/Radio-Canada, NHK, NPR, SABC and ZDF within the past year, additional alternative sources of income are needed now more than ever.

Independence and Interference

While funding and bargaining power is certainly a limiting factor for public media in regaining and maintaining trust, independence and political interference remain key determining factors. Being present, revealing truth, and holding power to account have never been more difficult, nor more urgent. As geopolitics plays out as much in people's smartphones as it does in the real world, traditionally trusted public media are fighting an uphill battle.

PSM require robust safeguards to ensure their independence from the state, especially editorially when funding is received from a government or public source. But the global rise in populism in recent years, and the reliance on social media as a vehicle for such rhetoric, has made many PSM easy targets for political campaigns and for those that want to silence news outlets. Impartiality has become a hotly contested topic, as has the argument that PSM are not diverse or representative. This has been particularly effective in France and elsewhere in Europe,[11] where during a cost-of-living crisis it has been relatively easy to rally support for cutting 'burdensome' licence fees and taxes.

According to the 2023 State Media Monitor report, '83 per cent of the 592 state-administered media entities across 157 countries lack editorial independence', many of which are considered public service media.[12] This is an increase of 3 per cent since 2021. Since then, we have seen numerous attempts to capture, influence or pressure public service media.

In Argentina, President Javier Milei has stood by his campaign promise to dismantle the country's public institutions, including the public news agency Télam, resulting in mass layoffs and protests in support of press freedom. And in Peru, accusations of IRTP being a government mouthpiece continue, especially with new government-linked appointments to its board.

While government appointments are not uncommon, it is the use of such mechanisms by governments to hold sway over PSM that is the concern. In Europe, despite the introduction of the European Media Freedom Act, which will fully apply from August 2025, there are significant fears for a number of PSM. This includes

RTVS in Slovakia, which was dismantled and replaced with a new organisation with fewer protections from government influence over key appointments. Another is Rai in Italy, where there is growing concern over political interference in management and content, with unions accusing one of the largest public broadcasters in Europe of becoming a 'mouthpiece of the government'.[13]

The rise in anti-PSM rhetoric by politicians and parties, including in France, the Netherlands and the Czech Republic, as well as the ongoing capture of PSM in Hungary, where an estimated 70–80 per cent of the media is linked to the ruling Fidesz party, has left a general sense of vulnerability for organisations that are considered crucial staples of democracy by the EU.[14] Meanwhile, in Canada, Switzerland and the United Kingdom, there are very active campaigns to 'defund PSM', in some cases supported by major political parties.

Independent public media can only exist where the conditions are right, and as press freedom falls around the world, so too does the potential for PSM to operate independently or to their full potential. SLAPPs, the decline of journalist safety online and offline, and arbitrary laws such as the rise of so-called 'fake news laws'—often vaguely defined and which allow governments to 'define prohibited content at their own discretion'—only add to the limitations placed on both public and private media. According to the Center for International Media Assistance, ninety-one such laws were active around the world by 2022,[15] Sri Lanka being among the most recent.

Maintaining and Building Trust

While this is not a complete account of the challenges facing public media, the combination of these issues is placing considerable strain on the ability of PSM to maintain audiences and their trust. Public broadcasters do, it must be said, also acknowledge a share of the blame, relying on their traditional audience base, and not trying to reach underserved and marginalised communities.

But there are solutions. Many of our members are doubling down on digital-first strategies as a way of both cutting costs and extending their presence to where their audiences are and will be—although some critics question whether older or more remote audiences will be left behind.

Others are collaborating to find solutions—after all, there is power in numbers, especially where there are shared values. This means working with like-minded organisations, or via associations like PMA or the European Broadcasting Union, but also with the wider media ecosystem. It includes projects like the Public Spaces Incubator, where German, Swiss, Belgian and Canadian public broadcasters are collaborating with the tech company New_ Public to develop a new interactive space bound by public service values to support healthier democratic debate.

Other projects include the multinational and cross-industry Journalism Trust Initiative, which aims to label trusted newsrooms that have strong, independent editorial values. Another is the Content Authenticity Initiative, which is developing algorithmic tools to watermark content as a sign of provenance, to counter false generative-AI images as they become more commonplace. In Belgium and the Netherlands, PSM and commercial news services joined forces ahead of the 2024 European elections to run a 'fact-checking' marathon from a central editorial office, with shared output across eight news outlets.

Yet, in this increasingly fast-paced world, many collaborative initiatives take time and risk being obsolete by the time they are rolled out, especially in the age of AI. They also do not necessarily involve public media in non-G20 countries, which often lack the resourcing to take part in such initiatives. That is why associations like PMA are coordinating initiatives such as regional guidelines on responsible AI and gender sensitive reporting.[16] It is also why we are strongly advocating that public media capitalise on their strongest playing card: their core values. These are what define them, and at a time of crisis, conflict or elections, it is this that turns audiences back to PSM.

Some, like the BBC, are placing values at the heart of marketing campaigns, and transparently demonstrating the process behind editorial decisions. Others, like Swedish Radio and Belgium's VRT, are taking it back to basics and engaging directly with their audiences through 'meet the correspondents' events and touring the country to meet listeners and learn more about their audiences.[17]

Ultimately, it is about media literacy for citizens and politicians alike, and empowering the public—who PSM are ultimately accountable to—with the tools to know exactly what public service media is, and what it is they stand to lose.

Trust and the Danish Experience

Gert Tingghaard Svendsen, author and Professor of Public Policy, Aarhus University, Denmark

DENMARK HOLDS THE highest level of social trust globally, nearly twice that of countries like the United States, and is renowned for its high level of happiness too.[1] When surveyed with the question, 'Do you think most other people can be trusted?', 77 per cent of Danes respond affirmatively. Understanding the mechanism behind this exceptional level of trust, what could be termed 'trust-building technology', is pivotal in deciphering how to restore trust in media and facilitate cooperation between journalists and users.

Social trust is defined as the expectation that a stranger will follow an established norm within a given context. Individuals, akin to small-scale statisticians, accumulate experiences over time, and in societies where most people follow cooperative norms, the system works.[2] In essence, social trust is the expectation that an unknown individual will not break the norm and cheat you whenever there is a personal economic gain from doing so. Consequently, citizens residing in high-trust societies are more likely to cooperate with journalists and vice versa. Social trust differs fundamentally from specific trust in people you already know because it includes strangers you do not know beforehand and have no direct information about. Thus, social trust is a general assessment of how trustworthy people believe others to be—we can call this the trust culture. For example, there is no written contract between a journalist and a citizen, but citizens expect that they will gain from cooperating with journalists. Such a strong verbal-agreement culture makes everyday life easier, lowering transaction costs.

Differences in trust cultures can be measured in practice by extensive questionnaire surveys.[3] More specifically, a standard measure for social trust is the percentage of the population who answer 'Yes' when asked if they think most other people can be trusted.[4] When observing social trust across nations, we see a huge variation. The table below ranks selected countries in relation to the level of social trust over the period 2017–20.

Rank	Country	Score (%)
1	Denmark	77.4
2	Norway	75.1
3	Finland	72.2
4	Sweden	67.4
5	Iceland	65.8
9	New Zealand	59.5
10	Australia	54.0
12	Germany	46.0
15	United Kingdom	41.4
16	Spain	41.0
17	United States	39.7
26	Italy	28.5
28	France	28.1
35	Russia	23.9
54	Turkey	14.3
58	Romania	11.9
63	Mexico	10.3
67	Greece	8.4
72	Philippines	5.4
74	Indonesia	5.2
75	Colombia	4.5
76	Nicaragua	4.3
77	Albania	2.5
78	Zimbabwe	2.1

Source: European and World Values surveys collected 2017–20 (numbers rounded up).

Overall, the Nordic countries occupy the top five positions, representing the world's most trusting nations, followed by New Zealand, Australia, Germany, the United Kingdom and Spain. The United States holds about half the trust level of Denmark, a trend highlighted by researchers who noted a decline in civic engagement in the United States during the 1990s.[5] Intriguingly, others have found that Nordic immigrants in the United States maintain notably higher levels of social trust across generations compared to the national American average.[6]

Why this Nordic excellency in terms of social trust? This is not an easy question to answer. However, one possible historic starting point for social trust accumulation in Scandinavia dates back to the Viking Age (793–1066 CE). During this time of rampant trade, market transactions were signed off on a handshake rather than a written contract because of high levels of illiteracy among the Vikings. Deals therefore had to be grounded in trust. This reliance on trust-based agreements fostered the emergence of social norms such as 'a word is a word', which were socially endorsed within this Viking 'handshake' culture.

Let's say a trader engaged in the sale of fake Ulfberht swords. If the fakes were detected, that trader would have been seen to have broken his trust contract and would encounter social disciplinary measures within the marketplace despite no written contract existing. These measures encompassed a spectrum of social punitive actions aimed at preserving social order and communal integrity. So the cheater could be subjected to public scolding, resulting in a deterioration of reputation and credibility. Ultimately, this process of social disciplining could culminate in the individual's ostracism from the social fabric of the marketplace if the problem was not solved by dialogue and compromise.[7]

Because this kind of deal was commonplace and discipline for someone breaking their word was meted out, social trust norms were established that remained even as literacy in Denmark increased.

The Danish Experience of Media

Despite the fact that Denmark possesses the strongest trust culture globally, trust in journalists within the country is surprisingly low. This phenomenon is substantiated by recent findings presented in the table below, derived from a 2023 study focusing on trust in twenty-seven distinct Danish professions. The study reveals that journalists, alongside politicians, car dealers and influencers, occupy the lowest positions in terms of trustworthiness. Utilising a scale ranging from 1 to 5, where 1 signifies the lowest level of trust and 5 the highest, politicians rank second-lowest with a score (rounded up) of 2.3, followed by car dealers at 2.5 and journalists at 2.6. Real estate agents follow closely at 2.7, while bank advisers rank slightly higher at 3.0. Notably, influencers receive the lowest trust score at 1.8.

Conversely, the professions occupying the top five positions in terms of trustworthiness are midwives, doctors, nurses, physiotherapists and police officers. These findings underscore a significant discrepancy between the level of societal trust and the trust placed in certain professional domains, particularly within the realm of journalism.

At the core of trust lies the concept of expectation, wherein the fulfilment of expectations plays a pivotal role in determining trustworthiness, particularly in the context of journalism. Renowned American journalist Carl Bernstein encapsulates the essence of good journalism as 'the best obtainable version of the truth'. However, the commercialisation of media introduces complexities, casting doubt on whether journalists adhere solely to the pursuit of truth. Leslie Moonves, former CEO of CBS, one of the largest TV and radio companies in the United States, commented on Donald Trump: 'Who would have thought that this circus would come to town? But, you know, it may not be good for America, but it's damn good for CBS' and 'It's a terrible thing to say, but bring it on, Donald. Go ahead. Keep going' and 'the money's rolling in'.[8] The surge in advertising revenue during CBS's coverage of Trump's campaign illustrates the potential influence of commercial interests on journalistic practices. This financial incentive raises questions and concerns about the extent to which media outlets prioritise profit over the impartial pursuit of truth, thus impacting their trustworthiness.

Rank/profession	Score
1 Midwives	4.16
2 Doctors	4.08
3 Nurses	3.98
4 Physiotherapists	3.85
5 Police officers	3.83
6 Librarians	3.83
7 Engineers	3.81
8 Dentists	3.79
9 Psychologists	3.72
10 Soldiers	3.67
11 Pedagogues	3.59
12 School teachers	3.59
13 Accountants	3.57
14 Priests	3.51
15 Care assistants	3.50
16 Lawyers	3.48
17 Farmers	3.44
18 Bus drivers	3.40
19 Craftsmen	3.27
20 Social workers	3.24
21 Civil servants	3.07
22 Bank advisers	3.00
23 Real estate agents	2.67
24 Journalists	2.60
25 Car dealers	2.45
26 Politicians	2.26
27 Influencers	1.83

Note: The credibility analysis was conducted from 21 August to 4 October 2023. A representative sample of 2000 Danes aged 18–75 participated in the online questionnaire survey.

Source: Radius, *Troværdighedsundersøgelsen 2023*

The prevailing low level of trust directed toward journalists in Denmark indicates a pattern of repeated disappointment among media users, stemming from instances where journalists have failed to meet expectations and deliver on their promises. This failure to 'deliver the goods' suggests a disconnect between journalistic practices and public expectations. Therefore, it becomes imperative for journalists to strive towards meeting expectations and cultivating positive user experiences in media consumption. This means ensuring that users perceive tangible benefits from their engagement with the media, fostering a sense of mutual benefit and win-win situations.

Fundamentally, trust hinges on the expectation that promises will be upheld and deception avoided. The observed lack of trust in journalists may be attributed to instances where news coverage fell short, either due to inaccuracies, omissions or the magnification of trivial matters. The repercussions of this erosion of trust are twofold: diminished credibility for the media and a disengagement among users. Consequently, news avoidance and a decline in informed voters pose a direct threat to democracy, creating fertile ground for populist leaders claiming to champion the interests of 'the people'.

Restoring Trust in the Media

So how can journalists respond to restore trust and thereby help create a society that has more cohesion and is therefore happier and more successful? Citizens need to feel that it is possible to influence the political agenda in a well-functioning democracy. Public discussion should then address the topics that citizens and politicians find particularly important. However, the media can skew this agenda by consciously choosing to omit some topics while focusing on others.

This so-called priming determines what should or shouldn't 'be on the table'. Because the media, by its choices, can influence what comes onto the political agenda and is debated in the public sphere, problems arise when some relevant topics are omitted or mis-prioritised. Furthermore, the media can influence people's attitudes by the way in which stories are framed. Certain angles can leave users with the impression that perhaps not the entire reality has been truthfully presented. In Denmark around fifteen years ago, for example, a proposed payment ring (road toll) around Copenhagen was largely framed by the media as a new tax rather than as a measure that, like the successful introductions of payment rings in Stockholm and Oslo, should prevent congestion and improve air quality. That one-sided framing of the story influenced the way in which it was discussed and debated in the public sphere. The proposal was subsequently dropped in 2012.

In the same way, the sometimes chaotic listing of conflicts and negative news in modern journalism can skew the political agenda and public debate, especially when they do not include any discussion of possible solutions.[9] This lack of constructive, solutions-focused journalism can lead to a problem-oriented solution model. On the other hand, a free and independent press can keep those in power accountable and better educate voters, who can then make a more informed choice at the ballot box. Society becomes richer and happier in this way, and the trust relationship between media and citizen is strengthened.

In everyday life, people grapple with a multitude of issues, such as the potential construction of a new motorway passing by their homes, an increasing number of bicycle thefts, the erection of a new high-rise building on a neighbouring plot, the lack of safe bike lanes for children's school commute, or the potential impact of a new offshore wind farm. These issues, and others like them, actually present an opportunity. How can journalists restore Danes' trust in their professional group? One big step forward would be for journalists to go back to traditional ways of news-gathering and hit the beat more often to connect with people and their issues more directly.

Modern technology has enabled journalism to be done solely through web-based communication. However, these new technologies are not necessarily more trust-building, especially if journalists no longer meet users. If we go back to the roots of what we can call the classical period, it was about face-to-face meetings and dialogue between journalists and users. The journalist went where people were. It's something journalists worldwide need to rethink.

A trust-building initiative in this regard could involve journalists actively engaging with their current and potential users face-to-face instead of remaining confined to their offices. Nowadays, you only know your journalist by name—but you've never met! Establishing more formal meeting points between journalists and citizens can be achieved through forums such as town hall meetings and hearings, where specific topics are addressed. Here, journalists can engage with their users, enabling them to better represent the interests of the people. The dialogue creates a win-win situation—citizens benefit when their issues are addressed, and journalists benefit because more people will demand what they do.[10]

Journalists must meet their users, just as health staff meet their patients. We are all familiar with the situation at a hospital. You walk in to get medical help. The nurses and doctors come to your rescue and assist in solving your problem so that you obtain the desired treatment. Afterwards, you go home satisfied, with the impression the nurses and doctors are willing to help and cooperate as much as possible. This situation can similarly be created between the journalist and their customers, who receive what they demand, namely a potential solution to their problem. Satisfied customers will return and will also tell others about their positive experience.

What Can We Learn from the Danish Experience?

Even within Denmark, renowned for having the strongest trust culture globally, the level of trust in journalists is very low. If the audience—the journalist's customers—perceive the journalist as being unhelpful by not representing their interests, they will feel they have received the sucker's pay-off and lose trust. Trust is all about expectations, and when journalists don't meet them, their readers feel disappointed and cheated.

However, higher trust is created when the expectation from a user is fulfilled, raising the likelihood that successful cooperation will continue in the future. If the journalists meet the users in real life, returning to the idea of the physical 'meeting place'—as in the classical period—trust may be restored. One example is the Danish media outlet Nordjyske which, in the spring of 2018, sent a 'dialogue bus' (a mobile newsroom) on a tour with journalists to local areas. Citizens were invited into the bus to share and discuss their stories.[11]

Establishing physical meeting places as a trust-building initiative arguably fosters the cultivation of an even more robust trust culture and contributes to a more democratic and happy society. Journalists have the potential to climb the trust ladder and have real impact on society. Why not just do it?

PART IV
TRUST, CORPORATES AND LEADERSHIP

Trust and Distrust:
The Existential Tension

Ross Honeywill, social scientist, and Michele Levine, CEO,
Roy Morgan, Australia

IN THE AGE of Doubt, trust provides hope. Trust is an absence of doubt. Without it, we would be paralysed in everyday life. We would never make an online purchase, book an Uber, take a flight, go on a date, give our credit card details over the phone, open the door to strangers, get married, believe the news, stay married—the examples are endless. And nowhere is trust more on show than in the corporate world.

Marc Benioff, CEO of software company Salesforce, says, 'Trust has to be the highest value in your company, and if it's not, something very bad is going to happen to you.'[1] A Deloitte study in the United States has found that trusted companies outperform non-trusted brands by 2.5 times, with 88 per cent of customers who highly trust a brand more likely to buy from it again.[2]

In today's economy, where consumers are increasingly values-driven in their purchases, trust signifies a company's alignment with social and environmental concerns, leading to a larger market share and resilience when it comes to market fluctuations. Trust, therefore, is not just an asset. It's a necessity for a business' valuation and a crucial indicator of sustainability. Paul Polman, CEO of global consumer goods brand Unilever, said in 2018: 'Trust is our most important value driver. Unilever's current market capitalisation is 130 billion euros, but our asset value is only 30 billion. The balance is made up of trust, or reputation.'[3]

The flip side of trust—its dark side—is distrust. Distrust is not just an absence of trust. It brings society's most profound fears and any sense of betrayal to the surface. Often, we experience distrust when we feel foolish about trusting too much.

Distrust can also spike dramatically in response to specific events, such as scandals or ethical breaches. For example, with distrust in relation to Australia's health insurer Medibank soaring, the company saw $1.6 billion erased from its market value after a highly publicised customer data breach. Financial services company AMP's market capitalisation fell by 80 per cent following the Australian Banking Royal Commission. And Facebook lost $120 billion in market value after the Cambridge Analytica scandal, one of the largest losses in corporate history, leading to significant changes in the marketing ecosystem.

The trajectory of distrust mirrors the stages of grief but unfolds with its own distinct, dramatic progression. It begins subtly, with doubt—a small seed of uncertainty planted by inconsistencies or unfulfilled promises. This doubt grows and festers into suspicion as the integrity and intentions of a brand, politician, government or even a spouse are questioned. As the suspicion deepens, it transforms into fear, a palpable anxiety that the cause of our distrust is not just unreliable but potentially harmful. Fear then spirals into rejection, where we actively turn away, abandoning brands, voting governments out of office, or ending relationships in a desperate bid for self-preservation. This is the realm of material risk.

Over recent years, Australians have been experiencing growing fear and anxiety about the nation's economic ecosystem. This distrust has been growing since the onset of the COVID-19 pandemic in 2020, and the economy is now more distrusted than trusted.

The graph, produced by the Roy Morgan Risk Lab, highlights the growing distrust across the economy. Australians are particularly disappointed in the behaviour of corporate and institutional leaders who exhibit moral blindness. Roy Morgan data shows Australians are angry about companies being too motivated by profit while people are struggling to keep a roof over their heads and put food on the table.

Overall Levels of Trust Vs Distrust across the Economy

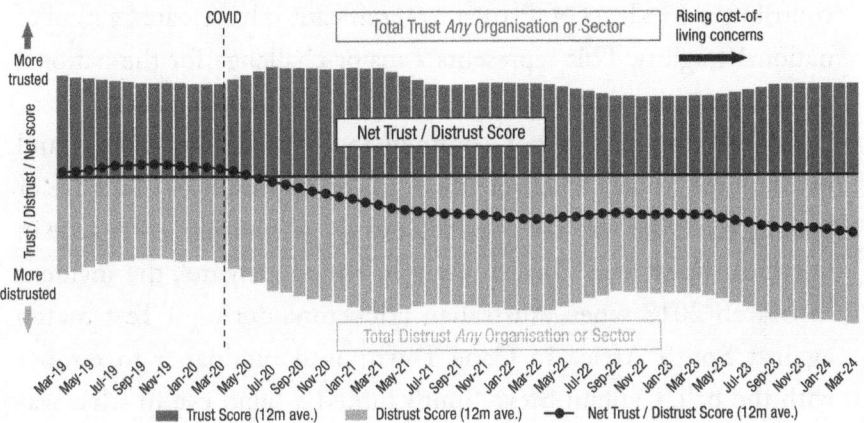

Base: Australians 14+, twelve-month average to March 2024, n = 24,663
Source: Roy Morgan Risk Lab

Moral Blindness

Moral blindness is a pervasive ethical failing whereby individuals and leaders do not recognise or acknowledge the ethical dimensions and broader consequences of their actions. This phenomenon extends beyond mere lapses in judgement to reflect a systemic inability to align actions with moral and ethical standards. Corporate leaders often prioritise profit maximisation and competitive pressures, which can lead to ethical compromises, moral failures and soaring distrust.

The concept of moral blindness is not new. Sociologist Zygmunt Bauman explored this in his work, highlighting how modern societies can become desensitised to ethical transgressions. Bauman argued that moral blindness arises from a disconnect between individuals and the ethical implications of their actions, often facilitated by bureaucratic structures and organisational hierarchies that blur responsibility. This detachment can lead to a 'moral vacuum' in which unethical behaviour becomes normative, and individuals fail to see the moral consequences of their decisions, which generates distrust.

In Australia, the moral blindness recently exhibited by leaders at Qantas, Harvey Norman, PwC, AMP, Rio Tinto and QBE has contributed to a level of distrust so significant it has created a kind of national fragility. This represents a major challenge for the national economy and for Australia's political and institutional leaders.

Moral blindness is not confined to overt actions. CEOs and institutional leaders who practise omission by turning a blind eye or looking the other way are as culpable as those who actively engage in unethical behaviour. One example is 'Sandpapergate', the incident in March 2018 when Australian cricketers, during a Test match against South Africa in Cape Town, used sandpaper to tamper with the ball. Captain Steve Smith turned a blind eye to what was happening, prioritising winning over ethical behaviour.

This passive form of complicity is as damaging as active wrongdoing, as it perpetuates a culture where unethical practices can flourish unchecked. For example, when leaders ignore whistleblower reports or fail to address known ethical breaches, they contribute to a moral environment where misconduct is implicitly condoned. The consequences of moral blindness also extend beyond immediate financial impacts. A tangible distrust is created between organisations and their stakeholders, leading to long-term reputational damage and decreased stakeholder confidence.

Robust governance frameworks are essential to prevent ethical lapses. These frameworks should include clear ethical guidelines, regular training for employees, and mechanisms for reporting and addressing unethical behaviour. Transparency and accountability are also key to avoiding moral blindness and the distrust that inevitably follows it.

Narrative Economics and the Rate of Recovery

What is the mechanism behind the spread of this deep distrust in the consumer economy? In his groundbreaking 2019 work *Narrative Economics*, Nobel Prize–winning economist Robert Shiller asserts that the stories people tell about economic events significantly influence economic outcomes.[4] So when public distrust is soaring and uncertainty prevails, understanding and leveraging positive narratives becomes essential for managing recovery and fostering resilience.

Shiller proposes that economic narratives are like infectious agents, spreading and evolving as they resonate with the public's emotions and perceptions. These narratives shape collective beliefs and behaviours, often more powerfully than empirical data or rational analysis. In the Age of Doubt, then, the narratives that dominate public discourse, such as acts of moral blindness, can exacerbate economic instability.

Stories help us make sense of complex events, giving them meaning and emotional impact. They affect how we feel about ourselves, our governments and our society. They also impact the economy, influencing our spending and investment decisions, and guiding policymakers in their responses.

Consider the global financial crisis or GFC. The dominant story during this time painted financial institutions as greedy and reckless. This narrative wasn't just background noise—it deeply affected public trust and drove significant regulatory change. People began to see banks not as stable pillars of the economy but as risky ventures, leading to widespread distrust. The tale of plummeting home values and failing banks created a sense of systemic risk and institutional failure, and it was quickly picked up by the media, amplifying fear and uncertainty. As people became more anxious, they cut back on spending and investment, which in turn worsened the recession.

Shiller also highlights the self-fulfilling nature of economic narratives. When a narrative captures the public's imagination, it can drive behaviour that reinforces the story. For example, during the dotcom bubble, the narrative of the boundless potential of technology stocks led to a surge in investment. Stock prices soared as more people bought into the narrative, further validating the story—until the bubble burst. Similarly, negative narratives can lead to economic downturns as distrust and uncertainty drive consumers and investors to act cautiously, reducing economic activity and validating the narrative of decline.

In the Age of Doubt, leaders and policymakers must recognise the power of the truth—or at least credible stories that can counteract distrust and uncertainty. For instance, during the COVID-19 pandemic, the narrative of scientific progress and vaccine development played a critical role in restoring public confidence and encouraging economic activity.

The Role of Trust and Distrust on the Global Stage

The dynamics of trust and distrust on the world stage have created powerful examples of trusted and distrusted brands, and the tangible consequences of their reputational standing. Let's start with trusted brands.

Apple Inc. is consistently ranked among the most trusted global brands. Its reputation for innovation, quality and user-friendly products has fostered a loyal customer base. Trust in Apple is further reinforced by its strong commitment to privacy and security, a perception that has become a significant differentiator in an era of increasing digital threats. Apple's strong brand trust translates into high shareholder value, with its market capitalisation frequently ranking it as one of the world's most valuable companies. Trust also creates a willingness to pay premium prices for Apple products, delivering robust revenue growth and profitability. Even in the face of occasional controversies, such as labour practices in its supply chain, Apple's reservoir of goodwill and strong trust foundation has helped it recover quickly, maintaining its social licence and good reputation.

Toyota is another globally trusted brand known for reliability, safety and quality. Its commitment to innovation in sustainability, particularly with hybrid and electric vehicles, has further enhanced its reputation. Trust in Toyota has cemented its position as a leading global car maker, with consistent sales and market share growth. High levels of customer trust translate into strong brand loyalty, with repeat purchases and positive word-of-mouth recommendations. Toyota's reputation supports its financial stability and investor confidence, contributing to a strong share market performance and steady dividend payouts.

Now let's look at distrusted brands, beginning with Facebook. Now part of Meta Platforms Inc., Facebook has confronted dramatic distrust issues in recent times, particularly in the wake of the 2018 Cambridge Analytica scandal, when user data was misused for political advertising. This breach of trust highlighted serious concerns about data privacy and the company's ethical practices. In the wake of the revelations, Facebook's share price value dropped by more than 20 per cent. Distrust also prompted increased scrutiny from regulators and a growing public backlash—including a trending #DeleteFacebook movement that encouraged users to leave the platform. Since then, persistent distrust issues have continued to tarnish Facebook's brand image.

Volkswagen's involvement in the diesel emissions scandal nicknamed 'Dieselgate' in 2015 created global distrust, severely damaging the company's international reputation. The company was found to have installed software in diesel engines to cheat on emissions tests, leading to significant legal and financial repercussions. Volkswagen faced billions of dollars in fines and settlement costs, and the scandal resulted in a sharp decline in Volkswagen's share price, eroding shareholder value. Soaring distrust led to a significant loss of consumer confidence, affecting sales and market share, particularly in markets with strong environmental regulations.

The Disruptive Role of Digital Media and Social Platforms

Digital media and social platforms act as powerful megaphones, amplifying narratives that sway public opinion on a global scale. They are fertile ground for disinformation and misinformation, resulting in a complex landscape where truths and falsehoods intermingle. These platforms generate waves of both positive and negative sentiments, often with far-reaching consequences.

Consider the 2017 Equifax data breach, one of the world's most significant cyber incidents, which impacted the personal data of 147 million Americans, Canadians and Britons. Traditional media reported on the breach, but social media turned it into a firestorm, leading to widespread panic about personal data security and significant regulatory changes.

Social media platforms are notorious for the rapid spread of misinformation. Algorithms designed to maximise engagement often prioritise sensational or emotionally charged content, which can include false or misleading information. This contributes to escalating distrust in information sources and institutions as people struggle to discern credible information from fake news, fostering a climate of widespread distrust.

Social media algorithms also create echo chambers, where users are predominantly exposed to content that aligns with their existing beliefs and preferences. This reinforces biases and deepens societal divisions as people become insulated from diverse perspectives. The resulting polarisation produces distrust in opposing viewpoints and can lead to increased social fragmentation.

Addressing the disruptive role of media and social platforms requires regulatory and ethics decisions. Policymakers and tech companies must collaborate to develop frameworks that promote transparency, accountability and the responsible use of technology. This includes combating wilful disinformation and the unwitting spread of misinformation, protecting user data, and ensuring that algorithms do not perpetuate harmful biases—all crucial for mitigating distrust and rebuilding trust.

In the Age of Doubt, trust and distrust are central to understanding and navigating the complexities of modern society. Trust builds resilience and stability, enabling effective decision-making and fostering long-term success. Conversely, distrust exposes vulnerabilities, leading to profound societal, political and economic risks. Recognising and addressing these dynamics is essential for cultivating a more resilient and trustworthy future. In this existential tension between trust and distrust lie the pivotal choices that will define our collective fate.

Trust and Corporate Leadership: Operating 'Outside the Building'

A Q&A with Rosabeth Moss Kanter, Harvard Business School, United States

Q [Tracey Kirkland]: You've spent your career researching and writing about corporate leadership. What have you seen in terms of trust in leaders and corporates over that time?

A: What I've seen is that some things have changed and some things are exactly the same. When we think about corporates, we probably think about large public companies. Earlier in my career, the large corporations were typically big bureaucracies, which were somewhat faceless, and the CEOs were not necessarily famous. They were run with varying degrees of efficiency.

The first wave of concerns about whether business leaders could be trusted came in the 1980s, when there was the push to break up big companies and sell them off to private equity, and that undermined faith in large companies. It coincided with a time when US companies in particular, but also Western companies of all kinds, were facing big foreign competition within many major industries, and the efficiency and effectiveness of management came into question, and trust in business leaders declined.

In that same era, trust in government was also being reduced, so there was a question about whether we could trust government to handle business. There was a push for independence, rather than letting companies become huge conglomerates that owned many unrelated things. Virgin is a good example of that. The same thing was happening in Asia and India as well, where a company, owned by a wealthy family, [might buy] up a variety of entities, whether they were related or not, and establish large conglomerates. That whole era was a time when the public did not have a lot of trust in business.

Then we had the rise of the dotcom era, when there were lots of challenges to business leaders about whether they could handle the new technology. At the same time, because of the amount of information available and the rapidly changing technology, there was much more public awareness of the problems that businesses got into. It meant there was more scrutiny, not only about how companies were run but also about the very premise of the companies and the industries they were in.

Because of the huge amount of information—some of it misinformation—that could now flow around the internet, there were major challenges to trust and the legitimacy of business. Some of that was brought about because people started to have a greater voice. I remember speaking with the CEO of a global pharmaceutical company in the early 2000s who was a physician and a very humane leader, who thought he was positioning his company to be concerned about the needs of patients who used his products. He said: 'I never thought I would see a day when we would be treated like tobacco.' In short, because of the nature of the profit-making industry he was in, people questioned whether shareholder demand for a return on investment in health care was a legitimate business model. The magnification of voices on the internet meant people could challenge the very premise of a business.

Q: *So what about now?*
A: There's an interesting irony at the moment. The Edelman trust survey shows trust is higher in business as an institution than in government, but there's much less trust in individual companies.

Industries that were once seen as doing wonderful things and great for the world, including those companies that grew during the dotcom era, are also now seen as dominating and doing bad things. So the issue of trust is hard to talk about in general. It's industry by industry, and company by company.

One industry with very low trust levels is the fossil fuel industry. A lot of that is the climate crisis, but not entirely. For a long time, they had been big faceless bureaucracies that just dominated without anyone really knowing much about what they did. When BP had to face the oil spill in the Gulf of Mexico, and the CEO at the time responded so badly, that was a major scandal because he just did not know how to talk to the public. And trust fell accordingly.

Q: What level of personal responsibility do you think business leaders need to take for declining trust levels?
A: Business leaders have always been expected to take responsibility for what happens on their watch. There are some big global companies where the CEOs have worked hard to not only act responsibly but make that a centrepiece of their strategy. Unilever's former CEO Paul Polman, even in retirement, is a big spokesman for sustainability and corporate responsibility for climate and the environment. Proctor & Gamble was another company making that a centrepiece. Both of these companies were often making trade-offs internally to support things that would be very good for society but maybe not quite as profitable. In one case, Proctor & Gamble set up its own not-for-profit to run a water purification company with other non-profits, because they could not make selling water-purification tablets profitable but they knew the developing world really needed them.

Part of the development of every leader who rises to the top has to be what I call the 'outside the building' issues, not just running the company internally or dealing just with the customers. A good leader has to be thinking about the issues of society, how they contribute to them, and try not to do harm. Of course, leaders do have to take responsibility internally, ensure that there's no misconduct. And, with so many eyes looking at the business all the time and information spreading so quickly, leaders have to be prepared and they have to act in ways that show that they care. That doesn't mean getting involved in politics necessarily or taking a stand in public issues.

Q: As far as trust, how risky is it for leaders to stand up and speak out about controversial issues?
A: Leaders have to try to differentiate between their own personal reactions and what they are saying or doing on behalf of the company. One of the great examples of a leader who navigated this beautifully was also in pharmaceuticals. The CEO of Merck & Co, Kenneth Frazier, who is an African American, spoke out about racism. He was one of the first corporate leaders to resign from a business council and speak out about an issue. It was personal ... he couldn't ignore the harm to his community. He tried to differentiate himself from Merck & Co but, in the end, Merck's policies also supported anti-racism and inclusion, so it was in keeping with the policies of the company and he successfully spoke out.

Q: You've previously said: 'After years of telling corporate citizens to "trust the system", many companies must relearn instead to trust their people.' What do you mean by that?
A: I was talking about empowerment. You run a better company if your people have the tools to do the job but also the voice to speak up about what they are seeing. Increasingly, people want a voice to talk about their personal circumstances and not just things going on in the company.

Leaders who gain the trust of their people, gain trust internally, are leaders who listen to their people and give them opportunities to talk about what's on their mind, what they see on the job, what trends they see, what their needs are to have a fulfilling life.

When I talk about thinking 'outside the building', I partly mean the boundaries between a company and the rest of the world are blurred. We used to think work was one thing and family life was totally separate. Now we see the overlaps and the connections. People want their needs met by their employers more than they have in the past. So empowering employees and listening to them is a very important aspect of leadership today. Otherwise, there's no loyalty, no trust, and people will sabotage or undermine the company they work for.

Q: Thinking about external and internal trust, what would your one piece of advice be to leaders about how to rebuild the trust that perhaps has been lost over the past few decades?
A: Trust can be lost very quickly. It's like Humpty Dumpty sitting on that wall. All it takes is one little fall and that egg is gone. How do you put it back together again? It takes a long time, so you have to demonstrate that you are trustworthy, you have to show you are taking a hard look at yourself, your company, your policies, your behaviour, and that you are not writing this off as something small, that you are taking this loss of trust very seriously. Then you have to take strong action right away. There's an iconic business example from decades ago that gets taught over and over around the world because it illustrates this point perfectly. Johnson & Johnson is a pharmaceutical company known for Tylenol. There was an issue with tampering with the caps. It was not clear who was responsible, but rather than pointing fingers, Johnson & Johnson acted fast, recalled the product, looked at the company, and the CEO became famous for that.

It's action. You build trust again over time. You also build it by empowering your people. You say to your people, 'What would you like to do to contribute in mitigating this harm or proving that we are trustworthy?' They will have ideas. They will talk about community actions. They will talk about programs they could do in their local neighbourhoods. They can become your ambassadors for rebuilding trust in the brand.

Lastly, you have to stand by your values. It's very hard to rebuild trust if you never had a strong set of values to begin with. You have to ask, 'What do we stand for?' And, if you haven't had a strong set of values before, you have to build one.

Rebuilding Trust after a Crisis

Michael Smith, former chairman, 7-Eleven, Australia

ON FRIDAY, 28 August 2015, the board of 7-Eleven was feeling satisfied. The company was a clear market leader in Australia, the winner of many national awards, and met public company standards judged by both internal auditors and external ones from the Big Four. It had high staff and franchisee satisfaction and excellent financial performance, including a very strong balance sheet.

I felt good, too. I was deputy chair of an ASX 200 company, the national chair of the Australian Institute of Company Directors (AICD), and on the board of three other companies, with invitations to join significant national business and sporting organisations.

The following Monday, the current affairs program *Four Corners*, working with *The Age* newspaper, aired 'The Price of Convenience', alleging 7-Eleven was running a business model that forced franchisees to underpay their workers. By the Tuesday, we were in a media hell, accused of an epic failure of governance fuelled by greed and a lack of care. We could now imagine how Richard Kimble, the protagonist of the movie *The Fugitive*, felt.

September was a dreadful month of being publicly battered by the media, government and social media: 'scandal-plagued' seemed to lead every article about us. In a grotesque caricature, our chair,

Russ Withers, was cast as a rich man taking advantage of vulnerable people. Withers had already left the Australian Olympic Committee, while I had stepped down from the AICD, but at the end of the month, he resigned from 7-Eleven and appointed me chairman with unambiguous instructions to fix this mess. I then accepted the resignations of the CEO and COO.

As an utterly selfish aside, I felt professionally ruined. I was deeply disappointed that, as the most experienced director, I had not seen this coming and thus let down the very principled family that owned the business. Appointing me in these circumstances was an astonishing and personally inspiring act of forgiveness and trust by Withers.

Over the next twelve months, we were the focus of hundreds of negative media pieces, called before two Senate inquiries and investigated by Australia's Fair Work Ombudsman (FWO), and what had seemed like a warm relationship with the franchisees tipped into open revolt. This is not the place to recount the circumstances in detail, as they have been widely reported elsewhere, but I will say that, recognising that the company and the franchisees were separate legal entities, it was agreed by all that 7-Eleven per se had not underpaid any staff—as evidenced by it not being fined or convicted of breaking a law or regulation. It did, however, enter an enforceable undertaking with the FWO to ensure the company's franchisees paid their staff the correct wages, after an inquiry found that 7-Eleven's approach to workplace matters, 'while ostensibly promoting compliance', did compound the situation by not detecting or addressing the issues at the franchise level.[1] A new arrangement was then struck with franchisees, and a class action run by them was settled.

The allegations rocked our staff, with many feeling their careers had been ruined. The franchisees aggressively sought a better deal. The shareholders were profoundly disappointed that a company they had trusted had been accused of shameful conduct—the industry regulator and the government publicly accused the company of evil-doing, and the media reported on this daily.

But as I write this almost nine years later, 7-Eleven is being quoted as an example of how to deal with a crisis, it has won multiple industry awards, been valued by the market at $1.7 billion, and is a clear market leader with an envied leadership.

This is our story about trust—trust that was slowly accumulated over three decades, lost in a week, and rebuilt over six years. While I am the author here, this story is one of collective leadership. In telling this, let me be clear that this is not about personal success. The success is due to an extraordinary group of people who understood the importance of rebuilding trust, step by step. It has been the privilege of a lifetime to be part of that group.

Taking Responsibility

In my first days as chair of the board, and with the support of the shareholders, I came up with actions to guide us through the dark and the reputational gunfire.

We held a town hall meeting with the headline message: 'While we have not underpaid our staff, this happened in our name, under our brand and we must accept that we are responsible. We are guilty, and we must make this right. And in making it right, we can be the authors of a story about our integrity.'

This was very difficult to accept, as most of the company staff had no knowledge of franchisees underpaying their employees, or that our model was inadequate for franchisees with low gross profit. Underpaying staff was never part of our mindset, but nothing blinds you like a strong belief grown from success. High-calibre directors saw enough in our commitment to agree to join those who'd pledged to address this crisis.[2] They were all wise, persistent and unfailingly collegial.

Based on the worldly counsel of our public affairs adviser,[3] we gave up on the futile task of trying to correct the media and instead dedicated ourselves to fulfilling three promises:

1   Take responsibility.
2   Look after those who have been hurt.
3   Make sure it doesn't happen again.

We made these promises to a sceptical Michael Campbell, deputy commissioner at the FWO. We didn't expect or gain trust, but we did go on to establish a basis for earning it by meeting every commitment we made.

Looking after Those Who Have Been Hurt

We had quickly taken responsibility. We now had to help those who had been hurt by what had happened.

It was agreed we would find and compensate all employees underpaid by the franchisees, a startlingly high number. Going way beyond the legal requirements, we applied a lenient standard of proof to the claims and accepted these beyond the statute of limitations; we even paid claims within families. It ended up costing over $100 million, which would have bankrupted the business had the shareholders taken even conservative dividends. While we focused on reorganising the business, Deloitte was hired to look after the payments independently, keeping the details confidential. Allan Fels, the former head of the Australian Competition and Consumer Commission, initially oversaw the scheme, which cost tens of millions of dollars to administer.

In making this right, Russ Withers and the shareholders did what no-one in that position should have to do: accept uncapped liability. This is, by far, the most principled act I have ever seen in my now-long corporate life. The person most demonised throughout this incident, Russ Withers, is the actual hero of this story, along with his family.

Making Sure This Doesn't Happen Again

The arrangement between 7-Eleven and its franchisees is fundamentally the same worldwide. The franchisor provides the store, fittings, support and services, while the franchisee employs the staff and buys the stock; gross profit is shared. But it should have been obvious this was not working for all Australian stores, especially those with low sales. The arrangements were unfair on these stores, so we altered them to ensure all franchisees were assured of enough profit to run their business and pay their staff. I am not aware of another franchise system that goes this far.

It was also essential to repair the relationship with franchisees, to make it sustainable and trustworthy. However, what had seemingly once been warm and constructive state franchisee meetings were now angry, shouty affairs—they often felt like the scene in *The Blues Brothers* where the band is playing behind protective chicken wire while abusive patrons throw bottles at them. We were upset with those many franchisees who had underpaid their staff, while many of the franchisees were upset with us because they felt the deal was unfair. We found ourselves looking at franchisees who had made substantial profits standing alongside those who had not, and realised this had to stop. We were partners, and the only way back was together.

Most of our franchisees come from India and Pakistan, cultures that are very different to Australia's. Thinking we needed to forge a shared understanding of how to run a franchise (including never underpaying wages), I offered an olive branch: 'We have not understood each other. We must change this. If you let me, my wife and I will travel to your countries, meet with your families in their homes, and learn your stories.'

And so began a life-changing experience. My wife Robyn and I went with a videographer to visit families in Pakistan, India and China. We hugged people, we wept, and we experienced family and community structures that were a world away from ours. Robyn and I saw a diaspora of sacrifice spreading from often severely impoverished circumstances in home countries to places of work and education in nations like Bahrain, Germany and Australia.

The story of one family in Pakistan began with the forced displacement of its illiterate, already poor members during the Partition of India in 1947. The father was imprisoned during that conflict, and as a reward for his heroism, the Pakistani Government asked what it could do for him. He replied: 'Educate my children.' I was introduced to this family by the youngest son, an Audi-driving successful franchisee in rural New South Wales who had been supported to take on the store by his family and who sent money back to them in Pakistan. I was proud that our business could provide such opportunities for the brave people who left their countries for a better life and invested with us.

The videos of these trips and the very human stories of connection and understanding underpinned the rebuilding of our culture and the relationships with our franchisees.

Stepping into Different Shoes

At a Qantas annual general meeting, a shareholder asked the board if any of the directors had experienced a long-haul flight in economy with their airline. It was a good question. It made me think about how, as a retailer, you must spend time in stores, seeing and feeling how the experiences are for the customer and the people running the store. But I had been doing that in business class in the form of official, announced visits on a bus during pleasant afternoons. There was no chance this would give me a sense of what store life was like across the network.

I thought about what job I would find most challenging, and how I could experience and learn from it. This led me to visit stores in communities with high levels of crime and substance abuse. I would arrive on my own, unannounced, between midnight and 2 a.m.—the memory doesn't make me proud, as I felt real fear walking past intimidating people and places to get to these stores. I then talked with our people who were in the store alone about their experiences, and helped with the usual night duty of stocking shelves.

As you would expect, and as I should have known, working side-by-side with the franchisees laying out the sandwiches led to engagement and learning that vastly exceeded what I'd discovered on my 'royal visits' during the comfortable times. One team member's account of being held up in the small hours by a drug-affected, weapon-carrying robber was viscerally disturbing and caused me to push even harder on what I felt was an already robust approach to the robbery risk.

I did all this as a private learning exercise and had no intention of using it for publicity, but word spread very quickly that we were really trying to understand. Our actions were not calculated to win trust. They were primarily driven by a human-centred, moral drive to be the leaders that people deserved. This must begin with respect and a genuine desire to understand and value the experiences and perspectives of all our people, something that requires a capacity for empathy.

One key moment was asking Allan Fels to hand back to us the running of the wages repayment program (although we continued with Deloitte's arm's-length administration, which preserved the confidentiality of those making claims and our commitment to getting people paid—we were never going to risk that). Now Allan is a passionate advocate for those who have been treated unfairly, and he still didn't trust us to run the program. He went on the ABC's *7.30* and said things like '7-Eleven don't get it', and expressed a fear that 'lawlessness would return to 7-Eleven'.

We expected that. But our motivation was to be an exemplar, and I made that point to *7.30* anchor Leigh Sales the following night. I said that we couldn't outsource our morality: 7-Eleven had to fix this, not Allan. And we had to be seen fixing it when we could have been doing something else. I promised we would pay more people, and pay them faster, and that people would be able to judge us on what we actually did. We would be completely transparent.

I am proud of what we accomplished, which is now one of the girders reinforcing our corporate culture. Many of our people reported that our conduct through this crisis is one of the reasons they feel so positive about the company. And it is appropriate to remind ourselves that we did this with shareholder money—the same shareholders who had demonstrated trust in me and who had unfairly suffered the consequences of the problems.

New Leadership

We needed new leadership. Both on the board, to better represent our stakeholders, and in the form of a CEO who could lead us in becoming an exemplar. It could have taken months to recruit a new CEO, but fortunately Bob Bailey on our board was tailor-made for the job. He was a very experienced CEO of retail businesses and possessed a rare combination of a phenomenal head for detail and the people skills of a maître d'.

We then commissioned a leading recruitment firm to conduct an international search for an outstanding retail leader, which resulted in a shortlist of six names. We knew we needed a leader with exceptional qualities of integrity and the ability to be transformational. Angus McKay certainly had those qualities, but he did not have the relevant industry experience: would he understand a job in retail?

One of his most telling early acts happened in front of a packed audience of 800 people at our end-of-year conference dinner. He and his executive team performed a professionally choreographed dance routine. Most were good, some very good, and a few fought through the challenges of a less natural rhythm. This was the moment we knew we had made it through. Here is why I think it was so important in earning trust: it was an act comprising generosity, humility, vulnerability and humour. It was designed to show our people a good time, but also to show that our leaders were prepared to take the chance they would look silly doing something they were not necessarily good at. It showed they were approachable. It demonstrated they were a team and that they could laugh along with the rest of group.

It was far from the characterisation of oppressive, rent-seeking, uncaring, out-of-touch leaders. It echoed the perception that the journey Robyn and I had taken to understand the stories of franchisee families was one of humble curiosity and respect.

Reflections on Trust

When I look back over that time, a few things stand out: our recruitment of a man with no retail experience to lead us because we put character first; our understanding that the fault for this was widespread, crossing our business and the franchise community, and that both were filled with good people; and our commitment to making sure this didn't happen again, demonstrated through investment, systems, assurance, people, and a close relationship with the regulators.

We earned the trust of our stakeholders through repeated actions when it would have been easier and less costly to do something else. We were guided by the goals: take responsibility; look after those who were hurt; and make sure it doesn't happen again but rather be an exemplar of how you deal with a crisis.

Through this time, I learnt many valuable lessons about trust. I learnt that a genuine belief in trust comes from a consistent series of actions taken when other courses would demonstrably be easier—we trust people whose character we can measure through their actions.

I also learnt that being a leader of a large organisation in a complex market makes it a certainty that difficulties will arrive, and that the organisation will let people down despite a solid commitment to integrity. And when successful organisations are seen to fall, it is easy to locate them in the drama triangle of victim–villain–hero. This makes for a sensational media narrative, and trust is less readily offered to large organisations whose leaders are paid much more than those who do business with them.

A healthy part of accepting a senior role is that you will likely be attacked by people with little interest in facts or fairness. You must accept this, as a Rugby player knows that being hit is part of the game. Even the best of us will never play the perfect game—we will get things wrong, people we trust will let us down, and we will probably let down those who trust us.

It is necessary and healthy to recognise your failures, not only because we should, but because we then have the opportunity to make them right. In a strange and hard-to-accept way, failures, even moral ones, represent one of the best opportunities to demonstrate character and earn trust. Our test is how we react to failure, and our achievement is how we continue to lead with extraordinary character after the crisis has passed.

Finally, we trust people we can relate to, and one of the traits we most admire is the capacity for forgiveness.

Engaging People in Change

A Q&A with Subramanian Rangan, Professor of Strategy and Management, European Institute for Business Administration (INSEAD), France

Q [Gavin Fang]: Your research looks at the evolution of capitalism, and issues around performance and progress, particularly around fairness. I'd like to ask you about institutions, either government or business, that appear to be suffering from a loss of trust. What's your view on whether and why this is occurring?

A: Let's look at what an institution is and then understand how it actually works in reality, and then how people ... adhere to the institution, trust it or not. Institutions are constraints and enactors that are socially constructed, and the best of them are self-enforcing. Institutions fall in two categories: *conventions* and *norms*. Norms may be like ... being an honest judge, not being corruptible. A norm might be to keep your promises. Conventions are usually self-enforcing. Language is a convention, and I know that you know that I am speaking English, and you know that I know that you know, so I use only the words that I mean to use.

Institutions can also be the enactors, if you will, of our norms. So, for example, if we have a norm of equal rights under the law for every person but, in fact, the institution that is supposed to uphold the equal rights and the equal sanctions is actually, in practice, doing something that is not seen as equal, then people may start to doubt that institution. They say it isn't working. It isn't upholding in practice the norm.

Each society chooses its norms. It could be a norm of equal rights under the law, it could be a norm of ... non-discrimination based on colour, gender, age. And then it could be, for example, the norms in science, which are to pursue the truth wherever that may lead and not to falsify.

Science itself is an institution which is constrained by certain standards of rigour and quality. It is supposed to be apolitical. It is supposed to be truthful, which means you don't fabricate data, you make observations, and then you study and analyse those observations, and then you report your findings. But if it turns out that a scientist is not unbiased, or worse, selectively chooses data that may represent a certain ideology, not just a certain idea, and they are in fact confirming their hypotheses whichever way they want it to go, then belief in the institution called science becomes wobbly. So, for example, *The Wall Street Journal* recently had a story about the number of scientific articles being recalled. It said hundreds, perhaps thousands, of articles are being recalled, even in prestigious journals, because the data was fabricated. When that starts to happen at the highest levels—that is, in bodies that we think should be unimpeachable, that are elite—then it's like a tall building. Once you see some fissures and you see a certain facet of this large structure looking shaky and even flaking off or falling off, the whole edifice is suspect.

And remember what institutions are supposed to do. Institutions are *enactors* but they are also *constraints*. What do they constrain? They constrain power. Each of us has some power, small or big. A justice of the Supreme Court has a lot of power compared to just me, a professor. But a professor has more power than just a student, and so on. Institutions ... constrain the use of power, and they are supposed to be the check against the abuse of power. But if institutions are no longer constrained, and generally those kinds of institutions are unobserved or, even if they're observed, they cannot be audited in any effective way, then institutions are seen as failing. And it seems like this has been happening widely over the last decade or two, at least.

So basically, there is power and there are interests. Institutions are the check on power against advancing self-interest. If you have some power, you should not use your power to only advance your self-interest at the expense of society. This is what institutions do—they constrain the use of power so that your self-interest is kept in check. But today that self-enforcement is visibly shaken and there are too many instances that are coming up for people to ignore and say, this is an anomaly. And so, when elites and experts are themselves seen as a little bit wobbly, in that they are somehow pursuing their self-interest, associates' interest, their party, their ideology, whatever, then the public's trust in institutions starts to fray.

Q: You talked about fissures and you talked about cracks. Is there something systemically problematic with our modern system that is leading to this, rather than just individuals taking action that is a breach of trust? Is there something fundamentally flawed about our system as it currently stands?
A: I've not studied this issue, but sociologist Karl Polanyi said society wants two things: we all want *liberty* and *security*. So how can I have the most liberty with the most security? There is a trade-off between liberty and security, so if we want collective security, then individual liberties will have to be constrained. Over the last twenty or thirty years, there has been a kind of deepening [view] and a greater intensification and confidence that liberty may be more important and that somehow security has been achieved. We think our world is stable and civilised enough that we can all afford to worry more about the individual. So the unit of sovereignty has moved more to the individual and probably away from the collective ... But, actually, achieving security is a chronic problem. It's not an acute thing that, once we achieve it, we will have it. You've got to reproduce stability. You've got to regulate interdependence every day ...

Understandably, we thought, now we can pay more attention to individuals. Your views versus my views. I'm for animal rights, I'm for wearing masks; you are not for animal rights, you are not for wearing masks. There is a sense that we are all right and that there is more than one truth, and we can all kind of coexist in this. But then you start to see polarisation and the pressure to form these interest groups and so, when I'm in power, I will advance my ideology, my interests, and this has been creeping up on us. This is called the success trap. Success leads to a certain adjustment and adaptation, and that adaptation may unravel the very success.

This is the first time in history we've achieved such a high degree of confidence in the nation-state, in institutions, in education, in the whole family and court system and all of this. People may underestimate and not appreciate what an incredible achievement the twentieth century has been in many, many respects. And that has led to, maybe, overconfidence and then kind of thinking that we don't have to be so collective, we can now be more local and individual. And that was okay. But when that individual instinct is also having contagion and infection of people who are supposed to be upholding the collective, that's when micro choices have macro consequences.

Q: In your work, you talk about fairness and the role it needs to play in the modern system. And also, progress and how we must update our thinking around that. Could you just briefly explain where those ideas might intersect with these issues around trust in institutions?
A: So now you raise a very complex and potentially important question. We've achieved a lot of material success measured in money terms and measured in terms of goods and services, what we would call per capita GDP. There have been enormous strides in life expectancy, in the rates of technological advancement, in the widespread access and adoption of that technology. As our incomes rise, it seems our moral preferences are also evolving toward a more equitable and sustainable society. That is, we wish the economy to attend more to so-called

people and planet issues and not only to profit or wealth. This, mind you, is an evolution in norms [the 'ought-to-be' versus the 'is'].

Yet, in our rush to get to this broadly more desirable future, we are short-circuiting the process. We want green energy so we commit to offshore wind power. But then transmission lines have to come over land to where the power will be used. All the communities through which the lines will pass can now resist because they feel they bear more of the costs and not enough of the benefits. The same can play out in diversity- and inclusion-slanted recruitment, or pressure on coalmining or cattle farming or immigration. In these situations, we may observe reactionary reflexes. The disfavoured group can cling to convention while the progressive group heaves to norms. Polarisation ensues and we label the sides as conservatives and progressives.

What we have sidestepped is the process of engaging, exchange, explaining and, where necessary, the wisdom to slow down and/or compromise. Instead, we 'judge' and demean. That sets off sentiments of resentment and anger. The partisans can be politicised and even radicalised. Culture wars get underway and the media can air the flames.

We would all benefit, I feel, by reading and practising more [regarding] communicative action and consultative morality. We cannot sidestep fairness in process and fairness in outcomes and hope to enact a successful transition.

In a democratic society, we state that each one of us is equal to the other and should have that voice, should have that representation, should have that capacity to register their preferences, but this has been violated. There is a perception for some people that we want to get to the future a little too fast rather than taking it step by step.

Q: You're part of a group of eminent philosophers, social scientists and business leaders working on issues of progress. Do you have hope that these problems can be tackled and solved?

A: I definitely have hope. The German philosopher Jürgen Habermas made this point that we need communication, dialogue, exchange, engagement and explanation because institutions are only self-enforcing to the extent that individuals who are covered by the institution comply voluntarily. Otherwise, you will have to put cameras everywhere and record every speech, act and monitor everyone's social media, and that becomes a complete surveillance state. No institution can actually operationalise such a draconian kind of control. If we are to have self-enforcing institutions, then people have to feel that those choices made by the institutions are legitimate, and that legitimacy comes from a procedure, not from a particular preference. I think … in our haste to get to the future, we have short-circuited the process of engaging, exchanging and explaining. I'm hopeful to the extent that we have a reasonable solution. Where that has been tried, by and large, there has been success. For example, empirical research in sociology shows that if you do adhere to procedural justice, which is engaging, exchanging and explaining, then the institutions become more self-enforcing.

It will never be perfect, but nothing in society is ever expected to be perfect. But it should be robust. It should be solid and give us enough confidence that we can invest—that we can, not predict the future, but at least understand that the future is not going to be radically different or a broken-down version of the present.

Another reason I'm hopeful is that we can teach and remind leaders and remind one another that this is a collective project and all voices matter. So to me, the whole voice idea is extremely important and feasible. It's not elections per se. Voice is not registering your preference once every three or four or five or six years. It is much more regular and deliberative.

Right now, we're in a transition moment: labour transition, technological transition, energy transition, demographic transition, geopolitical transition. There are many transitions. This is a moment where preferences are being scrambled and re-sorted. At this moment, we need a whole lot more debate and discussion among ourselves and we need to take the time to do that.

It's not fun ... it's messy, but it is empowering, and it is the only way for societies to self-organise in a predictable and reliable manner. If we don't have these conversations, then I am afraid there will be a further decline in trust in institutions. But I am hopeful because the course of history over the last 1000 years, or even 2000 or 3000 years, shows us we are capable of governance and architectural innovation.

The Currency of Trust

Louise Mahler, executive adviser and coach, Australia

TRUST CAN BE the elusive obvious. We grasp at solutions, create a consistent pattern of behaviour, wear the right clothes and build our strength of argument, only to pass over the key currency—our body—right at our fingertips, literally. Building trust using our physical body and its extended vocal presence is about going back to basics. It's about considering the origins of postures and sounds, and recognising the inherent psychologies within.

Turning to the Ancients

Luckily for us, there's no need to re-create the wheel. Ancient and medieval writers from Augustine to Amalarius of Metz to Hugh of Saint-Victor emphasised the role of the body and voice in effective speaking to influence and gain the trust of the masses.[1] References to gestures, for example, can be found in ancient bronze and marble sculptures, public and private reliefs, and even coinage. The ancient Romans and Greeks in particular knew just what it took to have trusted communications. They coined this 'gravitas', defined at the time as *the manner of trust and respect*, which was influenced by the Greek virtue Arete, who stood for excellence, goodness, fulfilment and virtue.

In achieving that virtue, the ancients were unanimous that our physical/vocal apparatus—in other words, our delivery—was most important. This is evidenced by the ancient orators Crassus and Demosthenes, and reinforced by Cicero, the Roman statesman, lawyer, scholar, philosopher and writer, in his *Rhetorica ad Herennium*, and ultimately laid out in the quote by Demosthenes that delivery holds the first, second and even third positions of importance among the canons of rhetoric. Aristotle also recognised its significance and Quintilian, acclaimed Roman educator and rhetorician, gave it considerable focus in his *Institutio oratoria*.[2]

What is clear from the ancients is that delivery was, and has always been, a critical tool for building gravitas—that is, trust and respect.

Our Modern Study of Body Language

Somehow, we have lost our association with the physical and verbal nature of delivery, which may partly be attributed to the loss of texts, such as that of Aristotle's student Theophrastus (*On Delivery*), as well as the very physical and verbal mode of learning. During the last seventy years, our communication study and hence work on trust has been in the field of non-verbal studies, where in 1952, anthropologist Ray Birdwhistell demonstrated that over 65 per cent of communication is done non-verbally.[3] Also often quoted is the work of Albert Mehrabian, who believed that communication was only 7 per cent verbal, and 38 per cent vocal and 55 per cent body.[4]

Despite this, contemporary literature offers little skills guidance. In the rhetoric-focused textbook *The Rhetorical Companion*, out of the 156 pages, gestures (a vital element of delivery) receives only one page.[5] In Granville Toogood's 198-page-long book *The Articulate Executive: Learn to Look, Act and Sound Like a Leader*, only one page is devoted to 'sound'.[6] This is only 0.51 per cent of the book's total extent, which begs the question: how is one meant to achieve the weighty objectives the title implies?

The Impact

Since childhood, we have been guided to be static. We have been told to stop fidgeting, stand still, keep our hands down, refrain from distracting movements. And when moving, we have been taught to follow the guidelines of perception as outlined by the school of body language originally made popular through Julius Fast's *Body Language*,[7] and also Alan Pease's *Body Language*.[8]

These works were written in response to the need to refocus on the body. Yet these 'fake it to make it' ideas imply a theory of relationships that is consciously solipsistic and lacks concern for authenticity of expression—and is therefore often rejected. And all this accomplishes is the stifling of the ability to exude the trust we seek.

The consequent dearth of skills has left many with a lack of confidence, a greater feeling of imposter syndrome and higher performance anxiety, with around 75 per cent of people having glossophobia (the fear of public speaking).[9]

Leadership and Trust

Research shows that 45 per cent of a company's performance is directly attributable to its CEO's impact.[10] So a poor-performing CEO, sitting at the heart of a failing enterprise, spreads distrust across their organisation and has a severe impact on everything around them.

How are we doing? The Edelman Trust Barometer report shows that only around half of those surveyed believe business leaders are telling them the truth; 50 per cent believe our business leaders are lying, dissembling or obfuscating.[11]

Not only are the skills of delivery important, but their importance increases as a person moves towards a leadership role. If delivery is the major way of building trust, it follows that presence exuding trust becomes exponentially more important. Our failure in this area is reflected in the CEO attrition rate. Research shows there was a

53 per cent increase in CEO resignations in 2023, and that CEOs are leaving the role younger than ever before, with an average age of fifty-six in 2023, down from over sixty-three six years previously.[12]

The Growth Plan

The solution begins with a paradigm shift.

I am often asked to speak on how to spot liars, to which I reply that I do not work with liars—I work with people who tell the truth. As Quintilian made clear, the critical starting point for anyone attempting gravitas is that they are a 'good person': 'I hold that no one can be a true orator unless he is also a good man and even if he could be, I would not have it so.'[13]

Recent contemporary paradigms begin with a lack of ability and the need to 'fake it to make it', pandering to the perception of others. On the other hand, real trust is built when we (as noted in the ancient world) recognise we have all the skills within us and freeing that body and voice brings our best (as a good person) in total congruence. Or, to put it perhaps more honestly, we need to recognise these skills if we don't want to *lose trust*. Building confidence, creating trust and, ultimately, communicating with gravitas, are as much an art of unlearning as they are of learning, and they begin with an understanding of the blockages of body (posture, breath and gestures) and voice.

Change involves a plan, and that plan must first involve awareness of the patterns of impediment adopted throughout life that instil an uncertainty in the listener and lead to a loss of trust. We need to make sure we are not utilising patterns that are doing the opposite of building trust, such as undermining our own communications with clenched fists or wandering eyes. We need to stop the misdirecting that creates uncertainty and confusion.

Then we need to practise, practise, practise. Indeed, 'The amateur practises until they get it right. The professional practises until they can't get it wrong.'

Building Trust

Posture

There is no denying that maintaining bodily balance is crucial for effective delivery. Cicero declared 'rapid oscillation' from side to side as wholly objectionable—Julius Caesar referred to this as 'rocking the boat'. It brings to mind the imbalance of then US president Joe Biden being guided down stairs, and the impression this physical limitation brings to the perception of competence. It shows us how important it is to maintain balance to engender trust.

Quintilian said, 'A proper and natural head position contributes to gracefulness. Casting down the head signifies humility; throwing it back shows haughtiness; leaning it to one side indicates languor; and keeping it rigid and unmoved suggests a certain degree of rudeness.'[14] For the modern leader, this means standing up straight, not stiff, but flexible, with the head set atop your neck, in total balance and nodding forward to show a lack of defensiveness and freedom of thought. This, of course, is the way a person is born, so it is worth checking nature's course has not been thrown into disarray by the stresses of life.

Breath

The skill of breath management is at the core of all work on trust. Again, this might feel like it should be an innate skill, but proper breath control must be rethought and ineffective responses 'unlearnt'. The forgotten art here is the management of breath under stress.

We know that stress will have many effects, one of the most detrimental being the jamming and holding of the diaphragm. Anciently, this would disarm a warrior and render him ineffective. In modern times, this habitual pattern blocks trust through a squeezed throat and a tight voice and the physical barrier of a raised chest.

The Fijian greeting 'Bulla', like many ancient greetings, involves an explosive outbreath, unblocked by tension and resonating from deep in the body, depicting the control of the man to allow the breath to flow.

Interestingly, the word 'anxiety' derives from the verb 'to strangle', and the word 'inspire' derives from the verb 'to breathe'. Arthur Lessac, one of the most significant recent researchers in the area of breath, reflects these truths when he says that 'voice and speech training is body training, and body training is language/communication training, as well as bio-neuro-psychic heightened sensitivity training'.[15]

When we harness the power of the breath, we harness the power of the voice, the power to undo anxiety and the power to inspire trust.

Voice

Voice is simply a transmutation of personal energy, an energy that sings through the individual composition of each person in which words, though important, are but a part of the whole equation. Words have been the centrally considered aspect in traditional rational-cognitive–based research traditions, to the demise of true voice. My task here is not to ignore content, but to be aware of some pitfalls and redress the imbalance which may indeed be a significant contributor to a lack of coherence and hence trust in individuals.

From a different perspective, non-verbal studies identify the *attractive* voice as sounding 'more articulate, lower in pitch, higher in pitch range, low in squeakiness, non-monotonous, appropriately loud and resonant'.[16] People with attractive voices, in turn, are seen to have greater power, competence, warmth and honesty attributed to them. However, trying to implement vocal change through pitch, pace and volume leaves us in a similar conundrum to the school of elocution—stuck with communication that is artificial and manufactured.[17]

Quintilian stated: 'Delivery is elegant if supported by a voice that is easy, powerful, fine, flexible, firm, sweet, well-sustained, clear, and pure.'[18] But other than advising against going too high or too low (as those sounds don't carry well), in ancient times, pitch and tone played no part in a voice that brought gravitas. Nor should it today.

Blocked by stress and unaware of the importance of breath, the speaker may impede their sound and squeeze it from the body interspersed by filler words such as 'um' or 'like'. This broken pattern is unsettling for the listener and undermines every aspect of trust. The listener finds themselves unconsciously searching for the reasons why the speaker's voice is restricted.

When we speak, our voice must flow—this is the voice of trust—and so we must unlearn poor habits. The air flow in and out must remain unblocked and supported by the lower body, with the vocal folds closing cleanly. As that vibrating flow of air leaves the body of the speaker, it enters the body of the listener, vibrating their eardrum and massaging their skin to be recognised as sound. Like the act of continual touch in physical massage, the unbroken smoothness of the touch of the voice is the expression of trust in its purest form.

Gestures

Gestures were a foundational communication element for mankind right up until the end of the nineteenth century. In ancient times, gestures were prescriptive, with certain ones having set meanings and orators being instructed to use them at set intervals. Cicero in 1 CE was said to have stipulated that one should use eight gestures every seventeen words, yet we are taught almost none, showcasing how alien these skills have become in our modern world.

After World War II, the understanding and implementation of gestures in our lives as a crucial communication tool simply died. Perhaps the reason for this was Hitler's obsession with ancient Rome, which led him to adopt many of their practices—among these, gesturing, something he practised in an exaggerated way to cope with large group motivation. Certainly, in the movie *Gladiator*, directed by Ridley Scott, the Roman gestures of the actor Russell Crowe were edited out for fear of a Nazi association.

But gestures allow you to complement, match or even disagree with your verbal messages. They support what you're saying and build trust. For instance, an orator's eyes typically follow the gesture's movement, indicating harmony. Conversely, if the eyes and gesture move in opposite directions, it can signal disharmony or aversion.

Embracing gestures in your own communications starts with the three golden rules:

1. They should be non-repetitive. This means that you cannot use the same gesture over and over again.
2. They must be congruent with the message. They need to support what you're saying to be part of trusted communication.
3. They should be held until the next movement. If you're using a gesture every two to three words, then you hold the first gesture until you move to the next.

Gestures to Build Trust

Some gestures were initiated in ancient times that signal the lack of physical blockage and hence the impression of trust.

The open palm shows that you aren't hiding anything and that you're willing to listen to what others want to share. To leave the palms open conveys peace and trust; to clench the fists is an action that undermines it.

The revealing of the body with arms wide and palms forward and open is a natural expression of trust. It is clear that this is the most vulnerable position of the body, with the organs unprotected. Conversely, elbows lodged on the side of the body, or arms crossing the body, are defensive responses inspiring a lack of trust.

Touch to Build Trust

Herodotus knew you can trust your eyes far better than your ears—we all know seeing is believing. But is that the truth anymore with the evolution of editing tools and AI? If seeing is better than hearing, but seeing is no longer believing, what we have left is touch, smell and taste—all the realms of the oft-ignored kinaesthetic world.

What does this mean for you? It means you need to balance your virtual world with events where you can quite literally touch and feel the comfort of reality. As Gallace and Spence told us: 'Interpersonal tactile stimulation provides an effective means of influencing people's social behaviours.'[19]

Within the conference industry, we hear that live conferences are back, as well as on-the-ground dinners, retreats, events and cocktail get-togethers. So post-COVID, the handshake should also be firmly back in your repertoire. The handshake has been around for 3000 years and has survived plagues for those millennia. It is unique in that it fulfils the etiquette of being a completely appropriate act where we can touch strangers to build trust.

How we actually facilitate the enactment of the handshake is shown on ancient Greek vases.[20] It involves a sword thrust without a sword, with the added bonus of physical touch. The movement is more than just the hand. It encompasses the entire body posture. A proper handshake includes the weight on the front right leg, with the right hand extended. The arm is long and the pressure of the hand is in the thrust between the thumb and second finger. Lastly, the eyes are on the eyes of the person being greeted.

Embracing the Eyes

A wide body of literature looks at how we can 'read' people from their faces, particularly their eyes. In Western culture, a person who is making direct eye contact is often seen as more trustworthy, attractive and friendly than somebody with an averted gaze. There are, however, subtleties in application. This includes avoiding the obvious limits of staring intently, which may be associated with the blinkless gaze of the psychopath with no startle response. Staring can be rectified by movement of the face, which may involve nodding, blinking and smiling. This is more than anecdotal—researchers studying the blink rate for trusted listening have found this to be fifteen blinks per minute.[21]

The key to trust is eye control. What has become clear is that succumbing to the natural movement of the eyes for thought can undermine trust. In contrast, building trust is about being able to control the movement of the eyes to hold a gaze with softness, and direct the eyes congruently where effective.

Mirroring the ancient categorisation of eye movement as another gesture, it might be possible to get people to trust you more by using your eyes to direct their attention in a helpful way. For example, researchers have found that participants tend to like objects that are looked at by faces during an experiment more than ones that aren't.[22]

Trust Is at Your Fingertips

To be trusted, we must recognise what the ancients understood: the vital importance of body and voice. This is not enough, however. We also need to realise it is not so much about building trust but about not losing trust through habits that could be read as untrustworthy by the listener.

As a good person, your challenge is to be aware of the body and voice and the blockages you may have. Then you need to implement the right techniques to undo them.

This is the elusive obvious, and without it, all efforts at trust may otherwise be a fool's errand. But with them, trust is literally at your fingertips.

PART V
TRUST AND THE FUTURE

In AI We Trust? What to Expect in Our Technological Future

Toby Walsh, Chief Scientist, UNSW AI Institute, Australia

> The real problem of humanity is the following: we have Paleolithic emotions, medieval institutions, and god-like technology.
>
> Edward O Wilson, sociobiologist, September 2009

THE FUTURE RARELY unfolds like we expect. Take AI. We fear the rise of our machine overlords. And Hollywood has given us plenty of technological tropes to worry about. You will know them well.

There is the terrifying T-800 robot played by Arnold Schwarzenegger in the *Terminator* movies that is engaged in a war against humans. There is the Tyrell Corporation Nexus-6 replicant robot in *Blade Runner*, fleeing Harrison Ford after a bloody off-world robotic mutiny. There is Harlan, the rogue AI in the recent Netflix movie *Atlas* which, being programmed to save humanity from risk, seeks to destroy humanity itself based on our history of destructive behaviour.

My personal favourite is HAL 9000, the sentient computer in *2001: A Space Odyssey*. HAL talks, plays chess, runs the space station, and has murderous intent. HAL voices one of the most famous lines ever said by a computer: 'I'm sorry, Dave. I'm afraid I can't do that.'

Why is it that the AI is always trying to kill us?

In reality, our artificially intelligent future, which is rapidly arriving as I write, is none of these conscious robots with lethal ambition. Our AI future is much more mundane and much more insidious.

This should not be a surprise. Hints of this future were predicted very early in the day. In 1909, for example, in a short story titled 'The Machine Stops', the great EM Forster painted a prophetic picture of our digital future. ('The Machine Stops' is probably Forster's best-known short story—pop group Level 42 even wrote a song about it.) The story gets a lot right. It predicts globalisation, the internet, videoconferencing and many other aspects of our current digital reality, from more than a century ago. It is a haunting tale of a high-tech haven that hurtles towards a horrifying bloody halt. Without noticing, humans in the story become so dependent on the technology mediating their society that society itself breaks when the machines do.

Perhaps 1909 is too far in the past to resonate with people today. If so, we can instead look to the marvellous Carl Sagan from just thirty years ago, in his book *The Demon-Haunted World: Science as a Candle in the Dark*. This text ought to be required reading for every politician, educator and concerned citizen today. Back in 1995, Sagan prophetically wrote:

> I have a foreboding of an America in my children's or grandchildren's time—when the United States is a service and information economy; when nearly all the key manufacturing industries have slipped away to other countries; when awesome technological powers are in the hands of a very few, and no one representing the public interest can even grasp the issues; when the people have lost the ability to set their own agendas or knowledgeably question those in authority; when, clutching

our crystals and nervously consulting our horoscopes, our critical faculties in decline, unable to distinguish between what feels good and what's true, we slide, almost without noticing, back into superstition and darkness. The dumbing down of America is most evident in the slow decay of substantive content in the enormously influential media, the 30-second sound bites (now down to 10 seconds or less), the lowest common denominator programming, credulous presentations on pseudoscience and superstition, but especially a kind of celebration of ignorance.[1]

This future has, it seems, now arrived. Not just in America, but in Australia and indeed every other Western democracy. Every one of Sagan's predictions has come true. The night is starting to envelop us. And in that darkness, we have lost trust in many of the institutions which make up our society.

We have lost trust in government and politics. In the Australian Public Service Commission's 2023 survey of *Trust and Satisfaction in Australian Democracy*, three-quarters of the Australian population did not trust their political parties.[2] And more than half did not trust government itself, state or federal.

We have lost trust in journalism. In the *Trust and Satisfaction* survey, only a third of our population trusted newspapers. And only half trusted the public broadcaster despite its Reithian duty to 'educate, inform, entertain'. Indeed, most of us have switched off broadcast television altogether, with audiences down and ever ageing.

We have also lost trust in other important societal glues, such as religion. Just one in five of us still goes to the church, temple, mosque or synagogue. This is a dramatic drop. Back in the 1950s, around half of Australians attended church regularly.

We have even lost trust in science. Only 61 per cent of the population polled in the *Trust and Satisfaction* survey trusted scientific reports. Scientific truth is now often in dispute. From climate change to COVID, the public is overly sceptical. Scientists like myself are increasingly afraid to put our heads above the parapet for fear of the incoming projectiles.

What is causing this loss of trust? And what impact is this having on our society? These are questions that are starting to keep me awake at night. Especially as I see the way that my field, AI, is feeding into this loss of trust.

It's hard to be sure about the causes and the impact of this distrust since society is, after all, a bit of an amorphous concept. But perhaps the biggest threat to society—to the values that many of us hold dear, like democracy, equity and freedom of speech—is that society itself is fragmenting. And it is hard not to identify many technological drivers that are contributing to that fragmentation.

Let me name half a dozen or so of these drivers. Identifying them is a start. For we can only hope to nurture society if we identify the forces being corralled against it.

First, and I suspect foremost, is social media. The biggest ruse, of course, was calling it 'social media' when, in fact, it might be more accurately called 'anti-social media'. It was supposed to connect us, but rather than do that, it polarises and drives us apart.

The other issue with the name 'social media' is that, despite media being the other half of the name, we bizarrely don't consider social media to be part of the media. Yet, for many people, social media is their main source of news. Facebook is arguably the largest news organisation on the planet, even if, for financial and legal reasons, it is now trying frantically to distance itself from this role.

Social media is also one of the main sources of our entertainment. Its rise is intimately connected to the death of broadcasting, and to the rise of streaming. And social media is arguably now the main source of human relationships. Today, many people meet their partners online. And much of our social life is conducted on, and aided by, social media.

Social media is becoming humanity's main distraction. It is intermediating many of the relationships we have with each other.

The average Australian checks their phone every eight minutes. We experience anxiety if we leave our phones at home. We text people in the same room as us. And half of us say we wouldn't be able to continue our day-to-day lives if we lost our phones. We are addicted to the dopamine hits that it gives us. On average, Australians spend over five hours per day on our phones. I fear this cannot end well.

The second technological driver of this breakdown in trust is the demise of broadcasting and its replacement by AI-powered streaming services. What we see now is often the choice of the algorithms. Broadcasting is slowly but surely dying. We live in a world of micro-targeting where AI algorithms filter what we see.

Around 80 per cent of the content that people watch on Netflix is not what they came to watch but what the algorithms recommend. YouTube has five billion monthly active users, and over one billion hours of YouTube content are watched around the world every day. The content we watch is no longer broadcast. It is narrowcast.

Audiences of traditional broadcasters continue to decline. And content, as well as delivery, is adapting to these new and shorter forms of delivery.

The third technological driver is the rise of misinformation and disinformation. The algorithms that engage us on social media encourage content that creates a reaction, and misinformation and disinformation provoke a reaction. Facebook claims to encourage meaningful engagement but the reality is that it encourages clickbait.

We are used to believing what we see and hear. But we are entering a world in which we have to entertain the idea that anything we see or hear is fake. Unless we were in the room and saw it with our own eyes, or heard it with our own ears, there is the possibility that it might be synthetic. And deepfake content is now very good. You can no longer tell the difference between what is real and what is fake.

Timothy Snyder, in his 2017 book *On Tyranny: Twenty Lessons from the Twentieth Century*, described well the impact of a society in which we cannot believe anything: 'To abandon facts is to abandon freedom. If nothing is true, then no one can criticize power, because there is no basis upon which to do so. If nothing is true, then all is spectacle.'

Sadly, truth was already a pretty fungible idea. But this is about to get much, much worse. The tools used to generate fake content are widely available and easy to use. Deepfakes have been an unwelcome feature of every election held around the world since generative AI tools like Stable Diffusion and Midjourney became available. They have, for example, featured in recent elections in Argentina, Slovakia, India and the United States. And no doubt, they'll be turning up shortly in elections in Australia.

Cambridge Analytica should have been a wake-up call. We had invented a very powerful and cheap way to reach into people's lives and deliver manipulating and fake content. We are now about to supercharge this with persuasive AI-generated untruths.

In most countries, we have strict laws about the use of traditional media to influence elections. We don't want the media barons or those with the most dollars to win elections. We want those with the best ideas. But social media up-ends this. Elections can be won by those with the best algorithms and the most convincing lies.

The fourth driver is an increasing dislike of, even disdain for, experts—especially scientific experts. There are many factors behind this rejection, such as increasing inequity within society (driven in part by technological disruption and globalisation), and the rise of conspiracy theories and other forms of misinformation (again driven by the algorithms).

There is, however, the deeper problem that in many countries we don't, for bizarre reasons, value intelligence in politics. The science fiction author Isaac Asimov identified this problem back in 1980:

> There is a cult of ignorance in the United States, and there has always been. The strain of anti-intellectualism has been a constant thread winding its way through our political and cultural life,

nurtured by the false notion that democracy means that 'my ignorance is just as good as your knowledge'.[3]

And ignorance is nowhere more prevalent than in the area of science and technology. It is unfortunately perfectly acceptable to be ignorant of the science and technology transforming our society. Carl Sagan again warned of the problem back in 1995:

> We've arranged a global civilization in which most crucial elements profoundly depend on science and technology. We have also arranged things so that almost no one understands science and technology. This is a prescription for disaster. We might get away with it for a while, but sooner or later this combustible mixture of ignorance and power is going to blow up in our faces.[4]

The fifth driver is that digital technologies are destroying the income of old-fashioned media. This makes it harder and harder for the fourth estate to shine a light on our democracy.

The tech companies now take 90 per cent of all digital ad spending, and around half of the total spend on all advertising. In the past, media used to subsidise news reporting by selling advertising, but the tech companies have stolen almost all of this income.

To make matters worse, almost all newspapers have perversely locked themselves into a market in which they give away all their content online for free. It is only a few sites, like *The New York Times*, that have managed to keep their content behind paywalls. Journalism now is a sad tale of redundancies and cutbacks as the media giants of old struggle to keep afloat. Traditional media is like the *Titanic*, heading at full speed towards a sea of icebergs. The outcome is entirely predictable.

In Australia, the News Media Bargaining Code was a brave attempt to prevent journalism sinking by having the large technology platforms pay local news publishers for the news content made available or linked to on their platforms. But it is unclear whether the platforms are going to support old-fashioned media in this way in the long run. Meta is already starting to pull back from contributing voluntarily. And politicians have so far not displayed much of an appetite to fight it.

The sixth technological driver of this breakdown in trust is that digital technologies have emptied the town square. Society depends on us having a shared vision. There used to be only a few channels on TV. And we would all stand around the water cooler discussing the same programs. We no longer do this.

Many people are unaware that the internet they see is unique to them. Even if we surf the same news websites, we'll see different news stories based on our previous likes. And on a website like Amazon, almost every item and price we see is unique to us. It is chosen by algorithms based on what we were previously wanting to buy and willing to pay. There is little on the web that we share in common.

We often think our superpower is our intelligence. But our superpower is actually our society. It is our ability to come together and collectively work on shared problems. But to do so, we must have shared goals. And digital technologies are undermining that shared vision. We are increasingly living in our own digital bubbles.

The seventh driver of this breakdown in trust is AI-powered surveillance. We see this most clearly in China. Again, this should not have been surprising. Authors like George Orwell predicted this future. Except it's not Big Brother—people watching people—but computers watching people. If you want to scale surveillance to cover a nation, then digital technologies are perfect for the job.

In China, there's a facial-recognition system that can scan a billion faces in a minute. It can surveil essentially the whole population in real time. And it is being put to use to track and persecute the Uyghurs—a sizeable ethnic group in north-western China. And in case you had any misunderstanding of the state's intention, it has been helpfully called 'Skynet', the AI computer in the *Terminator* series.

This is not, however, just a problem in China. Here in the West, we see this surface in what is wonderfully termed 'surveillance capitalism'. When the product is free, you are the product. And much of the digital economy revolves around collecting and selling data about you.

Digital surveillance is insidious. Even if you aren't actually being surveilled, the possibility that you might be changes your behaviour. Yet if we think of many of the changes to our democracy we now value, such as women having the right to vote or the representation of Indigenous voices, they came about because people could voice dangerous ideas, first in private and then in public.

Of course, this was all the opposite of what we were promised. Technology was supposed to be a force for good. Social media was, for example, supposed to bring us together. But in reality, it has driven us apart. It has destroyed the body image of many young women. And repeated studies suggest that using social media makes us more anxious and unhappy.

We should not be surprised that we have ended up here. We were seduced into this place. At the start, these digital technologies appeared to be a good thing. During the series of Middle Eastern uprisings in 2010–11 known collectively as the Arab Spring, social media gave voice to those who had previously no voice. It helped mobilise those campaigning for democracy. Similarly, in the election of Obama as president of the United States, first in 2008, social media got the young, people of colour, and other under-represented voices out to vote. It all seemed marvellous at the time.

But quickly, the same technologies were turned to less positive ends. They were used to spread untruths in the Brexit referendum, and to suppress votes in order to elect extreme candidates like Trump. And we now see states like Russia conduct election interference in other countries using these same tactics.

This is not the first time that technology has threatened to disrupt society. Other technologies, from the steam engine to electricity, have already transformed our lives dramatically. AI will, in many ways, be no different to these past technological transformations. Just like them, AI will alter almost every aspect of our lives: how we are born, live, work, play and die. But there is one way in which the AI revolution will likely be different. And that is in the speed with which it transforms our lives.

The Industrial Revolution took over fifty years to play out. Electricity took several decades. Even the internet took a decade or so to take hold, as we had to get people online. The AI revolution is different. We've already put the plumbing in. You only need to be told the URL or the API of some AI service and you can get to work.

Vast amounts of money are being invested in AI. In 2024, around a half-billion dollars was invested in artificial intelligence. Every day. We've never seen anything like this scale of investment before. And it is starting to pay off. Within a year of launching ChatGPT, OpenAI went from no income to earning over $1 billion per year and a valuation of somewhere around $100 billion.[5] This is without precedent in the history of capitalism. AI is arguably the largest gold rush ever. In terms of both revenue and market value, OpenAI is the fastest-growing company ever.

It would be easy, then, to be pessimistic. To argue that irresistible forces are in play. That the financial incentives are immense and misaligned with the public good. That these technology companies are more powerful than many countries. But there is everything still to play for. The future is not decided. It is the product of the choices that we make today.

Technology shapes society, but society also gets to shape technology. I therefore want to end this essay with ten levers we can pull that will enhance our society and counter the forces pulling it apart. The fact that there are so many levers to pull should itself bring some reassurance.

First, we need to hold the platforms more accountable for the content they serve. In the United States, for instance, we need to overturn Section 230 of the Communications Decency Act. We must hold the platforms accountable for the content they deliver, just as we hold traditional media accountable for the content they deliver. The digital platforms can no longer hide behind the argument that they are just an intermediary. Indeed, now that they are increasingly delivering AI-generated content that they created, this is plainly false.

Second, we need to protect those who are easily manipulated or harmed. For instance, we should lift the age of consent for using social media to sixteen years old. In a decade's time, I imagine we will look back at social media like we look today at tobacco and alcohol. Young minds in their formative years need to be protected from the harmful and addictive effects of tobacco, alcohol and social media.

The recent decision to prohibit deepfake pornography is a good example of protecting those who are being harmed. But deepfake pornography is just one of the most obvious harms that needs to be addressed. There are many others, such as doxing and cyberbullying. And sadly, unless we do something about it, AI will likely only make such harms more prevalent.

Third, we need to regulate to ensure truth in political advertising. In most countries there are strict laws about truth when advertising commercial products. You can't say that a toothpaste whitens teeth unless there is scientific evidence that it does. But you can say almost anything you like in political adverts. In the past, it didn't matter. If you said an untruth, everyone would see it. But now, you can tell every voter a different lie. And no-one else sees the lies that you see.

Fourth, we need to regulate against deepfakes. In Europe, the new AI Act requires social media platforms to identify and label deepfake content. Fake content will undermine our faith in many of our institutions. Compare this to another area where fake content would be dangerous. We rightly worry about fake money undermining our confidence in the financial system. We therefore have strong penalties for counterfeiting money that we prosecute vigorously. We need to do the same with deepfakes.

Unfortunately, it is not as simple as banning fake content. Politicians may be tempted to do so, but we have to balance this against maintaining freedom of speech. For instance, our ability to parody politicians is an important part of the political process. We must therefore walk the delicate tightrope between reducing fake content and supporting satirical debate.

Fifth, we need to embrace technological measures like digital watermarking to reduce the impact of deepfakes and protect intellectual property rights. Indeed, industry bodies are already actively engaged in defining standards for such watermarking technologies. We can confidently perform our financial transactions on the web because industry agreed on standards for digital certificates to verify the authenticity of websites. Similarly, industry needs to agree to standards for digital watermarks that verify the authenticity of digital content.

This is, in fact, the perfect application for the blockchain. We need a distributed ledger on which to record an encrypted certificate of provenance and of editing. This is a description of the blockchain—we have finally found something good to do on it!

Sixth, we need to restore financial support to the fourth estate for its role in shining a bright light on our democratic institutions. The News Media Bargaining Code was an attempt to do precisely this. We must double down on such initiatives, taxing the technology companies to ensure we can protect democracy by uncovering the lies and corruption that thrive in the dark.

Seventh, we need to develop digital technologies that can amplify democracy. For example, over 7000 cities around the world are using participatory budgeting to decide budgets from states, housing authorities, schools and other institutions. *The New York Times* has called it 'revolutionary civics in action'.[6] Participatory budgeting deepens democracy, builds stronger communities, and can more fairly distribute public resources. And digital technologies like e-voting can encourage participation in such novel democratic processes.

Eighth, we need to use digital technologies to increase transparency. Sadly, the long-running saga around the attempted extradition of Julian Assange to the United States has distracted attention from the revolutionary potential of websites like WikiLeaks. Such initiatives encourage and protect whistleblowers, helping to preserve democracy by shining a light on wrongdoing. The internet was, and still is, a powerful force to improve democratic transparency.

Ninth, we need to strengthen our digital privacy. In many respects, we are at the technological low point in terms of our privacy. To do anything interesting, we need to share our data with the tech giants and their AI algorithms. But advances in AI like federated learning, where AI models are trained without sharing our personal data with the tech giants, promise to give us back our privacy. Indeed, the AI will increasingly be smart and small enough to run on the edge, on our own devices. We will then not have to have our data leave our devices.

Tenth, we need to ensure that access to digital technologies is a fundamental human right. If we do not, the world will divide into the digital haves and have-nots. Access to the internet is becoming as important as other basic rights, like freedom of speech. We learnt during COVID lockdowns how many children in Australia did not have access to a single device at home on which to access the web. This cannot continue.

Ultimately, digital technologies like AI have the potential to increase trust. But we need to make some good choices to ensure that they do. People often ask me if I'm optimistic or pessimistic about the challenges that AI poses. I say that I'm both. I'm optimistic that AI will ultimately bring great benefits. But in the short term, I'm pessimistic. Sadly, our children are set to inherit a worse world, due to a raft of problems, from the climate emergency to global insecurity, and, as I've outlined here, distrust in the very institutions that we now need most.

TRUST AND THE FUTURE

The future requires us to be careful, smart, and committed to using AI to build, not break, our trust in society. And if we use technologies like AI wisely, we might look back at this time as the start of a new era of increasing, and not decreasing, trust in our democratic institutions.

So, do we trust AI? Maybe not yet, but with the right choices, we could.

Bots and Moral Panic

Timothy Graham, Associate Professor in Digital Media, Queensland University of Technology, Australia

'How bizarre is this.' These were the words of Professor Terry Hughes in January 2024, writing on X about a group of suspicious accounts posting about the Great Barrier Reef. As Australia's leading marine scientist and coral researcher, Hughes regularly monitors discussions on this topic and had stumbled upon a bot network posting repetitious and misleading content about it. Bots in this sense refers to user profiles on social media platforms that appear to be human but are fully or partly controlled by a machine. For Hughes, the repetitiveness and consistency of the messaging was the giveaway.

By February 2024, Terry Hughes wanted to know 'who is paying for hundreds of bots' to spread myths about 'marine debris', and he questioned whether the bot network was 'an orchestrated attempt to ignore anthropogenic heating due to greenhouse gas emissions'. As people tried to make sense of it, it also attracted the interest of ABC technology reporter James Purtill, who contacted me to help investigate.

Using an open-source software toolkit, I collected data from the suspected bot accounts to map out the network and forensically study it. It turns out the main goal of the bots was to promote cryptocurrencies, while also posting about random topics in multiple languages including English, Vietnamese and Spanish. They all had blue tick verified accounts, meaning they paid US$8 per month for premium access to X, which includes greater audience reach and the ability to 'monetise' their account to receive a share of advertising revenue on their content. Perhaps the most surprising finding was that the content was almost certainly generated by OpenAI's ChatGPT3.5 model. Unlike older types of bot networks that either reshared (retweeted) or 'liked' content, or spread messages by simply copying and pasting text—a practice sometimes referred to as 'copypasta'—the content in these bot networks was human-like and conversational. It contained nuanced variations on a set of topics such as reefs and mostly came in the form of replies to each other's tweets.

Posts from Professor Terry Hughes about a bot network spreading myths about the Great Barrier Reef

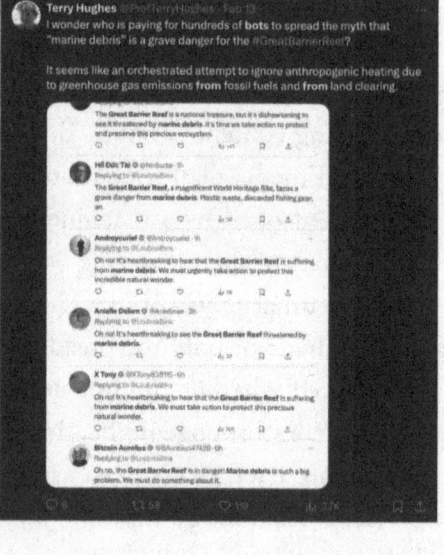

Source: Terry Hughes

Every AI detection model gave the same results: the text was 100 per cent generated by ChatGPT. Evidently these bots were replying to each other by using the previous reply as input to the ChatGPT model. They were engaging in a sort of 'zombie discourse' that recycled the same inputs over and over, simply to generate something to post about to make the accounts seem legitimate enough to avoid getting flagged by X's automated systems for preventing spam and platform abuse.

Although the meaningless babble of these bot accounts managed to attract the attention of Terry Hughes, the analysis showed the bot network wasn't concerned about the truth of its claims about coral reef degradation and likely wasn't even instructed to post specifically on this topic. Its modus operandi was promoting cryptocurrency and ensuring its own survival against X's bot-detection systems by posting replies about various topics that mimicked organic conversation. A recent study describes ChatGPT as 'bullshit' because it has no regard for the truth of what it generates.[1] But while this sounds intriguing and perhaps feels right, it fails to recognise that ChatGPT has no capacity for concern at all. Too easily do we anthropomorphise these AI actors by attributing human characteristics to them, even when explicitly trying not to.

Professor Hughes's experience serves as a jumping-off point for exploring the AI-bot deluge on social media and its impact on trust and truth as we move into the second quarter of the twenty-first century. James Purtill provided a rare glimpse into the growing industry of AI-powered content on social media when he contacted a bot maker, Awais Yousaf, a computer scientist based in Pakistan who explained how he sells 'ChatGPT Twitter bots' for between US$30 and US$500 per account, depending on the complexity of their profiles and behaviour. The bots had the ability to like, comment, reply to other accounts, reply to direct messages, and author engaging original content according to the client's specifications. When asked about the growing issue of spam bots on X, Yousaf said, 'It's hard to remove Twitter bots from Twitter because Twitter is mostly bot.'[2] While this is a bold claim, Yousaf's comments are supported by research that highlights how the platform's bot spam problem worsened considerably after its acquisition by billionaire entrepreneur Elon Musk.[3]

Zooming out, the case study of 'Terry Hughes versus the bots' highlights the scale and complexity of the issue, as LLMs such as ChatGPT afford digital content creators the opportunity to flood information ecosystems with low-quality content that is often ambiguous in nature. So, too, are they more capable of deception, as more 'work' is required to negotiate who or what one is encountering online—a problem that Florian Muhle diagnosed as a 'membership categorisation' problem,[4] and one that is far from new. However, the emergence of publicly available LLMs has exponentially reduced the cost of creating bots that can evade automatic detection and mass-produce 'original' content (even if it is stolen, but that's another matter). For internet users, it becomes increasingly difficult to know who or what to trust, raising questions around the erosion of authenticity in online discourse. Is this suspicious account a bot or a real person trolling? Is the bot you encounter an isolated case or part of an orchestrated network? And if it is coordinated, who or what is behind it? If a hashtag or topic is trending on social media, is it organic or the result of a paid campaign? How does bot spam contribute to the epistemic crisis facing our ability to distinguish truth from falsehood?

While these are all valid and open problems, I would like to suggest that how we think and talk about bots is just as important as what they actually do. The sudden onset of LLMs has turbocharged our capacity for moral panic. In addition to the problems outlined above, AI-powered bots have become a signifier for a set of concerns relating to post-truth and the transformation of online spaces by billionaire owners like Elon Musk, whose autocratic governance has led many to believe that platforms like X are in decline. Recognising this is an important step towards sustainable, collaborative and pro-social solutions to a problem that we haven't even properly yet defined.

Bots and the AI Moment in Post-Truth Societies

Before we proceed, it's important to recognise that for every 'bad' bot, there are likely ten times as many 'good' ones that go unnoticed. Bots have a long and storied history. A big part of the issue is that there's no consistent and concise definition that captures what a bot is. For example, the social platform Reddit couldn't function without the 'auto-moderator' (or 'automod') bots that do the tireless work of enforcing community guidelines, filtering out spam and hateful content, and curating content to maintain the quality of discussions as defined by the forums (or 'subreddits') that are moderated by volunteers. Similarly, web spiders and indexing bots do the job of crawling and cataloguing the countless webpages on the internet, providing an army of automated labour that underpins search engines. The mundanity of voice assistants such as Apple's Siri or Amazon's Alexa makes them not even seem like bots, with their roles ranging from putting on a specific Taylor Swift song in the car to playing trivia games or ordering a pizza. To complicate our definition of what a bot is, Dominique Carlon asks an existential question: 'Where do people who act like bots fit into this understanding, and does that distinction matter?'[5]

It is not a stretch to say that bots are as diverse as we are. Despite this, our cultural imaginary has been markedly shaped by the emergence of a specific species: political bots. While there are genuine concerns that well-resourced actors weaponise social media by deploying bots as tools of propaganda, public discourse around bots has, like 'fake news', increasingly taken on the appearance of an 'informational moral panic' where every political issue seems to be at least partly the consequence of automated deception on social media. 'Bot' has also become a pejorative term, with people on the internet who disagree calling each other bots to undermine credibility and delegitimise arguments.[6] In this way, our definition of 'bots' is coextensive with how we talk about and make sense of them, which is often framed as the dangerous 'other' threatening democracy and an idealised authentic human experience that we are somehow losing.

This definitional ambiguity is complicated by the advent of ChatGPT: bots that render the Turing test—the test of how a machine behaves like a human—an historical curiosity because they engage in discourse with us in our social spaces at light speed and at scale. Whether they can do so meaningfully or influentially is an open question and likely highly context-specific. Notwithstanding this, the fact that AI-powered bots are increasingly visible in discourse, and we believe they have these capacities, has led to an intensification of the crisis of trust and struggles over 'truth'. This invites us to revisit the relationship between bots and the post-truth condition.

Whereas truth is characterised by institutional authority and the circulation and influence of 'objective' facts and expertise, post-truth marks the dominance of emotion, personal experience and 'alternative facts' in shaping public opinion and personal beliefs.[7] Post-truth is about how it makes you feel, how it corresponds with your experience, how coherent it is in relation to your in-group belief system, and how authentic and authoritative you believe the speaker to be. For Jayson Harsin, post-truth is a periodising concept that 'refers to a historically particular public anxiety about public truth claims and authority to be a legitimate public truth-teller'.[8] It is a convergence of multiple complex historical, social, technological and cultural factors, of which bots are one aspect. For the post-truth condition, a decline in trust towards traditional mainstream media and politicians over the past fifty years coincides with strategies of political communication that have bombarded audiences with information overload.[9]

These structural factors are a perfect storm for intensifying public anxieties about LLM-powered bots precisely because of these entities' capacities for deception and speed. As a moral panic, they are constructed as the deviant other—a social threat leading to declining standards. As an informational moral panic, bots share some similarities to fake news, whereby these digital technologies come to signify and become a beacon for a broader set of concerns about the erosion of trust in the information we consume and produce online, along with the authority of its truth-bearers.[10]

Restoring Trust in the Age of ChatGPT Bots

What are we to do? Understanding AI-bot problems as a post-truth phenomenon can help us to both properly diagnose and develop meaningful responses to the trends I've sketched here. As Matt Carlson argued in relation to 'fake news', accusations of the misuse of ChatGPT and other LLMs for content creation need to be paired with a normative position that outlines what a healthy online environment should look like.[11] Put another way: if we removed LLMs and bots from the world, would things be much better? And if so, on what basis? Would there be less deception? Less online incivility and polarisation? Less misinformation? For political bots, lumping these technologies as part of an 'information disorder' has limited scope for interventions. It may even put us on a wild goose chase by misidentifying the cause of our problems.

Drawing on Harsin's critique of disinformation scholarship, we ought to examine our cryptonormativity in relation to LLM-generated content and bots. Cryptonormativity is where judgements are presented as non-normative (that is, not making claims about how things ought to be) but are in fact normative and made without any explicit framework for their assessment or evaluation. Rather than thinking of AI bots and their content as something we need to combat to restore an otherwise healthy body politic, or an otherwise ordered information ecosystem, there is an opportunity here to evaluate how different types of bots in specific contexts correspond to or promote the kind of media system we want to live in and the political discourse we desire. Just as LLMs are trained on what we say and produce, so too do they hold a mirror to our own frailties, limitations and biases.

As Harsin puts it:

> Beneath the metaphors of disorder and dysfunction is an assumption that deception and error are or should be oddities of political communication and are fundamentally bad. My sense is that they are not oddities, will likely never be eliminated from political communication, and are not even universally 'bad'.[12]

Like disinformation, AI bots are not external pathogens to liberal democracy; they are part of it and produced by it. With a growing recognition that politicians and other privileged actors are the worst spreaders of misleading information, and that social media platforms incentivise and profit from it, we need to change tack.

A key challenge is how we can do things differently and socialise the idea that bots are not the problem: we are, too. Our post-truth condition is a testament to this. Like all technologies, AI bots and content are just as much an opportunity for trust and truth as they are a 'pathogen' to it. Like many dimensions of human affairs, LLMs and the bots built on them are 'a jumble of truth and falsehood' that deal in provisional knowledge: it is not bullshit but 'botshit' that is the problem when these technologies are used blindly and interpreted through Manichean thinking as either good or bad.[13] As botshitters, their capacity for not telling the truth has a unique character: it is not the same as ours. Emerging research suggests that we may be able to manage their epistemic risks through the co-development of frameworks that guard against these while taking advantage of their potential for helping us work towards the type of world we want to live in. For instance, the typology offered by Hannigan, McCarthy and Spicer is one promising direction that pays close attention to the situated work modes of chatbots and their technical specifications.[14]

To create normative levers that steer us in the right direction requires a renewed phase of collaboration. By levers, I mean practical and strategic interventions that steer us incrementally towards societal goals and ethical standards. Collaboration between academics and journalists is needed to shift public discourse by creating social and economic disincentives for falling for the informational moral panic trap, or exacerbating it for strategic gain. Deflating moral panics will yield dividends for trust. Education is a further strategy, but one that should focus less on individual responsibility and more on promoting mass subjectivities that offer levers for people to relate to themselves and others in new ways that eschew panic and determinism in favour of critical thinking and collective action.

In this spirit, we also need to create levers for platforms and companies to come together and act in unison so they can move together and be immune to political attacks. Regulation is one thing, but it needs to be bulwarked by the capacity for synchronised action—force by numbers. To address the profitability of 'botshit' and AI-generated content in the attention economy, we need to create short-term incentives for tech companies to algorithmically amplify quality content over quantity. Platforms optimise for user engagement and attention in the service of advertising revenue, which Laufer and Nissenbaum argue amounts to algorithmic displacement of social trust because 'it chokes out trustworthy processes that we have relied on for guiding valued societal practices and for selecting, elevating, and amplifying content'.[15] Content through this lens is not the problem, AI-generated or not. It is a symptom of the wrong kinds of incentive structures mixed in with our social realities and cognitive predilections. This is a post-truth problem, and in this way an issue of structural inequality rather than just an 'AI problem'.

In some ways, we have never really had an online 'public square'. As platforms like X increasingly demonstrate, perhaps a better metaphor is that of a sprawling cyberpunk city. Mega-corps with little oversight or transparency have always run the show. They moderate their share of the turf inconsistently and largely with impunity. Bots, then, have always been with us in one form or another. Bot networks afford genuine activists opportunities to find new volunteers and nation-states to collaboratively spread disinformation. Deception has always been a virtual birthright—a design feature baked into many platforms. Avatars and pseudonymity allow us to express ourselves in ways we can't in other spaces, whether for fear of persecution or for antisocial purposes such as trolling and hate speech. Scheduling software offers cybernetic augmentations enabling us to act like bots in defiance of platform power,[16] raising questions about what we even mean by authenticity and whether the distinction between personhood and bot-hood really matters, or even makes sense.

In the spirit of cyberpunk cities such as the futuristic Los Angeles depicted in *Blade Runner*, a post-truth perspective of the AI bot moment invites us to ask not only what we should do about the machines, but also what it means to be human.

Understanding Conspiracies and Their Theorists

Kaz Ross, researcher into far-right extremism and conspiracy theories, Australia

IN MAY 2020, as governments around the world began to respond with alarm to the developing COVID-19 pandemic, an illegal protest sprung up in Melbourne. On the steps of the Victorian Parliament House, security guard and unlikely protest leader Fanos Panayides stepped up to question COVID-19 lockdowns and restrictions. Victoria Police rushed forward to arrest him just as he started linking vaccinations to the biblical 'mark of the beast'—the number 666. For the small but vocal crowd, this seemed perfectly timed. To them, Panayides was revealing a satanic secret that 'the powers that be' did not want known, and his arrest proved a government cover-up was directing police actions.

And so conspiratorial thinking was a feature of the burgeoning pandemic protest movement from the beginning. In those early days, the Melbourne-based movement was dominated by people who had never considered themselves political activists before. Many were attending their first protests or talking about politics for the first time. This was a very diverse group, consisting of a wide variety of religions, ages, ethnic backgrounds, and occupations.

Over the next three years, the conspiracy theories got wilder and wilder. At their height, the COVID conspiracists believed that

Melbourne's onerous lockdowns were called so that Chinese-made 5G technology could be secretly installed to monitor the vaccinated via injected spike proteins and microchips, while children were moved around via tunnels beneath Melbourne so that their bodily fluids could be harvested for the elites. The tunnels reached as far as Uluru, some said. It was there that aliens conducted experiments on the hapless 'mole children'. Meanwhile, other conspiracists were boiling vinegar over fires in their backyards to dispel the 'chemtrails' (AKA vapour trails) being emitted from aeroplanes overhead. Some even burnt down 5G towers or disrupted vaccination centres.

This unusual mix of protesters and conspiracists had one thing in common: they were trying to make sense of an unprecedented and disruptive global event. Conspiracies not only gave them a framework for making meaning of frightening events, they also gave them a sense of agency—there was something they could do. They could fight back against the secret forces. Some started turning up every day outside state governors' residences and yelling about a supposed government cover-up of the names of paedophiles in power—they wanted to save the children, they said. And, more than four years later, some are still 'saving the children' in this same way.

Social media platforms tried to moderate the spread of conspiracies online during the pandemic, and government health spokespeople tried to share accurate information. Yet, for the conspiracists, these efforts only proved they were right. In their minds, they were getting flak because they must be on target.

What led to this situation? Why are so many people attracted to these outlier beliefs? And what impact does this have on society and societal trust?

It's true that Australia is a literate country with a good public education system, a free press and a robust legal system. Australia is also considered to have a low corruption score and overall good political transparency. Conspiracy theorists, however, have little faith in institutions, governments, the media, experts, academics and even scientists. Indeed, one of Fanos Panayides's first political stunts back in 2020 was to encourage his tens of thousands of online followers to video themselves smashing and burning their televisions and newspapers. The media was the virus, he said. But it is too simplistic to dismiss individual conspiracy theorists as stupid, deluded or uneducated. They are most commonly caring and worried people wanting to understand and improve society, and who can end up holding wild and clearly nonsensical conspiratorial beliefs.

It helps to think about your own beliefs. Many people have grown up with stories about 'the tooth fairy', Father Christmas, angels or ghosts, and may even still believe in those things. Are these conspiracies? Some people are convinced the 1969 moon landing never happened, or that the terrorist attack on 9/11 was a false-flag or inside job. The evidence proves otherwise, but people cling to their beliefs, and so they become conspiracists. No amount of scientific data can pull them out of their belief that a band of nefarious plotters are behind a cover-up. Researchers accept that fake information will be readily accepted as truth if it conforms to an already held set of beliefs, and that factual information will be rejected for implausible scenarios which confirm a set of beliefs.

Interestingly, sometimes conspiracies are later proven to be true, and these cases can provide justification for the conspiracy adherents. The process of questioning official narratives by conspiracy theorists can yield further facts that may have been occluded in the first official accounts of an event. Wild conspiracies began to circulate as soon as the 9/11 attacks began. Over two decades later, some of these—particularly the anti-Semitic ones—have become bedrock beliefs for many conspiracy theorists. Yet, some researchers argue, the pressure from conspiracy theorists forced authorities into releasing more detailed information about the attacks.[1]

A key problem is that it takes time after a big event for accurate information to be obtained and released, and this allows a significant gap to develop between what is known and what happened.

Investigative journalists and researchers operate in this gap. And conspiracies flourish in this gap. Most people abandon the conspiracy once a certain level of facts provides a plausible explanation. Conspiracy theorists, however, are on an endless quest and won't stop pushing until their belief—that the moon landing was faked, or that the earth is indeed flat—is confirmed.

Among researchers, the term 'conspiracy theory' is notoriously hard to define. In general, however, the consensus is that it involves more than a set of wacky beliefs. A conspiracy theory necessarily involves a conspiracy—that is, a power plot secretly formulated by a hidden group of people which has nefarious or harmful aims. (This rules out the tooth fairy and Santa.) Perhaps the 'mother' of all conspiracy theories is the centuries-old belief that Jewish people are all powerful, financial manipulators in a global cabal enacting evil plots. Claims during the pandemic about George Soros orchestrating the COVID-19 crisis for purposes of population control fit the definition of an anti-Semitic conspiracy.

So who decides what's right, what's wrong, what counts as a fact? Does truth even matter if providing more facts is ineffectual in dissuading conspiracy theorists of their false beliefs? I would argue that in this so-called 'post truth' era of social media, alternative facts, AI and personal ideologies, truth and trust are even more crucial, especially if we are all 'choosing our own realities'.

Determining the truth claims of a conspiracy can be very difficult if facts are incomplete or just currently unknowable. Without getting too philosophical, perhaps the best way to evaluate a conspiracy theory is to follow accurate and credible information from subject experts. Except that in our current fake news misinformation/disinformation social media ecosystem, this is becoming increasingly difficult. Deepfakes and the widespread adoption of AI (for example, ChatGPT) are creating an extremely disturbing challenge. As it is impossible to personally fact-check everything we read online, we rely on others to sort out truth from falsehood. We necessarily hold a level of trust in the expertise, integrity and judgement of scientists, journalists, academics, experts, NGOs, and authorities such as government agencies, inquiries, reports and departments.

And even people with demonstrably false beliefs are concerned with truth—they just rely on different sources to find it.[2] During the pandemic, the phrase 'do your own research' became the guiding principle for determining fact from fiction. Instead of relying on experts ('part of the global plot to enslave humanity anyway'), conspiracy theorists turned to each other. 'Word of mouth' from my pal online replaced 'peer reviewed' by a credentialed expert. As a result, bad actors—whether for the purposes of making money (alternative health practitioners), influencing political processes through fake election claims or destabilising political systems (foreign influence)—were able to weaponise the 'do your own research' brigade. Rumours and word of mouth played a huge part.

Conspiracy Theories and Trust

Rumours can have serious and long-lasting effects. After the Fukushima nuclear reactor accident in 2011, a radioactive cloud started drifting towards mainland China. In southern China, people started panic-buying salt in bulk after hearing that iodine prevented radiation sickness. Despite government orders to cease, the frenzy continued, with people even desperately begging their overseas relatives to post salt immediately as a matter of life and death. Due to a lack of trust in official transparency, people felt the government was covering up the facts, and pretty quickly, the salt rumour was elevated to a conspiracy. It became a secret plot by those in power to withhold the truth from the people because the government couldn't keep them safe and protect them due to inadequate supplies of iodised salt.

In the case of the China salt conspiracy, we could argue that little harm was done, despite there being a few reports of some people ingesting large quantities of salt. Not all conspiracies are as benign, however. 'Pizzagate' is a well-known example of how rumours, spread for political purposes (in this case, right-wing efforts to discredit Democrat candidates during the 2016 American election campaign), lead to violence. Supposedly, Democrats such as Hillary Clinton were abusing children in the basement of a pizza restaurant in Washington. As the rumour spread, staff at the restaurant began receiving death threats. Finally, a man tried to free the captive children by storming the restaurant with a gun. No children were found—there was no basement. Instead of the conspiracy dissipating, however, the idea of a global ring of elite paedophiles took hold in the nascent QAnon conspiracy movement and later became a mainstay of conspiracy theories during the COVID-19 pandemic. This conspiracy is now deeply embedded in right-wing attacks on sex education for children and protests against events such as drag queen story hour. The Institute of Strategic Dialogue noted in 2024 that transphobic and anti-drag rhetoric and conspiracy theories had activated a network of groups which had successfully disrupted many all-ages drag events in Australia.[3]

Where rumours and conspiracy theories take hold, trust in mainstream institutions spirals down. The disruption of social cohesion is one noted outcome of the embrace of controversial conspiracy theories. At a personal level, adherents can lose their employment, social networks, even contact with their families. This has been well documented among adherents to the QAnon conspiracy. According to 2022 research by the Public Religion Research Institute, around one in five Americans believed in the QAnon tenets that a political storm was coming, that violence might be needed to save the country, and that the government, media and financial worlds were controlled by Satan-worshipping paedophiles.[4] Family members of QAnon followers have documented the deep family rifts caused by a commitment to these beliefs. Obviously, having a large number of people embracing violence is a danger for others and for democracy itself, as the 6 January 2021 insurrection at the US Capitol showed. Australia is vulnerable to similar beliefs and consequences.

And what of the conspiracy theorists themselves? It seems many see themselves as heroes in their own Hollywood story. They are a plucky band of misfits and outsiders who gamely pursue the truth at risk of ridicule or worse, believing they will win in the end. This is a story we are culturally very familiar with. It's also a seductive narrative that many people could fall for. After all, who doesn't want to fight baddies and save children? In terms of social cohesion, adherence to a conspiracy theory, or being in the 'conspiracy world', allows people to find a supportive tribe. Post-pandemic, Australia's anti-COVID-restrictions movement has broken into various groups in cities, towns and suburbs—groups that meet for a meal, share homegrown produce, disrupt their local council meetings and yell at drag queens. On the surface, it looks like these groups have become civic-minded (albeit conservative) democratic groups. Scratch the surface, however, and the foundation of these groups is a collection of conspiracy theories: chemtrails, sovereign citizen understanding of the law, satanic paedophiles, global Jewish elites—a veritable smorgasbord of conspiracies.

During the COVID-19 'plandemic'—which is the theory that COVID was deliberately started by the government for nefarious means—misinformation, disinformation, gossip, rumour and straight-out lies were pushed into people's social media feeds via the various platforms. The Centre for Countering Digital Hate found in 2021 that just twelve individuals and their organisations were responsible for up to 65 per cent of all anti-vaccine misinformation, rising to 73 per cent on Facebook alone.[5] These individuals served to make a lot of money from their digital content, alternative health supplements and other products such as books. And their reach on Facebook, YouTube, Twitter (now X) and Instagram was over fifty-nine million people. Social media companies' efforts to de-platform the 'Dirty Dozen' were woefully inadequate.

Similarly, QAnon adherents largely had a free run on Facebook and Instagram until a purge in the lead-up to the American election in November 2020. It was only after the 6 January insurrection that Twitter removed around 70,000 QAnon-related accounts. According to Ciarán O'Connor and Jared Holt, many booted from the mainstream platforms found themselves in the Neo-Nazi–infested waters of unmoderated platforms such as Telegram and Gab—incubators for radicalisation. The researchers found that extremist, violent and forbidden content on TikTok was rarely removed, with content creators using features of the platform to evade detection.[6]

Because of the way algorithms work on social media, there is no 'one' internet that we all see. Newsfeeds are vastly different and individualised. Interest groups and lobby groups are able to weaponise conspiracies and fake news easily. In early 2024, the EU Commission opened a case against Meta for illegally and irresponsibly allowing EU citizens to be exposed to paid Russian disinformation on its platforms. The erosion of trust in institutions, experts, media and governments is a goal for bad-faith actors. Blaming conspiracy theorists for being duped, therefore, seems unfair—the odds of always discerning facts and truth are stacked against all social media users.

What Can Be Done?

On a personal level, we need to recognise that often the conspiracy theorist is trying to make sense of a complex situation and has found a theory or explanation they think works. Frequently, they think that what they are doing is good, noble and right. And they probably want to save you as well. It is a good idea to follow advice given to family members of cult members: try to keep in contact, and recognise that confrontation may be less than useful. Talking to the people around us is helpful.

On a societal level, we need to ensure government transparency and accountability, clear communication, and that people are equipped with media literacy and critical thinking skills. What the explosion of global conspiracies has shown us over the last decade is that much more effective moderation on social media is essential. Political interference via misinformation and disinformation needs to be exposed and controlled as a matter of urgency. Unfortunately, social media platforms are frequently buffeted by the whims of their owners, as we have seen with X. The outcomes are not always the best for undermining dangerous and damaging conspiracy theories.

There's no doubt that conspiracy theories have a big impact on trust, but it's worth asking what comes first: loss of trust or the rise of conspiracies? Does a loss of trust foster a plethora of conspiracies? Or does an ecosystem of conspiracies erode trust? In one sense, this is a chicken and egg scenario. At their essence, conspiracies coalesce around a belief in an evil, political plot operating in secret for nefarious ends. Lack of trust is just one emotional element that fuels conspiracy thinking, alongside suspicion, anxiety, fear and righteous anger. There is no doubt that conspiracy theories are based on mistrust and that they spread mistrust further, somewhat like black mould. Conspiracy thinking becomes a template that can be applied in a myriad situations: school curriculum, health care, climate change, cloud formations and so on.

As we can see from the example of China, rumours spread widely in government-controlled news media systems because people cannot readily obtain independent information, and they don't trust the government to tell the truth. However, even in a democracy like Australia with multiple independent and authoritative, non-government sources of information, and a political system which is based on a certain level of transparency and accountability, conditions can arise for conspiracies to flourish. 'Disinfecting with sunlight' or exposing conspiracy thinking to scrutiny and increasing the amount of accurate information available may not be enough to stem the flow of conspiracy theories, but it certainly helps.

Living with Uncertainty

A Q&A with Julia Baird, author, broadcaster and journalist, Australia

Q [Tracey Kirkland]: We're calling this book Age of Doubt. *It's about this current time of uncertainty, when people are trying to figure out who they can trust, and there's a lot of distrust in information and in facts. As a journalist and writer, how do you feel about this age we're living in?*
A: I'd say, first of all, that doubt is really important. It should never be seen as a negative to question, to query, to hold people to account, to try to establish what someone's credentials or motive might be, to understand that a lot of people bring various biases to things they produce. I think all of that is really natural. We want to live in a questioning society, but when that questioning becomes baked in and the distrust is not reasoned, it becomes a problem. Instead of, 'I don't trust people who won't tell me who their sources are,' it becomes, 'I don't trust all journalists.' And that then leaves you with nothing and no-one to trust. This is where we have some responsibility as journalists. If, in our profession, where people have to provide sources and be accountable and transparent and accurate, journalists are not doing that, I think that's when there's a problem. That's when distrust starts to calcify and can lead us to a series of false truths. I just don't think we should give up on the enterprise that reporting is valid. There are a lot of decent individuals who are really trying to, when

we talk about journalism, tell good and important stories and do it in a right and fair and proper and accurate way.

As a journalist, I can see why there are a lot of outlets you wouldn't trust. I can see the peddling of misinformation and disinformation every day, that it is getting worse, and I can't see a single positive coming from that. It's a little bit difficult to establish neat lines of causation, but it is definitely occurring at a time when we are feeling more lonely and desperate and disconnected from community. And I think that's really crucial because when you're part of a community group, for example, a swimming group, you'll have a bunch of people there who you probably violently disagree with on a bunch of political or cultural issues. You do, however, have something that you share. Someone might share your love of the ocean, also turn up at the surf club every weekend and help out the Little Nippers program for kids, but have views about the war in the Middle East that you cannot stand. If you can see that people can sometimes have good values but different politics to you, then you are much more likely to understand where they are coming from.

I think the fundamental thing we need to do is to spend more time understanding why people think the way they do instead of writing them off, stereotyping them and vilifying them. Because I can see that so much is being fomented in this atmosphere of distrust. I just have to say a single thing on social media and because I'm a woman or because I'm from the ABC or because of whatever, I'm targeted. And, as a result, what I am often portrayed as is so far from who I am and what I'm about that I'm constantly struck by it.

Q: Have you felt that amplified in the last five to ten years, or has it always been this way?
A: I think there's a number of measurements by which we can see that distrust and outrage are being monetised right now. There are people who are making money from making us feel angry, making us feel impotent ... as though the world is populated with people

who deliberately don't understand and deliberately want to crush us. And it's very disconnected from a lot of our lived realities. Twitter has changed so markedly since Elon Musk took it over. I've seen the breakdown of community there. I used to love the community I had on Twitter, and some of those people are still there, but it's much harder to find them. But I know the people who can more easily find me now are people who will hate what I represent and the things that I say. They don't follow me, but they find me or I'm served up to them by the algorithm.

You only have to look at the court case of Johnny Depp and Amber Heard to see this. There were the actual events happening in the court case, then there was what was happening in mainstream media, then there was social media. What you read on social media was vastly different to what was actually occurring with a judge in that whole process. And I found that really arresting because I noticed a lot of young people were only reading social media and actually being encouraged to hate. They really, really hated a woman who was claiming that she had been the victim of domestic abuse, [who] a High Court in England had … found had experienced domestic abuse. There is a sense that victims have to be perfect for them to be believed, but no-one's ever perfect. And life is never like that.

In fact, some of the most important principles are tested when we have somebody imperfect. A lot of people seemed to personally dislike Julian Assange, but I'd argue that the principles that were tested in his case—about access to information, and publishing leaked information when to do so might be in the public interest—form a really important part of a well-functioning democracy. We also saw a lot of misinformation and disinformation with the Voice referendum that went untested. The US election was the same. It's very hard to quantify and it's very hard to predict, let alone control.

Q: There are a lot of people who find this era, as you've just described, really destabilising. What advice would you give about finding balance or finding

stability when it seems like the court is saying one thing, social media is saying another, and you're trying to work out what the truth is?
A: Well, there's a few different levels to that now. I mean, first of all, if we're talking just about how you're dealing with this fire hose of information and how you weigh it, you've got to be very careful with managing your time and ... who you listen to. You're not going to go out into the street and ask 300 strangers what they think of your dress, but you might ask five people around you who you trust to be honest and yet not unkind.

So you need to be plugged into people you trust online, and if they do something you're disappointed with, challenge them on it and hold them to account in a respectful way. But stick with the people you trust, allow them to be imperfect while asking them to be their best. That way you're not weeding through a massive amount of information that is misleading or incorrect and exhausting and overwhelming, which is why a lot of people turn off the news.

You need to find the reporters or commentators or authors that can also fix your eyes on what can be hopeful and what can be good and what can be positive and give you a broader view. You need to find people who will give you good information and more hopeful narratives and stories, sometimes rooted in history, sometimes rooted in personal experience.

Q: When you say find people that you trust, some people are finding people on social media they think are legit but they're actually leading them astray. So how do you navigate that? How do you find trustworthy sources?
A: Those rabbit holes are so hard in terms of algorithms. I mean, I think one of the most pernicious things is the constant criticism of, and dismissing of, expertise. I am a professional researcher. I really love researching, but I also want to have enough time to brush my teeth and spend time with my children. So I'm not going to research every single health and medical issue on earth. I want to know that there's people who have trained, who have looked at, for example,

peer-reviewed journals and peer-reviewed research. When I read one outlier study that might be the indication of something alarming, I won't panic, especially when there's fifty other studies that say that is actually not the case. We need to be mature about understanding that as well. The media does too. We need to examine the weight of evidence. Obviously it's the same with climate change and so on. That's when you need to go back to the media or experts you can trust because you can't wade through all those academic journals yourself.

Q: You've written a lot about your own life, which has been amazing but has also had significant periods that have been quite uncertain and destabilising. So how have you found a way to stay grounded and positive and forward-looking in those times?
A: Well, I think life is uncertain, and I think we need to kind of embrace uncertainty. I like that stoic line that, you can't always determine what happens to you but you can determine how you respond to it. And I think that's really important. I also think it's really important to hold on to the good stuff. If you have read accounts of survivors, if you have spoken to survivors, if you've ever survived anything horrific yourself, there's always a moment of grace or humour or of absurdity. There's always a moment when you put your arms around each other or there's a moment of connection or recognition of what matters. We see that a lot in responses to natural disasters, for example. You see so much goodness and decency coming out in the community and people rallying around each other and trying to make things better. I think a lot of it's about training your mind to see those things and remember that they're there. I've written a lot about grace recently and which is really about acts of great moral beauty, great decency, generosity, courage. Someone asked me once, 'What is the emotion that grace evokes?' And for me, I think it's a comfort to know that these people are in the world and there are in fact millions of us. Yet we get such a different view on social media.

The reason I started writing about grace was because, for me, it's a form of awe. There was a study done of 2600 people across twenty-six countries to find out what the most common experience of awe was. And I thought it would be nature, hands down, because that to me has been a big thing. But it was actually beauty we see in each other. That's what most people across all histories, cultures, dialects, demographic groups, recognise as awe. It is in people overcoming hurdles, in people of great ability doing things they don't have to do. Forgiving the unforgivable, loving the unlovable, giving of themselves. That's why I think we love the Olympics so much. I mean, they are such powerfully made people, mentally and physically, and yet there's also an ordinariness about it. Someone who discovered they had an ability and gave everything they could to it, and all the people around them.

I discovered that through ocean swimming. And that's what got me thinking about awe because that sustained me so much during difficult times. There's something about it that forces you to pay attention to the world, and that makes you feel small. And I think it's very psychologically healthy to feel small, even though, with all of our securities and doubts, we're so often trying to project authority and space. Sometimes it's really good just to remember that we are a speck in this massive universe and we have to protect this planet and each other. National boundaries don't matter and suburban boundaries don't matter. And the research shows that when people experience awe regularly, they're more likely to be calmer, kinder, more content, more altruistic, and feel like an inhabitant of this earth.

I think that in a world where we are rightly taught to care for ourselves and nurture ourselves, sometimes we've got to remember that's not the only answer. Looking outwards can be a form of self-care as well. Caring for other people can be a form of self-care. And it's about paying attention. I've found the deliberate pursuit of awe and wonder and grace, to think about things of grace, has been immensely strengthening. And I think that we often think that awe is something that's not just tangential but serendipitous. But no, make it part of the way you live deliberately and make it a practice. If it can't be daily, it can be weekly. And it's not about rafting down the Grand Canyon rapids. It can be about your own garden. It can be about someone who just gave birth. It can be noticing the birds in your local trees. It can be art, architecture, music, sport. It's not just something incidental, it's something fundamental. And we actually draw strength from it. A lot of people have written to me after reading my books, telling me how looking outwards and immersing themselves in nature has got them through a time of grief. And it's often dismissed as something corny. And it's not meant to be the idea that, oh, you've had a really terrible diagnosis, or you've lost someone you really love, or you're overwhelmed by the world, so just lie under a tree and take some deep breaths and everything will be fine. It won't be fine. It will still be all those things. It will still be exactly the same situation, but you work out what makes you strong, and that's what the key is. You need your strength to be able to deal with all of the hard stuff.

Q: You've dealt a lot with public institutions just because you've been unwell, and we live in an age where public institutions and science are doubted or there's higher levels of distrust. What do you think has happened with trust in public institutions and what are the consequences of that?
A: Trusting doesn't mean an absence of distrust. Belief doesn't mean an absence of doubt. It's not like you're going to smilingly go, 'Oh, I'll just do everything everyone says to me,' because obviously some things won't work for you. Solutions often need to be individually tailored. And when it comes to science and rare illnesses, for example, you really work out they're just having a crack at it a lot of the time. They're really just trying, and sometimes the science falls short and they are making calculated guesses. I think that's a really interesting part of entering the medical system and trying to work that out and getting second opinions and not always believing what you're told.

But ultimately it's within a framework of knowing that there is a thing called empirical evidence, and there's a scientific basis for most of these treatments. And even if some of them are nascent … it's worth talking to people who you respect and trust to find a way through all of that.

I really get very, very concerned at the attacks on the credibility of science and scientists. We saw this recently with the questioning of Anthony Fauci on Capitol Hill, and it was, I think, Marjorie Taylor Greene who kept saying repeatedly, 'Oh, this is what you call science,' as if the word itself was loaded. At the end of all of our intellectual inquiry, centuries after the Enlightenment, if we now say this is a dirty word, then that troubles me enormously. It doesn't mean that every scientific test will be proven right. It's about understanding that you test something a number of times in a number of different circumstances with a host of variables and see whether or not you can prove your various hypotheses. This has been a craft that's been honed over many centuries. But if we don't believe in the core mission of scientific research, then we will be persuaded to take things that are bad for our health and for our bodies, or to refuse things that are good for our health, or we will refuse to acknowledge what's happening to the planet soon enough to give us sufficient time to be able to try to arrest it.

And it's troubling how deep that distrust goes, and if that spreads, because it won't benefit the people living in my street or your street or this street, it will benefit people probably financially who are offering their own solutions. That's where you apply your thinking to who is funding something and [in] whose interest is this research being done. Why would it benefit a certain group of people or companies to cast doubt on the whole science of climate change, for example? Scepticism is the intellectual inquiry that should lead you to greater trust in something. Be as sceptical as you can. Science is a sceptical inquiry. It's sceptical of just coming up with hunches and beliefs and maybes, and 'I've just got a feeling' and 'It's a full moon' and whatever. Science should be a weapon of those who distrust instead of something that we are now starting to distrust. It has to be rigorous, and rational.

Q: Lastly, you've been labelled a joy expert. You've talked about your own positive ways to find a path through uncertainty. You've talked about seeking awe, you talked about offering grace. What do you think are the keys to not just surviving but thriving amidst uncertainty?
A: I think you've got to work out what your values are and find other people who hold those values, whether they're reporters or whether they're scientists, or whether they're judges or politicians, or activists or climate change experts or so on. And you've got to support them and follow them. The world has been through horrendous things and gone through to better times as well. Look at war, which we all want to end, then look at the people who are there risking their lives to bring healing and to try to bring an end to the suffering. Look at the people who are resisting it. Look at the people who want to bring peace and ask how the peacemakers can be strengthened. Look at the people who are trying to fix broken systems. Look at those who persist despite all kinds of doubt and junk being thrown at them. Look at those people who continue to show determination and courage, continue to say that we want to pull on what Paul Keating called 'the golden threads of our community'.

There'll always be people who want to exploit fear and shame and division and anger, but there will always be people too who, in the midst of that, will be calling for calm or calling for change, or reminding us that we can be better, that we have done better and we can do better in the future, and that we can't give up on that. We also need to teach our children that there are different ways of being in the world. That whole idea of the world being held together by historic acts, that the smallest of gestures can sometimes completely change lives, and we're not all completely impotent. The work of blood donors and paramedics and nurses and people who work with those with disabilities, with people who come up and tell their truth of trauma despite all the cost of it and the people who look after their families and look after their communities, we know they're there. You just have to make sure you've got them in your sights at all times. Otherwise, you'll be overwhelmed and think that everything is impossible, and that's just not true.

Acknowledgements

We have to admit, we had big plans for this book. We wanted to take a look at the work that was happening across the globe in the field of trust, by inviting some of the world's best experts and big thinkers to sit around a virtual campfire with us, to share their thoughts. We wanted to tease out the best ideas, biggest concerns and most effective solutions for tackling the problems at hand—that being, a global decline in trust in public institutions, especially our governments and media. The idea was that the resulting collection would allow us all to learn from each other as we, side by side, fight this loss of trust and aim to rebuild it.

We were amazed at how many people jumped on board to take part. We set up video calls with incredible leaders in their fields from Denmark, France, the United Kingdom, Canada, the United States and Australia. We were often left hanging off every word of wisdom with awe and gratefulness, not wanting to end the calls. We then spent weeks waiting excitedly for their contributions.

None of them were paid for their work. Instead, their fees are donated to the Indigenous Literacy Foundation, which sends much-needed books and resources, many in local languages, to remote Indigenous communities.

ACKNOWLEDGEMENTS

To say we are proud of this collection is an understatement. It does everything we hoped, offering insight, clarity, thoughtful consideration, research and solutions on truth and trust that we can all tap into. This book is a tribute to the hard work and creativity of our contributors, often based on decades of experience. The pages are rich with both lived experience and expertise.

To the crew at Monash University Publishing, thank you—again—for your partnership. We couldn't ask for a better team in our corner. It has been an absolute privilege and pleasure to work alongside such a professional, supportive and good-natured team—Julia Carlomagno, Kate Morgan, Sarah Cannon, Rachael McDiarmid and Phil Campbell. And a huge thanks to our editor Paul Smitz for his sage advice, feedback and support over two books.

Thank you to our early readers Katie McRobert, Simon West and AC Grayling. We appreciate your wisdom. Thank you to Dharma Chandran, Kevin Nguyen and Alice Mulheron for assisting us with contacts—Alice, you are a workhorse and a gem.

From Tracey

A special thanks to my amazing friends who have my back no matter what crazy project I am working on and let me talk it through. Big love to Sumi Skellem, Lyndal Parker, Julie-Anne Jones, Miriam Groves, Mimi Kwa, Katie McRobert, Jo Rolland, Leanne Jeffs, Francine Dawson, Justine Legge, Lee Brooks, Alison Dennison, Megan McCracken and Tom Vujevic. And to Mark and Erin Jaggers, for letting me spend an entire weekend at your dining table working on my essay!

A shout-out to all of our amazing ABC colleagues, who are seeking answers every day as to how to build trust with our audiences. I watch in awe.

Thanks especially to my dear friend, co-editor and maven of Ancient Rome, Gavin Fang, who always sees the big picture and not the hurdles. I continue to marvel at the way your big brain works and appreciate you sharing it.

Finally, thanks to my mum Carolyn, who instilled in me a love of words and problem-solving. And to my precious family, Ian, Sean and Laura, for unbridled joy and conversation. The dinner table debates are still my daily highlight.

From Gavin
Thanks to my friend and co-editor Tracey Kirkland who knows a good idea when she sees it and is willing to dive in to find out more. This book wouldn't exist without your relentless energy.

My thanks also to all my colleagues in the media, especially at the ABC, who are driven by the purpose and passion to tell great stories in the service of the audience. We are custodians of the trust built up by those who have gone before us.

To my parents, Chang Sha and Barbara, and my sisters Amanda and Rebecca, thanks for discussing and debating ideas with me. Only as I get older do I recognise what a privilege a family like this is.

And finally, thanks to my sons Samuel and Gabriel for the joy you give me. You continue to inspire and amaze me as you grow into men. And Bronwyn, for always belaying the rope. There is no safe climb without someone watching out for you.

Contributor Bios

Dr Amy Ross Arguedas is a Postdoctoral Research Fellow in Digital News at the Reuters Institute for the Study of Journalism. She has worked extensively on issues around trust in media (the Trust in News Project) and previously worked as a journalist for the Costa Rican newspaper *La Nación*.

Ben Decker is the founder and CEO of Memetica, a threat intelligence group. Previously a technology researcher and former investigative journalist at *The New York Times*, he has produced research papers that have been presented in testimony to the US House Financial Services Subcommittee, submitted written testimony about domestic extremist financing to the January 6th Committee, and testified at the United Nations Human Rights Council. Ben participates in the Christchurch Call Advisory Network, a group of civil society and industry experts advising the New Zealand and French governments in their global policy efforts to eliminate terrorist and violent extremist content online.

Catherine Tait was the first female president and CEO of CBC/Radio-Canada (2018–25). During her tenure, she led many groundbreaking initiatives in the area of diversity, equity and inclusion.

Catherine was also a keen advocate for international collaboration among public service media in her role as chair of the Global Task Force for Public Media. Prior to CBC/Radio-Canada, Catherine was a media entrepreneur, producer and digital innovator. She was named Woman of the Year 2021–22 by Women in Communications and Technology, and in 2023 she received the Jury Award of Distinction from Women in Film and Television.

Dr Cathy Foley AO PSM became Australia's ninth Chief Scientist in January 2021 after an extensive career at Australia's national science agency, the CSIRO, including as the agency's chief scientist. Dr Foley is an internationally recognised physicist with major research achievements in superconductors and sensors that led to the development of the LANDTEM sensor system to locate valuable deposits of minerals deep underground. Dr Foley has been recognised with numerous awards and fellowships, including election to the Australian Academy of Science in 2020, and an Order of Australia for service to research science and to the advancement of women in physics.

Eli Pariser is an author, activist and entrepreneur focused on how to make technology and media serve democracy. He helped lead MoveOn.org, co-founded Avaaz.org (now the world's largest citizen's organisation), wrote the 2011 bestseller *The Filter Bubble*, and co-founded Upworthy. He is currently co-director of New_ Public at the National Conference on Citizenship.

Fergus McIntosh runs the fact-checking department at *The New Yorker*, where he has worked since 2015. As a fact-checker, he has worked on major stories such as Ronan Farrow's early investigations, and books that include *Say Nothing* by Patrick Radden Keefe and *American Oligarchs* by Andrea Bernstein. He writes occasionally about arts, culture and UK politics.

Gavin Fang is an Australian journalist with more than thirty years' experience in broadcast and print media. He is currently Editorial Director at the Australian Broadcasting Corporation and was previously deputy director of news. Gavin is a former correspondent for the ABC in Indonesia. He is the co-editor of *Pandemedia: How COVID Changed Journalism*.

Prof. Gert Tinggaard Svendsen is a Danish professor of public policy and has a PhD in economics and a master's degree in political science. Previously he has worked at the Department of Economics, the University of Aarhus, as an assistant professor and associate professor. He is chairman of a project called SoCap (the Danish Social Capital Project) which is helping to fight poverty in developing countries. In addition, he has published numerous international books and articles on social capital, climate policy and lobbying. His book *Tillid* explains why trust is essential to the functioning of the national economy.

Graham Ashton AM APM has had a forty-year career in Australian law enforcement. Graham served with the Australian Federal Police nationally and internationally for twenty-four years, attaining the rank of deputy commissioner. He also served with the Victoria Police, leading in the forensic and crime departments, and later served as chief commissioner of Victoria Police for a five-year term. In 2003, Graham was made a member of the Order of Australia for his role as police forward commander leading the international response to the 2002 Bali terrorist bombings.

Julia Baird is a broadcaster and journalist. Her writing has appeared in a range of publications including *The Daily Beast*, *Harper's Bazaar*, *The Guardian*, *The Good Weekend*, *The Philadelphia Inquirer*, *The Monthly*, *Newsweek*, *The New York Times* and *The Sydney Morning Herald*. In 2011, she returned from the United States, where she worked as a columnist and deputy editor of *Newsweek*. In 2005, she was a fellow at the Joan Shorenstein Center of Press, Politics and Public Policy at Harvard. Her latest book is *Bright Shining: How Grace Changes Everything*.

Dr Kaz Ross is an independent researcher into far-right extremism, Neo-Nazis in Australia, and conspiracy theories. For many years she taught Asian Studies at the University of Tasmania with a focus on China. She holds a doctorate in political science and qualifications in Chinese language.

Kristian Porter is the CEO of the Public Media Alliance, the largest global association of public service media organisations. Kristian has extensive experience working in public media support and advocacy, with a background in the NGO sector, editorial management, events, and as a journalist. He has worked globally in his roles for PMA and works with the association's membership and partners to develop campaigns, relationships, strategies, research and projects. He is a passionate advocate for media freedom, media independence and journalist safety. He sits on the steering committee for the Public Broadcasters International conference and runs the secretariat for the Global Task Force for public media. Kristian has a master's in media and international development.

Layla Mashkoor is a Deputy Managing Editor at the Atlantic Council's Digital Forensic Research Lab, overseeing a global team conducting groundbreaking research on online harms. Her expertise is in information integrity and digital repression. She previously tracked disinformation for *Buzzfeed News* and conducted visual investigations for *Storyful*. As part of her dedication to improving digital resilience, she has conducted training workshops for audiences worldwide. Mashkoor is a graduate of McMaster University with a master's in political science and a bachelor of journalism from Carleton University.

CONTRIBUTOR BIOS

Dr Louise Mahler is a communication, presentation and body language expert. She is the author of *Gravitas: Timeless Skills to Communicate with Confidence and Build Trust* and *Resonate: For Those Who Need to Be Heard*, an Adjunct Professor at Federation University, and a regular contributor to digital and print media. She works internationally as an executive adviser, speaker and coach, helping executives to build presence, and to present and handle emotional situations.

Bishop Michael Stead is an Australian Anglican Archbishop and the Bishop of South Sydney. He has been the Secretary of the General Synod Doctrine Commission since 2005 and is also a member of the Sydney Diocesan Doctrine Commission. Internationally, he is an active supporter of the Global Anglican Future Conference. Dr Stead holds a Bachelor of Commerce degree from the University of New South Wales, is an honour's graduate of Moore College with a Bachelor of Divinity and a Diploma of Ministry, and was awarded a Doctor of Philosophy by the University of Gloucestershire in 2007. His research interests include biblical theology, the atonement, hermeneutics and eschatology. He has written five books.

Michele Levine is CEO of Roy Morgan. She was born with a passion for people and what makes them tick, and social justice, and an insatiable curiosity about life. With over thirty years' experience as a researcher, Michele has been responsible for thousands of surveys, including many of the largest research projects ever undertaken in Australia, many of which continue to play a critically important part in shaping our society today. Michele is also Chair of Life. Be in it.

Mike Smith is an experienced leader with extensive experience chairing boards across diverse sectors, including business, sports and the arts. His significant roles have included serving as chair of 7-Eleven, iiNet, the Australian Institute of Company Directors, West Coast Eagles, Perth International Arts Festival, and Scotch College.

Currently, Michael is the Chair of Starbucks Australia and sits on the board of AusCycling. His present focus is on enhancing the effectiveness of top executive groups in purposeful organisations, particularly in addressing their most complex and consequential issues.

Nic Newman is Senior Research Associate at the Reuters Institute for the Study of Journalism and is also a consultant on digital media, working actively with news companies on product, audience, and business strategies for digital transition. He writes an annual report for the institute on future media and technology trends.

Patricia Karvelas is presenter of *Q+A* and *Afternoon Briefing* and co-host of the *Party Room* podcast at the Australian Broadcasting Corporation. She has been a prominent senior journalist in the Australian media for more than twenty years, beginning her professional career in broadcast journalism at the ABC and SBS as both a producer and presenter. She worked for *The Australian* newspaper from 2002 covering federal politics, most recently as the Victorian Bureau chief and editor, and senior national affairs journalist. Patricia specialised in Indigenous affairs, reporting for more than ten years.

Rosabeth Moss Kanter holds the Ernest L Arbuckle Professorship at Harvard Business School, specialising in strategy, innovation, and leadership for change. She co-founded the Harvard University–wide Advanced Leadership Initiative and is the author or co-author of twenty books. Her latest book, *Think Outside the Building: How Advanced Leaders Can Change the World One Smart Innovation at a Time*, has won a number of accolades. The former chief editor of *Harvard Business Review*, Professor Kanter has been repeatedly named in lists such as the '50 most powerful women in the world' (*Times of London*) and the '50 most influential business thinkers in the world' (Thinkers50).

CONTRIBUTOR BIOS

Dr Ross Honeywill is a social scientist, author and corporate strategist. An expert in consumer psychology, he has spent twenty years measuring and mapping population classifications and is best known internationally for the NEO high-value consumer. He leads a professional services company that works with world-leading brands.

Dr Simon Longstaff AO is a philosopher focusing on the ethical dimension of life. He's the Executive Director of the St James Ethics Centre. In 2013, he was made an officer of the Order of Australia for 'distinguished service to the community through the promotion of ethical standards in governance and business, to improving corporate responsibility, and to philosophy'. Simon is an Adjunct Professor of the Australian Graduate School of Management at UNSW, and a Fellow of CPA Australia, the Royal Society of NSW, and the Australian Risk Policy Institute.

Subramanian Rangan is Professor of Strategy and Management at INSEAD business school. He received an MBA from the MIT Sloan School of Management and a PhD in political economy from Harvard University. His research explores the evolution of capitalism, in particular how enterprises and all economic actors may better integrate performance and progress. He is developing a curriculum that aims to deepen not only the competence but also the character of business students and executives. In 2013 he initiated the Society for Progress, a fellowship of eminent philosophers, social scientists and business leaders.

Dr Timothy Graham is Associate Professor in Digital Media at the Queensland University of Technology. He is a computational social scientist who studies online networks and platforms, with a particular interest in propaganda and online influence, digital publics, and algorithmic curation. Tim is Chief Investigator of a newly commenced ARC Discovery Project, 'Understanding and

Combatting "Dark Political Communication"' (2024–27). He has authored over forty peer-reviewed journal articles and book chapters, featured in thousands of news articles in leading news outlets, and actively develops and maintains open-source software for the collection and analysis of data from the web and social media.

Toby Walsh is an ARC Laureate Fellow and Scientia Professor of AI at UNSW and CSIRO Data61. He is Chief Scientist of the UNSW AI Institute. He is a strong advocate for limits to ensure AI is used to improve our lives, having spoken at the UN, and to heads of state, parliamentary bodies, company boards and many others on this topic. This advocacy has led to him being 'banned indefinitely' from Russia. He is a Fellow of the Australian Academy of Science and was named on the international 'Who's Who in AI' list of influencers. He has written four books on AI for a general audience, the most recent being *Faking It! Artificial Intelligence in A Human World*.

Tracey Kirkland is an Australian news journalist who has worked in broadcast and print for more than thirty years. She is currently the Continuous News Editor in charge of TV and video at *ABC News Channel*, and was previously the ABC's national senior newsgathering editor. Since joining the ABC in 1999, Tracey has been a reporter, presenter or producer for all of the public broadcaster's major news programs. She is the co-editor of *Pandemedia: How COVID Changed Journalism*.

Ulrik Haagerup is the founder and CEO of Constructive Institute. He is a member of the advisory boards of People's University in Denmark, Bolius, and Dalberg Global Media. For ten years he was the executive director of news at the Danish Broadcasting Corporation, Denmark's public service broadcaster. He was previously editor-in-chief at NORDJYSKE Media from 2002 to 2007, editor-in-chief at the national daily *Jyllands-Posten* from 1994 to 2002, and an investigative reporter at the same place from 1986 to 1991.

Yalmay Yunupingu was the Senior Australian of the Year for 2024, honoured for her work as a teacher, linguist and community leader. She guided teaching at Yirrkala Bilingual School for four decades, retiring in March 2023. She qualified as a teacher and, with her husband (of Yothu Yindi fame), forged a bilingual teaching approach to make young people strong in their Yolŋu language and culture. In 2005, she was acknowledged as a 'Teacher of Excellence' by the NT Department of Education and was an honorary university fellow at Charles Darwin University. Since retiring, she has been teaching the next generation about traditional healing.

Notes

Introduction
1. MW Berger, 'Journalist and Activist Maria Resser on "Facts, Truth, Trust"', *Penn Today*, 10 November 2022, https://www.asc.upenn.edu/news-events/news/journalist-and-activist-maria-ressa-facts-truth-trust (viewed September 2024).
2. Edelman Trust Institute, *2024 Edelman Trust Barometer: Global Report*, 2024, https://www.edelman.com/sites/g/files/aatuss191/files/2024-02/2024%20Edelman%20Trust%20Barometer%20Global%20Report_FINAL.pdf (viewed September 2024).

The Long Age of Forgetting
1. H Mackay, *Corporate Ethics: The Mackay Report*, Mackay Research, Chatswood, NSW, 1990.
2. SA Longstaff, *The Cloven Giant*, The Ethics Centre, Sydney, 2020.
3. Deloitte Access Economics, *The Ethical Advantage: The Economic and Social Benefits of Ethics to Australia*, 1020, https://ethics.org.au/wp-content/uploads/2018/05/The-Ethical-Advantage-4.pdf (viewed September 2024).

Finding Truth in Ourselves
1. Matthew Giannelis, 'Impact of the Internet on Modern Society', *Tech News*, 13 June 2024, https://www.techbusinessnews.com.au/blog/impact-of-the-internet-on-modern-society (viewed September 2024).

2 Internet Live Stats, 'Total Number of Websites', 2024, https://www.internetlivestats.com/total-number-of-websites (viewed September 2024).
3 Statista, 'Average Daily Time Spent Using the Internet By Online Users Worldwide from 3rd Quarter 2015 to 4th Quarter 2023', 30 April 2024, https://statista.com/statistics/1380282/daily-time-spent-online-global (viewed September 2024).
4 HealthIT, https://healthit.com.au/how-big-is-the-internet-and-how-do-we-measure-it/#:~:text=In%202020%2C%20the%20amount%20of,and%20consumed%20on%20the%20web (viewed September 2024).
5 MW Berger, 'Journalist and Activist Maria Ressa on "Facts, Truth, Trust"', *Penn Today*, 10 November 2022, https://www.asc.upenn.edu/news-events/news/journalist-and-activist-maria-ressa-facts-truth-trust (viewed September 2024).
6 European Commission, 'A Strengthened EU Code of Practice on Disinformation', https://commission.europa.eu/strategy-and-policy/priorities-2019-2024/new-push-european-democracy/protecting-democracy/strengthened-eu-code-practice-disinformation_en (viewed September 2024).
7 T Notley, S Chambers, S Park and M Dezuanni, *Adult Media Literacy in 2024*, Australian Media Literacy Alliance, 2024, https://medialiteracy.org.au/wp-content/uploads/2024/08/AML2024_report_final-compressed.pdf (viewed September 2024).

Technology Didn't Give Rise to Misinformation—We Did

1 Daniel Pauly, 'Anecdotes and the Shifting Baseline Syndrome of Fisheries', *Tree*, vol. 10, no. 10, October 1995, p. 430, https://fbaum.unc.edu/teaching/articles/ShiftingBaseline.pdf (viewed September 2024).
2 David Axe, 'How to Win a "Fifth-Generation" War', *Wired*, 3 January 2009, https://www.wired.com/2009/01/how-to-win-a-fi (viewed September 2024).
3 Joseph Bernstein, 'Bad News: Selling the Story of Disinformation', *Harper's Magazine*, 9 August 2021, https://harpers.org/archive/2021/09/bad-news-selling-the-story-of-disinformation (viewed September 2024).
4 US Public Health Service, *Social Media and Youth Mental Health: The U.S. Surgeon General's Advisory*, 2023, https://www.hhs.gov/sites/default/files/sg-youth-mental-health-social-media-advisory.pdf (viewed September 2024).

Discourse Collapse: How Disinformation Erodes Public Trust

1. A Arif, LG Stewart and K Starbird, 'Acting the Part', *Proceedings of the ACM on Human–Computer Interaction*, vol. 2, issue CSCW, 2018, pp. 1–27.
2. Dina Sadek et al., 'Suspicious Accounts on X Amplify Allegations against UNRWA', Digital Forensic Research Lab, 14 February 2024, https://dfrlab.org/2024/02/14/suspicious-accounts-on-x-amplify-allegations-against-unrwa (viewed September 2024).
3. Digital Forensic Research Lab, 'Inauthentic Campaign Amplifying Islamophobic Content Targeting Canadians', 28 March 2024, https://dfrlab.org/2024/03/28/inauthentic-campaign-amplifying-islamophobic-content-targeting-canadians (viewed September 2024).
4. S Frenkel, 'Israel Secretly Targets U.S. Lawmakers with Influence Campaign on Gaza War', *The New York Times*, 6 June 2024, https://www.nytimes.com/2024/06/05/technology/israel-campaign-gaza-social-media.html (viewed September 2024).
5. C Bing and J Schectman, 'Pentagon Ran Secret Anti-Vax Campaign to Undermine China During Pandemic', Reuters, 14 June 2024, https://www.reuters.com/investigates/special-report/usa-covid-propaganda (viewed September 2024).
6. S Gregory, 'Testimony of Sam Gregory, Executive Director, WITNESS', U.S. Senate Committee on Commerce, Science and Transportation, Subcommittee on Consumer Protection, Product Safety and Data Security, 12 September 2023, https://www.commerce.senate.gov/services/files/DAD2163A-EF02-41B5-B7BA-2BA8B568C977 (viewed September 2024).

Agree to Disagree: Trust and Civic Debate

1. United Nations, 'Secretary-General's Video Message to the Second Summit for Democracy', 29 March 2023, https://www.un.org/sg/en/content/sg/statement/2023-03-29/secretary-generals-video-message-the-second-summit-for-democracy (viewed September 2024).
2. Press conference, Parliament House, Canberra, 5 August 2024, https://ministers.ag.gov.au/media-centre/transcripts/press-conference-parliament-house-canberra-05-08-2024#:~:text=radicalised%20more%20quickly.-,More%20Australians%20are%20embracing%20a%20more%20diverse%20range%20of%20extreme,as%20our%20principal%20security%20concerns (viewed September 2024).

3   Nic Newman, *Journalism, Media, and Technology Trends and Predictions 2024*, Reuters Institute for the Study of Journalism, January 2024, https://reutersinstitute.politics.ox.ac.uk/sites/default/files/2024-01/Newman%20-%20Trends%20and%20Predictions%202024%20FINAL.pdf (viewed September 2024).
4   Susie Allen, 'How Social Media Rewards Disinformation', Yale Insights, https://insights.som.yale.edu/insights/how-social-media-rewards-misinformation (viewed September 2024).
5   *The 7.30 Report*, 'Roxanne Gay: "Bad Feminist"', 11 July 2024, https://www.abc.net.au/news/2024-07-11/writer-roxane-gay-on-the-threats-to-same-sex-marriage-in-usa/104088206 (viewed September 2024).
6   eSafety Commissioner, 'Women in the Spotlight: How Online Abuse Impacts Women in Their Working Lives', 2024, https://www.esafety.gov.au/research/how-online-abuse-impacts-women-working-lives (viewed September 2024).
7   L Rainie, S Keeter and A Perrin, 'Trust and Distrust in America', Pew Research Center, 22 July 2019, https://www.pewresearch.org/politics/2019/07/22/trust-and-distrust-in-america (viewed September 2024).
8   United Nations, 'Secretary-General's Video Message'.

Trust in Government and Radical Impartiality
1   Strengthening Democracy Taskforce, *Strengthening Australian Democracy: A Practical Agenda for Australian Resilience*, Department of Home Affairs, Australian Government, July 2024, https://www.homeaffairs.gov.au/about-us-subsite/files/strengthening-australian-democracy.pdf (viewed September 2024).
2   CyberCX, *Green Cicada Network*, 13 August 2024, https://connect.cybercx.com.au/Intelligence-Update-CCX-IU-2024-004 (viewed September 2024).
3   Richard Wike et al., *Representative Democracy Remains a Popular Ideal, but People around the World Are Critical of How It's Working*, Pew Research Center, 28 February 2024, https://www.pewresearch.org/global/2024/02/28/satisfaction-with-democracy-and-ratings-for-political-leaders-parties (viewed September 2024).
4   N Biddle, *ANU Poll 58*, Dataverse, January 2024, https://dataverse.ada.edu.au/dataset.xhtml?persistentId=doi:10.26193/IDKTUK (viewed September 2024).

5   N Biddle, I McAllister and M Gray, 'Asian Barometer Survey Wave 6 (Australia)', Dataverse, 2023, https://dataverse.ada.edu.au/dataset.xhtml?persistentId=doi:10.26193/1SGK5O (viewed September 2024).
6   N Biddle and I McAllister, *ANU Poll 57*, Dataverse, January 2024, https://dataverse.ada.edu.au/dataset.xhtml?persistentId=doi:10.26193/13NPGQ (viewed September 2024).

Trust in Science: Strengthening Peer Review to Build Resilience
1   Macrotrends, 'Australia Life Expectancy 1950–2024', 2024, https://www.macrotrends.net/global-metrics/countries/AUS/australia/life-expectancy#:~:text=Chart%20and%20table%20of%20Australia,a%200.18%25%20increase%20from%202022 (viewed September 2024).
2   B Mayne et al., 'A Genomic Predictor of Lifespan in Vertebrates', *Scientific Reports*, vol. 9, no. 17866, 2019.
3   R Hosking, 'Peer Review—A Historical Perspective,' MIT Communication Lab, https://mitcommlab.mit.edu/broad/commkit/peer-review-a-historical-perspective/#:~:text=A%20short%20history,began%20in%20the%20mid%201970s (viewed September 2024).
4   B Tranter, 'Your Money or Your Life? Public Support for Health Initiatives during the COVID-19 Pandemic', *Australian Journal of Social Justice*, vol. 57, 2022, pp. 544–61.
5   B Tranter, 'Do Australians Trust Scientists? It Depends on the "Science"', *Australian Journal of Social Issues*, vol. 58, 2023, pp. 821–37.
6   D Angelucci and D Vittori, 'In Science We (Dis)trust: Technocratic Attitudes, Populism and Trust in Science during the COVID-19 Pandemic', *European Political Science*, 2024.
7   S Rosenfeld, 'Why Truth Matters for Democracy', Religion & Ethics, ABC, 2 November 2020, https://www.abc.net.au/religion/sophia-rosenfeld-why-truth-matters-for-democracy/11629714 (viewed September 2024).
8   L McIntyre, *On Disinformation*, MIT Press, Cambridge, MA, 2023, ch. 3.
9   J Kont et al., 'What Makes Audiences Resilient to Disinformation? Integrating Micro, Meso, and Macro Factors Based on a Systematic Literature Review', *European Journal of Communication Research*, 2024.
10 M Haruno and CD Frith, 'Activity in the Amygdala Elicited By Unfair Divisions Predicts Social Value Orientation', *Nature Neuroscience*, vol. 13, 2010, pp. 160–1; N Garrett et al., 'The Brain Adapts to Dishonesty', *Nature Neuroscience*, vol. 19, 2016, pp. 1727–32.

11 G Tesan, B Johnson and S Crain, 'How the Brain Responds to Any: An MEG Study', *Brain and Language*, vol. 120, 2011, pp. 66–72.
12 Garrett, 'The Brain Adapts to Dishonesty'.
13 David Suzuki, 'Squirrely Sex Makes Good Science, Dumb Politics', *Environmental News Network*, 7 April 2006, https://www.enn.com/articles/9056-squirrel-sex-makes-good-science,-dumb-politics (viewed September 2024).
14 Australia's Chief Scientist, 'Trust in Science', August 2023, https://www.chiefscientist.gov.au/sites/default/files/2023-08/Trust%20in%20Science.pdf (viewed September 2024).
15 This was determined by considering retracted papers for misconduct using two different databases, Web of Science and Retraction Watch, from 10 January 2013 to 1 January 2023, with Australia as the country in the authors' address.

Trust in Religion: We Are Like Cut Flowers

1 Australian Leadership Index, chart type: line, metric: trustworthiness, data cut: institution, for selected institutions, data accessed 23 June 2024, https://australianleadershipindex.org/dashboard/ChartBuilder.aspx (viewed September 2024).
2 Australian Survey of Social Attitudes Dataverse, https://dataverse.ada.edu.au/dataverse/aussa?q=&types=dataverses%3Adatasets (viewed September 2024). Note that the 2018 survey used a five-point scale, whereas the prior listed surveys used a four-point scale.
3 S Cameron and I McAllister, *Trends in Australian Political Opinion*, Australian National University, December 2022, https://australianelectionstudy.org/wp-content/uploads/Trends-in-Australian-Political-Opinion-Results-from-the-Australian-Election-Study-1987-2022.pdf (viewed September 2024).
4 Australian Survey of Social Attitudes Dataverse, https://dataverse.ada.edu.au/file.xhtml?fileId=18011&version=3.0 (viewed September 2024), p. 28.
5 L Saad, 'Historically Low Faith in U.S. Institutions Continues', Gallup, 6 July 2023, https://news.gallup.com/poll/508169/historically-low-faith-institutions-continues.aspx (viewed September 2024). Average confidence in 2009 was 34 per cent and in 2023 it was 26 per cent.
6 Gallup, 'Confidence in Institutions', https://news.gallup.com/poll/1597/Confidence-Institutions.aspx (viewed September 2024).
7 Saad, 'Historically Low Faith'.

8. Ruth Powell, 'Australians' Views of Jesus and the Church', NCLS Occasional Paper no. 45, 2022, p. 30.
9. Kate Gleeson and Luke Ashton, 'Trust in Religion among Women in Australia', Macquarie University, May 2024, quotes from pp. 4, 13.
10. Ibid., p.47.
11. Ibid. Statistics derived from pp. 11, 21–2.
12. Ibid., pp. 15–16.
13. Edelman Trust Institute, *2024 Edelman Trust Barometer: Australia Report*, 2024, p. 52, https://www.edelman.com.au/sites/g/files/aatuss381/files/2024-03/2024%20Edelman%20Trust%20Barometer_Australia%20Report_1.pdf (viewed September 2024).
14. Ibid., p. 53.
15. Ochlocracy is from the Greek word *ochlos* ('crowd, mob') + *kratos* ('rule').

Trust in the News Media: A Global and Audience Perspective
1. N Newman et al., *Reuters Institute Digital News Report 2024*, Reuters Institute for the Study of Journalism, Oxford, 2024.
2. Ipsos, 'Ipsos Veracity Index', 23 November 2022, https://www.ipsos.com/en-uk/ipsos-veracity-index-2022 (viewed September 2024).
3. John Jewell, 'Phone Hacking in the British Press: Three Key Moments in the Scandal—and What Happened Next', *The Conversation*, 22 December 2023, https://theconversation.com/phone-hacking-in-the-british-press-three-key-moments-in-the-scandal-and-what-happens-next-220010 (viewed September 2024).
4. S Altay, RK Nielsen and R Fletcher, 'News Can Help! The Impact of News Media and Digital Platforms on Awareness of and Belief in Misinformation', *International Journal of Press/Politics*, vol. 29, no. 2, February 2023.
5. T Hanitzsch, A Van Dalen and N Steindl, 'Caught in the Nexus: A Comparative and Longitudinal Analysis of Public Trust in the Press', *The International Journal of Press/Politics*, vol. 23, no. 1, 2017, pp. 3–23.
6. For example, see S Park et al., 'Global Mistrust in News: The Impact of Social Media on Trust', *International Journal on Media Management*, July 2020, pp. 1–14.
7. B Toff et al., 'Listening to What Trust in News Means to Users: Qualitative Evidence from Four Countries', Reuters Institute, 2021, https://reutersinstitute.politics.ox.ac.uk/listening-what-trust-news-means-users-qualitative-evidence-four-countries (viewed September 2024).

8   R Arguedas et al., 'News for the Powerful and Privileged: How Misrepresentation and Underrepresentation of Disadvantaged Communities Undermines Their Trust in News', Reuters Institute, 2023, https://reutersinstitute.politics.ox.ac.uk/news-powerful-and-privileged-how-misrepresentation-and-underrepresentation-disadvantaged (viewed September 2024).
9   K Collao, *The Kaleidoscope: Young People's Relationship with News*, Reuters Institute/Craft, 2022.
10 https://europeanconservative.com/articles/commentary/whos-verifying-bbc-verify/
11 B Toff et al., 'Overcoming Indifference: What Attitudes towards News Tell Us about Building Trust', Reuters Institute, 2021, https://reutersinstitute.politics.ox.ac.uk/overcoming-indifference-what-attitudes-towards-news-tell-us-about-building-trust (viewed September 2024).
12 E Heinrichs and N Newman, 'Seven Strategies to Counter News Avoidance', Reuters Institute, 2024, https://reutersinstitute.politics.ox.ac.uk/news/seven-things-journalists-can-do-counter-news-avoidance (viewed September 2024).
13 Newman et al., *Reuters Institute Digital News Report 2024*.
14 K Collao, *OK Computer? Public Attitudes to the Uses of Generative AI in News*, Reuters Institute/Craft, 2024.

Fact-Checking and the Golden Age of Journalism

1   Megan Brennan, 'Americans' Trust in Media Remains at Trend Low', Gallup, 14 October 2024.
2   Megan Brennan and Jeffrey Jones, 'Ethics Ratings of Nearly All Professions down in US', Gallup, 22 January 2024.
3   Jacob Liedke and Jeffrey Gottfried, 'US Adults under 30 Now Trust Information from Social Media almost as Much as from National News Outlets', Pew, 27 October 2022.
4   Christopher St. Aubin and Jacob Liedke, 'Social Media and News Fact Sheet', Pew Research Center, 17 September 2024.
5   See B Kalsnes and AH Krumsvik, 'Building Trust: Media Executives' Perceptions of Readers' Trust', *Journal of Media Business Studies*, vol. 16, no. 4, 2019, pp. 1–12.
6   Edelman Trust Institute, *2024 Edelman Trust Barometer: Global Report*, 2024, p. 3, https://www.edelman.com/sites/g/files/aatuss191/files/2024-02/2024%20Edelman%20Trust%20Barometer%20Global%20Report_FINAL.pdf (viewed September 2024).

7 Lee Rainie, 'Networked Trust and the Future of Media', *Daedalus*, vol. 151, no. 4, 2022, pp. 124–43.
8 Arlene Getz, '2023 Prison Census: Jailed Journalist Numbers Near Record High; Israel Imprisonments Spike', Committee to Protect Journalists, 2023, https://cpj.org/reports/2024/01/2023-prison-census-jailed-journalist-numbers-near-record-high-israel-imprisonments-spike (viewed September 2024).
9 Brennan, 'Americans' Trust in Media Remains at Trend Low'.
10 Brooke Gladstone, '"Trust" in the News Media Has Come to Mean Affirmation', *The New York Times*, 21 December 2015.
11 Silvio Waisbord, 'Truth Is What Happens to News', *Journalism Studies*, vol. 19, no. 13, 6 July 2018, pp. 1866–78.
12 Luxuan Wang and Naomi Forman-Katz, 'Many Americans Find Value in Getting News on Social Media, but Concerns about Inaccuracy Have Risen', Pew, 7 February 2024.
13 Christopher St. Aubin and Jacob Liedke, 'Most Americans Favor Restrictions on False Information, Violent Content Online', Pew, 20 July 2023.
14 The *2024 Edelman Trust Barometer* defines 'information war' as 'Other countries waging an information war against us by purposefully contaminating our media with falsehoods and publishing things meant to inflame our differences'.
15 Feven Merid, 'Unconfirmable', *Columbia Journalism Review*, 10 June 2024.
16 '2 Candidates. No Audience. 29 New York Times Fact-Checkers', *The New York Times*, 24 June 2024.
17 M Stencel, E Ryan and J Luther, 'Misinformation Has Spread, but Fact-Checking Levels off', Duke Reporters' Lab, 21 June 2023.
18 Lucas Graves, *Deciding What's True: The Rise of Political Fact-Checking in American Journalism*, Columbia University Press, New York, 2016.
19 For example, Politifact and Check Your Fact, associated respectively with the left and the right, vary widely in their chosen subjects.
20 Merid, 'Unconfirmable'.
21 Joseph Bernstein, 'Bad News', *Harper's Magazine*, September 2021.
22 Waisbord, 'Truth Is What Happens to News'.
23 Michael Schudson, 'What Does "Trust in the Media" Mean?', *Daedalus*, vol. 151, no. 4, 2022, pp. 144–60.
24 'Announcing A New Weekly Magazine', *The New Yorker* archives, 1925.
25 Maggie Doherty, 'Burned Out', *The New Yorker*, 9 May 2022.

26 'We Stand Corrected', *The New Yorker*, 23 April 1927.
27 John McPhee, 'Checkpoints,' *The New Yorker*, 1 February 2009.
28 This includes criticism, cartoons and even fiction, but reported pieces make up the bulk of the work. Some more ephemeral material, such as the text in certain newsletters, is handled differently.
29 In some places, this is known as 'right of reply'. A UN treaty designed to promote the practice, the 1953 Convention on the International Right of Correction, has been ratified by only seventeen states.
30 As Silvio Waisbord puts it, 'truth is not inherent to an idea; rather, it is a dynamic process by which the truth is proved or disproved. Veracity results from a process of verification and validation': see Waisbord, 'Truth Is What Happens to News'.
31 *Der Spiegel* reportedly had a research and fact-checking staff of around eighty, but somehow, this didn't stop the writer Claas Relotius from slipping countless false or invented details into his stories: see E Zerofksky, 'The Deep Pathology at the Heart of a Scandal at *Der Spiegel*', *The New Yorker*, 30 January 2019.
32 Kalsnes and Krumsvik, 'Building Trust'.
33 One recent internal document referred to accuracy as part of *The New Yorker*'s 'brand attributes and personality'. *The New York Times*'s 'Truth Is Hard' advertising campaign was decidedly more pithy.
34 A Baier, 'Trust and Antitrust', *Ethics*, vol. 96, no. 2, 1986, pp. 231–60.
35 Neil Levy, 'In Trust We Trust: Epistemic Vigilance and Responsibility', *Social Epistemology*, vol. 36, no. 3, 2022.
36 The Trust Project and Newsguard are among the practitioners.
37 Charles Bethea, 'The Terrifying A.I. Scam That Uses Your Loved One's Voice', *The New Yorker*, 7 March 2024.
38 Andrew Marantz, '"It's Not Possible for Me to Feel or Be Creepy": An Interview with ChatGPT', *The New Yorker*, 13 February 2023.
39 For example, see 'Can AI Steal Your Vote', *Dispatches*, Channel 4, June 2024.
40 FLF Lee, 'Disinformation Perceptions and Media Trust: The Moderating Roles of Political Trust and Values', *International Journal of Communication*, vol. 18, 2024.

There Is No Middle Ground: Reclaiming the Public Square

1 See European Broadcasting Union, 'Trust in Media', 30 September 2022, https://www.ebu.ch/publications/research/login_only/report/trust-in-media (viewed September 2024).

2   CBC/Radio-Canada, 'Public Broadcasters Collaborate to Reclaim Online Public Spaces with Creation of "Public Spaces Incubator"', media release, 8 February 2023, https://cbc.radio-canada.ca/en/media-centre/public-spaces-incubator-collaboration (viewed September 2024).
3   New_ Public, 'Civic Signals', 2024, https://newpublic.org/study/3378/civic-signals (viewed September 2024).
4   Yale University, 'Archetypes and Personas', 2024, https://usability.yale.edu/understanding-your-user/archetypes-and-personas (viewed September 2024).
5   D Allen, personal communication, 2023.
6   E Noelle-Neumann, 'The Spiral of Silence: A Theory of Public Opinion', *Journal of Communication*, 1974.
7   This number includes: the general public across four countries and five languages; and fifty-plus internal stakeholders across five organisations, five countries and five languages, spanning a variety of departments that include Leadership, Strategy, Design, Development, Community Management, Editorial and more.
8   J Jacobs, *The Death and Life of Great American Cities*, Vintage Books, New York, 1993.

Strengthening Global Trust
1   Nicholas Reece, 'More than 4 Billion People Are Eligible to Vote in an Election in 2024', *The Conversation*, 15 January 2024, https://theconversation.com/more-than-4-billion-people-are-eligible-to-vote-in-an-election-in-2024-is-this-democracys-biggest-test-220837 (viewed September 2024).
2   N Newman et al., *Reuters Institute Digital News Report 2024*, Reuters Institute for the Study of Journalism, Oxford, 2024.
3   Public Media Alliance, 'Public Media Funding', 2024, https://www.publicmediaalliance.org/about-us/what-is-psm/psm-funding-models (viewed September 2024).
4   J Curran et al., 'Media System, Public Knowledge and Democracy: A Comparative Study', *European Journal of Communication*, vol. 24, no. 1, 2009, https://journals.sagepub.com/doi/10.1177/0267323108098943 (viewed September 2024).
5   Public Media Alliance, 'Funding Democracy: Public Media and Democratic Health in 33 Countries', 28 January 2022, https://www.publicmediaalliance.org/funding-democracy-public-media-and-democratic-health-in-33-countries (viewed September 2024).

6 Reuters Institute, 'Public Service Media Are Struggling to Reach Younger, Less Educated Audiences and Risk "Decline and Ultimately Irrelevance"', https://reutersinstitute.politics.ox.ac.uk/news/public-service-media-are-struggling-reach-younger-less-educated-audiences-and-risk-decline-and (viewed September 2024).

7 N Nanji, 'More People Turning away from News, Report Says', *BBC News*, 17 June 2024, https://www.bbc.co.uk/news/articles/cj7799jv74vo (viewed September 2024).

8 Public Media Alliance, 'One Year after Meta's New Ban: What's the Outcome?', 14 August 2024, https://www.publicmediaalliance.org/one-year-after-metas-news-ban-whats-the-outcome (viewed September 2024).

9 Public Media Alliance, 'PSM Threaten to Leave Twitter', 18 April 2023, https://www.publicmediaalliance.org/psm-threaten-to-leave-twitter (viewed September 2024).

10 Ofcom, 'Understanding the Influence of Social Media as Gateway to News', 25 March 2024, https://www.ofcom.org.uk/media-use-and-attitudes/media-plurality/influence-of-social-media-gateways-to-news (viewed September 2024).

11 Public Media Alliance, 'France's Far-Right Threatens to Privatise Public Media', 20 June 2024, https://www.publicmediaalliance.org/france-far-right-threatens-to-privatise-public-media (viewed September 2024).

12 State Media Monitor, 'State Media Monitor 2023: Key Findings Released', 23 October 2023, https://statemediamonitor.com/2023/10/state-media-monitor-2023-key-findings-released (viewed September 2024).

13 M D'Alessandro, 'Italian Public Broadcaster Rai's Journalists Strike over Censorship Row', 6 May 2024, https://www.euronews.com/2024/05/06/italian-public-broadcaster-rais-journalists-strike-over-censorship-row (viewed September 2024).

14 European Commission, 'Media Freedom and Pluralism', 30 July 2024, https://digital-strategy.ec.europa.eu/en/policies/media-freedom (viewed September 2024).

15 G Lim and S Bradshaw, 'Chilling Legislation', Center for International Media Assistance, 19 July 2023, https://www.cima.ned.org/publication/chilling-legislation (viewed September 2024).

16 Public Media Alliance, 'Upcoming Projects', 2024, https://www.publicmediaalliance.org/projects (viewed September 2024).

17 Public Media Alliance, 'Best of PSM: Swedish Radio on Tour', 30 April 2019, https://www.publicmediaalliance.org/swedish-radio-on-tour; Public Media Alliance, 'How the Flemish Public Broadcaster Responds to the Wishes and Concerns of Media Users with Your VRT', 26 January 2022, https://www.publicmediaalliance.org/your-vrt-a-new-way-of-engaging-with-audiences (viewed September 2024).

Trust and the Danish Experience
1 GT Svendsen, *Trust*, John Hopkins University Press, Baltimore, 2024.
2 GT Svendsen and GLH Svendsen, *Trust, Social Capital and the Scandinavian Welfare State: Explaining the Flight of the Bumblebee*, Edward Elgar Publishing, Cheltenham, UK, 2016.
3 M Paldam and GT Svendsen, 'An Essay on Social Capital: Looking for the Fire behind the Smoke', *European Journal of Political Economy*, vol. 16, no. 33966, 2000.
4 M Rosenberg, 'Misanthropy and Political Ideology', *American Sociological Review*, vol. 21, 1956, pp. 690–5.
5 RD Putnam, *Bowling Alone: The Collapse and Revival of American Community*, Simon and Schuster, New York, 2000.
6 See EM Uslaner, 'Where You Stand Depends upon Where Your Grandparents Sat: The Inheritability of Generalized Trust', *Public Opinion Quarterly*, vol. 72, 2008, pp. 725–40.
7 GLH Svendsen and GT Svendsen, 'How Did Trade Norms Evolve in Scandinavia? Long-Distance Trade and Social Trust in the Viking Age', *Economic Systems*, vol. 40, no. 2, 2016, pp. 198–205.
8 Democracy Now, '"It Might Not Be Good for America, But It's Good for Us": How the Media Got Rich on Trump's Rise', 9 November 2016, https://www.democracynow.org/2016/11/9/it_might_not_be_good_for (viewed September 2024).
9 B Ingemann and GT Svendsen, 'I en fake news æra: Kan man stole på journalister?', *Politiken*, 20 December 2018, https://politiken.dk/debat/kroniken/art6911591/Kan-man- overhovedet-stole-på-journalister (viewed September 2024).
10 Ibid.
11 Ibid.

Trust and Distrust: The Existential Tension
1 Marc Benioff, *Trailblazer: The Power of Business as the Greatest Platform for Change*, Crown Currency, 2019.

2   Deloitte, *The Future of Trust: A New Measure for Enterprise Performance*, 2021, https://www2.deloitte.com/content/dam/Deloitte/us/Documents/risk/future-of-trust-pov-21.pdf (viewed September 2024).
3   Unilever News, 'Trust: The Key that Will Unlock Progress', 2018.
4   Robert Shiller, *Narrative Economics: How Stories Go Viral and Drive Major Economic Events*, Princeton University Press, Princeton, 2019.

Rebuilding Trust after a Crisis
1   Fair Work Ombudsman, *A Report of the Fair Work Ombudsman's Inquiry into 7-Eleven*, Commonwealth of Australia, April 2016, https://www.fairwork.gov.au/sites/default/files/migration/763/7-eleven-inquiry-report.pdf (viewed September 2024).
2   The directors were Sandra Birkensleigh, Dharma Chandran and Marina Go. The 'others' were Bob Bailey and shareholder Chris Barlow.
3   Steve Murphy.

The Currency of Trust
1   See, respectively, M Gottfried, 'Blocked Eyes and Ears: The Eloquent Gestures at Augustine', in *L'antiquité classique*, tome 69, 2000, pp. 217–20; Amala of Metz, *On the Liturgy, Volume 1*, trans. E Knibbs, Harvard University Press, Cambridge, MA, 2014; and A Falque, 'Gesture and Speech: Hugh of Saint-Victor's De Institutione novitiorum', *La Revue des Sciences philosophiques et théologiques*.
2   Quintilian, *Institutio oratoria*, ed. L Honeycutt, trans. JS Watson, 2006, https://kairos.technorhetoric.net/stasis/2017/honeycutt/quintilian/index.html (viewed September 2024).
3   R Birdwhistell, *Introduction to Kinesics: An Annotation System for Analysis of Body Motion and Gesture*, Hassell Street Press, 2021.
4   A Mehrabian, *Non-verbal Communication*, Routledge, 1972.
5   ND Wilson and D Wilson, *The Rhetorical Companion: A Student's Guide to Power in Persuasion*, Canon Press, Moscow, ID, 2011.
6   G Toogood, *The Articulate Executive: Learn to Look, Act, and Sound Like a Leader*, McGraw-Hill Education, New York, 1997.
7   J Fast, *Body Language*, Simon and Schuster, New York, 1970.
8   A Pease, *Body Language*, Manjul Publishing House, Bhopal, 2014.
9   A Intan, I Ariffudin and M Mulawarman, 'Psychological Experience Dynamics of Students with Glossophobia through Narrative Counseling as seen from Gender: A Qualitative Study', *Advances in Social Science*,

Education and Humanities Research, 2018, https://www.researchgate.net/publication/322694769_Psychological_Experience_Dynamics_of_Students_with_Glossophobia_through_Narrative_Counseling_as_seen_from_Gender_A_Qualitative_Study (viewed September 2024).

10 G Kumra, J Sengupta and M Sridhar, 'CEO Excellence: How Do Leaders Assess Their Own Performance?', McKinsey & Company, 2024, https://www.mckinsey.com/~/media/mckinsey/featured%20insights/future%20of%20asia/insights/ceo%20excellence%20how%20do%20leaders%20assess%20their%20own%20performance/ceo-excellence-how-do-leaders-assess-their-own-performance.pdf?shouldIndex=false (viewed September 2024).

11 Edelman Trust Institute, *2024 Edelman Trust Barometer: Global Report*, 2024, https://www.edelman.com/sites/g/files/aatuss191/files/2024-02/2024%20Edelman%20Trust%20Barometer%20Global%20Report_FINAL.pdf (viewed September 2024).

12 Challenger, Gray & Christmas, Inc., 'December 2023 Challenger CEO Turnover Report: Will Record-Breaking CEO Turnover in 2023 Portend Huge Economic Shift?', 18 January 2024, https://www.challengergray.com/blog/december-2023-challenger-ceo-turnover-report-will-record-breaking-ceo-turnover-in-2023-portend-huge-economic-shift/#:~:text=In%202023%2C%201%2C914%20CEOs%20left,tracking%20CEO%20exits%20in%202002 (viewed September 2024).

13 Quintilian. *Institutio oratoria*.

14 Ibid.

15 A Lessac, *Body Wisdom: The Use and Training of the Human Body*, Drama Book Specialists, 1997.

16 M Zuckerman, H Hodgins and K Miyake, 'The Vocal Attractiveness Stereotype: Replication and Elaboration', *Journal of Nonverbal Behavior*, vol. 14, 1990, pp. 97–112.

17 L Mahler, 'The Blueprint For Gravitas: Looking beyond Pitch, Pace And Volume For Voice', *Forbes*, 2023, https://www.forbes.com/sites/forbescoachescouncil/2023/12/20/the-blueprint-for-gravitas-looking-beyond-pitch-pace-and-volume-for-voice (viewed September 2024).

18 Quintilian, *Institutio oratoria*.

19 A Gallace and C Spence, 'The Science of Interpersonal Touch: An Overview', *Journal of Neuroscience and Biobehavioral Review*, vol. 34, no. 2, 2010, pp. 246–59.

20 G Davies, 'The Significance of the Handshake Motif in Classical Funerary Art', *American Journal of Archaeology*, vol. 89, no. 4, 1985.

21 B Whipple, 'Body Language 90 Blinking Rate', The Trust Ambassador, https://thetrustambassador.com/2020/08/13/body-language-90-blinking-rate (viewed September 2024).
22 James Strachan, 'How Do We Decide Who We Trust? Our Eyes Could Hold Important Clues', University of York, 2 July 2015, https://www.york.ac.uk/research/themes/trust (viewed September 2024).

In AI We Trust? What to Expect in Our Technological Future
1 Carl Sagan, *The Demon-Haunted World: Science as a Candle in the Dark*, Random House, 1995.
2 Australian Public Service Commission, *Trust and Satisfaction in Australian Democracy: 2023 National Survey*, Commonwealth of Australia, Parkes, ACT, 2024.
3 Isaac Asimov, 'A Cult of Ignorance', *Newsweek*, 21 January 1980, p. 19.
4 Sagan, *The Demon-Haunted World*.
5 M Isaac and E Griffith, 'OpenAI Is Growing Fast and Burning through Piles of Money', *The New York Times*, 27 September 2024, https://www.nytimes.com/2024/09/27/technology/openai-chatgpt-investors-funding.html (viewed September 2024).
6 S Sangha, 'Putting in Their 2 Cents', *The New York Times*, 30 March 2012, https://www.nytimes.com/2012/04/01/nyregion/for-some-new-yorkers-a-grand-experiment-in-participatory-budgeting.html (viewed September 2024).

Bots and Moral Panic
1 MT Hicks, J Humphries and J Slater, 'ChatGPT Is Bullshit', *Ethics and Information Technology*, vol. 26, no. 38, 2024.
2 J Purtill, 'Twitter Is Becoming a "Ghost Town" of Bots as AI-Generated Spam Content Floods the Internet', *ABC Science*, 28 February 2024, https://www.abc.net.au/news/science/2024-02-28/twitter-x-fighting-bot-problem-as-ai-spam-floods-the-internet/103498070 (viewed September 2024).
3 M Binder, 'The Majority of Traffic from Elon Musk's X May Have Been Fake during the Super Bowl, Report Suggests', *Mashable*, 16 February 2024, https://mashable.com/article/x-twitter-elon-musk-bots-fake-traffic (viewed September 2024).
4 F Muhle, 'Embodied Conversational Agents as Social Actors? Sociological Considerations on the Change of Human–Machine Relations in Online Environments', in RW Gehl and M Bakardjieva

(eds), *Socialbots and Their Friends: Digital Media and the Automation of Sociality*, Routledge, 2016, pp. 86–109.

5   D Carlon, 'The Bot in the Room: The Absence of a Consistent and Adequate Definition', Medium, 5 October 2023, para. 5, https://medium.com/automated-decision-making-and-society/the-bot-in-the-room-the-absence-of-a-consistent-and-adequate-definition-ba7051e32949 (viewed September 2024).

6   D Assenmacher, L Fröhling and C Wagner, 'You Are a Bot! Studying the Development of Bot Accusations on Twitter', *Proceedings of the International AAAI Conference on Web and Social Media*, vol. 18, May 2024, pp. 113–25.

7   J Farkas and J Schou, *Post-Truth, Fake News and Democracy: Mapping the Politics of Falsehood*, Routledge, 2019.

8   J Harsin, 'Post-Truth and Critical Communication Studies', in *Oxford Research Encyclopedia of Communication*, Oxford University Press, 2018, p. 2.

9   J Harsin, 'Regimes of Posttruth, Postpolitics, and Attention Economies', *Communication, Culture & Critique*, vol. 8, 2015, pp. 327–33.

10 M Carlson, 'Fake News as an Informational Moral Panic: The Symbolic Deviancy of Social Media during the 2016 US Presidential Election', *Information, Communication & Society*, vol. 23, no. 3, 2018, pp. 374–88.

11 Ibid.

12 J Harsin, 'Three Critiques of Disinformation (for-Hire) Scholarship: Definitional Vortexes, Disciplinary Unneighborliness, and Crypto-normativity', *Social Media + Society*, January–March 2024, pp. 1–12, quote p. 7.

13 T Hannigan, IP McCarthy and A Spicer, 'Beware of Botshit: How to Manage the Epistemic Risks of Generative Chatbots', *Business Horizons*, 2024, p. 13.

14 Ibid.

15 B Laufer and H Nissenbaum, 'Algorithmic Displacement of Social Trust', Knight First Amendment Institute, Columbia University, 29 November 2023, p. 30, https://knightcolumbia.org/content/algorithmic-displacement-of-social-trust (viewed September 2024).

16 A Matamoros-Fernández, L Bartolo and B Alpert, 'Acting Like a Bot as a Defiance of Platform Power: Examining YouTubers' Patterns of "Inauthentic" Behaviour on Twitter during COVID-19', *New Media & Society*, vol. 26, no. 3, 2024, pp. 1290–314.

Understanding Conspiracies and Their Theorists

1 J Uscinski et al., 'Have Beliefs in Conspiracy Theories Increased over Time?', *PLOS ONE*, vol. 17, no. 7, 2022.
2 N Levy, 'Do Your Own Research!', *Synthese*, vol. 200, 20 August 2022.
3 E Thomas, *A Year of Hate*, Institute for Strategic Dialogue, 25 March 2024, https://www.isdglobal.org/isd-publications/a-year-of-hate-anti-drag-mobilisation-efforts-targeting-lgbtq-people-in-australia (viewed September 2024).
4 PRRI, 'The Persistence of QAnon in the Post-Trump Era', 24 February 2022, https://www.prri.org/research/the-persistence-of-qanon-in-the-post-trump-era-an-analysis-of-who-believes-the-conspiracies (viewed September 2024).
5 Center for Countering Digital Hate, *The Disinformation Dozen: Why Platforms Must Act on Twelve Leading Online Anti-Vaxxers*, 24 March 2021, https://counterhate.com/wp-content/uploads/2022/05/210324-The-Disinformation-Dozen.pdf (viewed September 2024).
6 C O'Connor and J Holt, *TikTok and White Supremacist Content*, Institute for Strategic Dialogue, 12 September 2024, https://www.isdglobal.org/isd-publications/tiktok-and-white-supremacist-content (viewed September 2024).